Praise for *The Entrepre*

"Finally! Someone asks the million-dollar ques[tion] about CAN you be an entrepreneur? It is real[ly... en]trepreneur? You can spend thousands of dolla[rs] figuring it out. Or, you can read this book. Carol has been on all sides of entrepreneurship and objectively dishes out the cold hard truth—but in a way that leaves you feeling confident and empowered! A must-read for all would-be and all could-be entrepreneurs."

—SHAMA KABANI,
Author of the bestselling *The Zen of Social Media Marketing*
and president of the Marketing Zen Group

"Why do so many entrepreneurs fail? Because they receive bad or incomplete (read: typical) advice on how to start and grow a business. Instead of risking your savings or your [san]ity, invest in *The Entrepreneur Equation* so you understand what it truly takes to th[rive] as a business owner both now and in the future."

—ELIZABETH MARSHALL,
Co-a[uthor of] *The Contrarian Effect: Why It Pays (Big) to Take Typical Sales Advice and Do the Opposite* and founder, AuthorTeleseminars.com

---

"*The [Entrepre]neur Equation* is the reality check you need, plus the entrepreneur success to[olk]it you want—a must read!

In an [age] where ideas are heralded as the be-all, end-all of business, the importance lies in execution. Carol gives readers a roadmap to transform their dreams into viable businesses, allowing both aspiring entrepreneurs and small business owners the BEST chance to build successful, profitable businesses."

—CAMERON HEROLD,
Former COO of 1-800-GOT-JUNK? and CEO of BackPocketCOO.com

"*The Entrepreneur Equation* is a best friend's advice, risk management handbook and an entrepreneur's pre-qualification checklist all rolled into one. It's communicated in a heartfelt anecdotal style by someone who has been 'in the trenches' and who truly cares about the people who aspire to be entrepreneurs. In typical fashion,

Carol tells you what you need to know, then challenges you to take a hard look in the mirror before you make any decisions."

———————

"I wish I'd had *The Entrepreneur Equation* when I started my business. It would have saved a lot of time, stress, and heartache through the growth while I made a go of it alone. Carol Roth tackles the question, 'Even though I *can* be an entrepreneur, *should* I, now or ever?' with irreverence and a much needed dose of reality. If you're thinking about starting a business, already running a business that is not profitable, or you haven't been able to take your business to the next level, this book is for you."

———————

"Aspiring entrepreneurs and small business owners alike can generate the best return on their success simply by investing their time reading *The Entrepreneur Equation*. Written in Carol's frank and fun style, this book gives you the key tools that you need to stack the odds of success in your favor."

———————

"As an entrepreneur who's built a successful company with a bit of luck and a lot of perseverance, I know how important it is for business owners to have access to advice from someone like Carol. *The Entrepreneur Equation* will lead you down the right path as you ask yourself if you should be an entrepreneur and then do a true self evaluation of your potential for success."

———————

"Carol Roth leverages her experience as both an entrepreneur and a strategist for businesses to provide valuable and unique insights on entrepreneurship in today's business landscape. Whether you are an aspiring entrepreneur or even an existing business owner, *The Entrepreneur Equation* provides a roadmap to help you determine how and if owning your own business will help you achieve the American Dream."

—Adam Kaplan,
Chief Portfolio Officer, Banyan Mezzanine

———————

"I get asked the question 'Should I start my own business?' all the time, and I've never known what to say–until now: 'Read Carol Roth's book.' It's a no-brainer, 'must-read' for anyone who is even vaguely thinking of starting their own business.... In a sea of feel-good, 'yes-you-can' books that lure people into mindlessly wasting their limited time and resources on business ideas that don't stand up, *The Entrepreneur Equation* stands alone as a masterful, compelling reality check that every would-be entrepreneur disregards at their peril."

—Les McKeown,
Author of the *Wall Street Journal* bestselling book *Predictable Success*
and CEO of Predictable Success

———————

"Having run a publicly traded company myself, I know that taking the time to create a strategy for success is critical. By reading *The Entrepreneur Equation,* you'll not only think differently about what entrepreneurship means for you but also create an opportunity to get the best, most successful return on your investment. This book is a must-read for every would-be entrepreneur."

—Harry Schulman,
Past CEO of Applica, non-executive chairman of New Vitality
and director of Amoena, Hancock Fabrics, and Backyard Leisure

———————

"In *The Entrepreneur Equation*, Carol will help you confront what it really takes to be an entrepreneur and run a business for success (because there are no guarantees). In this book you'll ask yourself the most relevant question of all, 'Is this for me?' Reading this book is a critical step for anyone considering starting a business or re-evaluating their current business."

—Martin Chimes,
Serial entrepreneur, former CEO of Corporate Express Australia
and chairman of Unistraw International LTD

———————

The Entrepreneur EQUATION

Evaluating the Realities, Risks, and Rewards of Having Your Own Business

Carol Roth

BenBella Books, Inc.

DALLAS, TEXAS

BenBella Books, Inc.
10300 N. Central Expressway, Suite 400
Dallas, TX 75231
www.benbellabooks.com
Send feedback to feedback@benbellabooks.com

Printed in the United States of America
10 9 8 7 6 5 4 3 2 1
Library of Congress Cataloging-in-Publication Data is available for this title.
978-1-936661-86-2

Copyediting by Lisa Miller
Proofreading by Jay Boggis and Sara Cassidy
Index by Tracy Wilson-Burns
Cover design by Faceout
Text design and composition by John Reinhardt Book Design
Printed by Bang Printing

Distributed by Perseus Distribution
(www.perseusdistribution.com)

To place orders through Perseus Distribution:
Tel: 800-343-4499
Fax: 800-351-5073
E-mail: orderentry@perseusbooks.com

Significant discounts for bulk sales are available.
Please contact Glenn Yeffeth at glenn@benbellabooks.com or (214) 750-3628.

This book is dedicated to my mother, Sheri,

whose spirit endures every day.

Your love, natural curiosity, and really warped sense of humor live

on in me (although your domestic skills do not).

Acknowledgments

Writing this book has forced me to do two things that were previously way outside of my comfort zone: (1) promote my message and myself (instead of others) and (2) ask for help (instead of giving it).

There are so many people who have been of help and assistance, and while there isn't enough room to list them all, please know that I am grateful for every ounce of help and support.

I would like to give an extra special "thank you" to the following people:

To Alan Roby, without whom there would be no book. Your guidance and support have meant so much to me and have gotten me to where I am today.

To Tracey S., my original "editor in chief" and the world's greatest "elf," who read and proofread the original manuscript so many times that you are now a qualified business expert in your own right. Thank you for all of your help and hard work on this and other projects, as well as your support and love, which means so much to me—oh, and for your excellent use of commas.

To Elizabeth Marshall, my "quarterback," who has provided so much in the way of valuable feedback, insight, connections, and overall help. I can't begin to express my full gratitude.

To Liz Strauss, who has become a dear friend and mentor, and whose "blessing" gave me instant credibility with so many fantastic thought leaders. I adore you and thank you for all you have done for me.

To all of those dear friends and virtual strangers who were kind enough to help me in my "backward" quest to find a publisher and an agent: Harlan Cohen, Jason Seiden, Tracy Ketcher, Paula Pontes, Keith

Jaffee, Jeff Wellek, Shari Wenk, Deborah Johnson, Stacey Ballis, Paul Shrater, Marlene Franke, Mike Magnuson, Erik Castro, Lenny Dunn, and Ashley Chan.

To my actual agent, John Willig of Literary Services Inc., who "got" me and the book's message immediately. Thank you for believing in this first-time author.

To the wonderful staff at BenBella: Publisher Glenn Yeffeth, who believed in me as much as the book's message; you have truly been a pleasure to work with. Debbie Harmsen, my editor, who not only greatly improved the flow of the book but also indulged some of my, ahem, *particular* comments. Lisa Miller, who copyedited the book. John Reinhardt, who designed it. And Adrienne Lang, who helped on the marketing plan for the book.

To Michael Port, who enthusiastically embraced the message of this book. Thank you for your generosity and for providing such a thoughtful foreword.

To all of those who took the time to read the manuscript and put their reputations on the line in providing such wonderful and enthusiastic endorsements, including Cameron Herold, JJ Ramberg, Les McKeown, Loral Langemeier, Barry Moltz, Gini Dietrich, Shama Kabani, Harry Schulman, Laura Provenzale, Adam Kaplan, Martin Chimes, Paul Nizzere, and Scott Stratten.

To those who took the time to provide valuable feedback on the manuscript, along with their friendship, including Tracey Thompson, Ebony Thompson, and Ivan Wolfson.

To Rich Wolfson and Cathy Wolfson who, in addition to providing feedback, have provided unprecedented friendship and support on this journey and many others. You guys are the best.

To Suzanne Caplan, who managed to let me turn a reference check into a phenomenal working relationship, and whose support I truly appreciate.

To Steve Hofmann, for all of your hard work related to the book marketing and positioning.

To Luanne Rousseau, who has been an amazing resource and friend and whose general "fantasticness" has allowed me to spend time on this book.

To Alain Tremblay, Vaughn Sawyers, and David Buttry, who provide neverending comedy; although you all actually took me away from working on this book at times, working closely with you guys is totally worth it! And to Percy Newsum and the entire Newsum family, you have become a second family of sorts for me. And, of course, to all of you collectively for turning me into a fashion doll!

To Jason Wu, Stella Inserra, Joe Sriver, Wade Beavers, and Suzette Flemming, who shared your personal stories to help other aspiring entrepreneurs. I sincerely thank you for your time.

To Janice Marks, for your friendship and your help (including your styling!). Also to Rachel Hanel, who has helped me bring my personal brand to life in photos. And to Carol Woods, who did hair and makeup wonders in the cover photo.

To Mike Walsh, for all of your hard work, technical expertise, and willingness to fix issues that would otherwise take me forever, and for your excellent card-playing skills.

To my husband Kurt, you are my best friend and life partner and I thank you for your overwhelming love and support. You mean so much to me—no words here would be adequate.

And last, but not least, to my father Bernie, who has always provided unconditional love and support and would be proud no matter what I did...oh, and who also is potentially the only person in the University of Pennsylvania's history to tell his daughter to ask the financial aid office if they would accept food stamps in lieu of tuition payment. Somehow, we made it through.

Contents

2 B

Assessing Your Timing
93

2 C

Assessing Your Personality
129

SECTION THREE

Assessing the Business's Fit for You
159

3 A

Assessing the Opportunity
161

3 B

Assessing the Risks, Issues, and Rewards of Entrepreneurship
207

SECTION FOUR

Assembling Your Entrepreneur Equation, and a Few Reminders in Case You Get Sucked in By the Hype

275

Given the desire of certain parties and to preserve confidentiality, throughout the book, as noted, some names have been changed. Other identifying details and situations have also been modified to preserve the privacy of certain individuals and businesses referenced herein.

Foreword

I LOVE THIS BOOK. It's a well-written, straightforward exposé on what it takes to be successful as an entrepreneur by an author who's not only an experienced and trusted advisor but a woman of considerable character and integrity. I also love this book because it's a reality check. Most books on entrepreneurship are written from the perspective that anyone and everyone can do it, and it's super simple if you just follow these *three easy steps*. However, anyone who has built a remarkable business knows the truth. There are no three easy steps to your own business making a million dollars a day.

Carol Roth isn't trying to talk you out of starting your own business. Quite the contrary, she wants nothing more than for you to succeed—at whatever you choose to pursue. She is, however, trying to protect you, encouraging you to consider whether or not you *should* be an entrepreneur not whether you *can* be an entrepreneur. The difference may seem subtle, but it's significant. Anyone can be an entrepreneur, but should they? Should you?

In clever and cunning prose, Carol dissects how entrepreneurship has changed over the last seventy years. Yet most new business owners are wrong-headedly pursuing the American Dream as if it were still 1945, a paradigm that is no longer relevant or appropriate. Recognizing this paradigm shift alone is worth more than one hundred times the price of the book. It's just one of the many entrepreneurial misconceptions she reveals. As someone who's quick to buck common conventions, I know that demolition isn't hard; anyone can say that everything you've ever heard is wrong. The trick is building something better in its place. Carol does this well. The book is filled with stories about what works and what doesn't. It's fun to read and will challenge your thinking.

I love being an entrepreneur—most days. Other days, I feel like I own a business and I'm working for a lunatic. In order to succeed in business, one must master many technical skills as well as strategic concepts. Nonetheless, my experience has shown that my own business growth occurs at the rate at which I am able to grow emotionally and spiritually. Many venture capitalists say they invest in the entrepreneur as much, if not more, than the entrepreneur's business idea. This is why: one can only handle what one can handle. The reality is that many business problems are personal problems in disguise, to which I can testify. As I've increased my ability to handle personal problems, I've better managed my business problems and, as a result, have continued to see my business grow.

Being an entrepreneur takes enormous responsibility. Fortunately, *The Entrepreneur Equation* shows you exactly what you're in store for and helps you to determine if you're ready for it. If you are, you'll learn precisely how to prepare for success, which is a gift, because as Carol says, "If you fail to prepare, be prepared to fail." This book is also relevant to you if you are already an entrepreneur and need to reassess your current situation to create a better path forward.

If entrepreneurial success is something you long for, ask yourself:

- Do I want to make a living, make a difference, or leave a legacy?
- Am I done personally growing, or am I willing to let my business force me to continuously change and develop myself?

In my experience, many people skip these two essential questions and instead ask, "What can I do that is guaranteed to work?" Any trusted advisor worth her salt will tell you nothing is ever guaranteed. However, if you keep the above questions top of mind while reading Carol's book and following her sound advice, you can get pretty darn close to guaranteed success. Note, that I said, "pretty darn close." The future is always uncertain; you can't determine a result. You can, however, find business success, personal satisfaction and, yes, maybe even serenity, when you accept the things you cannot change and muster the courage to change the things you can.

Thank you for giving me the opportunity to be of service.

Think big.

—MICHAEL PORT,
New York Times bestselling author of four books,
including *Book Yourself Solid*
and *The Think Big Manifesto*

Introduction

READ THIS FIRST!
Do not pass "Go" and do not collect $200
until you read this Introduction.

———————

Matthew, a 33-year-old with shaggy brown hair and an impish grin, sat across from his financial planner. The planner pushed a glossy brochure across the table toward Matthew entitled "Financial Dreams Inc."

"How much is the investment?" Matthew asked.

It was $25,000, just about the amount Matthew had in his savings. He would also have to invest his salary every year as well. But the planner sang the praises of Financial Dreams Inc. and showed Matthew article after article about how Financial Dreams would give him a better life, with more control, more money, and more recognition.

Then the planner introduced Matthew to several other clients who had made a similar investment. Karen, a single mother, didn't have enough for the initial investment in Financial Dreams Inc. so she took out a personal guarantee against her house. Sam, a former lawyer in his fifties, had done pretty well for himself, so he was investing a few hundred thousand dollars. In each scenario, the client made a financial and emotional investment, plus their yearly salary, to get a piece of what Financial Dreams Inc. was promising them. Investing in Financial Dreams Inc. is something that up to six million people contemplate each year in the United States alone.[1] Of these investors, a small number do well. A fraction of a percent do extremely well. But up to 90 percent of those

1

who invest in Financial Dreams Inc. lose some or all of their investment within a few years. Yet each year, another several million people commit to the investment. You may be thinking that Financial Dreams Inc. is a scam or perhaps even a cult. But it is actually something very familiar; Financial Dreams Inc. is entrepreneurship.

Now that I have your attention, let me clarify that last statement. I am not suggesting that entrepreneurship is the same as a scam, cult, or Ponzi scheme. I am, however, suggesting that potential entrepreneurs are continually lured into businesses with a false picture (or at least a gross misunderstanding) of what entrepreneurship is, with unrealistic promises regarding the potential financial and other rewards they can gain from opening a business, and with no means to assess whether the investment justifies the risk, or if the opportunity is appropriate for them.

Entrepreneurs ask themselves, "Could I be an entrepreneur now," and the answer is yes, anyone *can* start a business at any time. However, the right question to ask is, "*Should* I be an entrepreneur now?" because in many cases, your possible payoff won't justify your risk or you may not have done everything you can to stack the odds of success in your favor. This is not theory, this is reality; while every entrepreneur dreams of success, statistics show unequivocally that the majority of new businesses fail and most entrepreneurs don't succeed. That is not what most new entrepreneurs believe they are signing up for and, I imagine, not your intended outcome for your new business.

The misconceptions about entrepreneurship are rampant. As noted by Professor Scott A. Shane in *The Illusions of Entrepreneurship*, "More people start businesses each year than get married or have children... and the typical start-up isn't innovative, has no plans to grow, has one employee, and generates less than $100,000 in revenue." Plus, the greater majority of entrepreneurs do not succeed. With so many people attempting entrepreneurship who are misinformed, underprepared, and generally a poor fit with that path, and with so many other choices available, how do we address this problem?

Perhaps you may think that there isn't enough information on how to be successful. That is clearly not the issue because there are hundreds, if not thousands, of books on how to "successfully" start and run a business. With that amount of information out there about what it takes to succeed in business, why aren't there more business successes happening?

Working from the Wrong Assumptions

Sometimes, the answer to a problem is so obvious that nobody sees it. This usually starts with somebody relying on an incorrect assumption. Have you ever been in an office where a copy machine isn't working? Your office workers start pressing all kinds of buttons, lifting up the lid to check parts (as if they would have any idea what to do with those parts once they saw them); they even shake the machine violently as if a good pounding was the key to optimizing copier operations. They check to see if there is paper in the machine—there is, and nobody can figure out why the darn machine isn't working. Then, someone comes along with the most obvious answer: the copy machine wasn't working because it was never turned on (or plugged in) in the first place. This sort of scenario happens all of the time—people take a base assumption as a given (in this case, the assumption that the machine is turned on) and start looking for solutions to other problems, when it was really the assumption that needed fixing.

To illustrate what this means for the new era of entrepreneurship, I refer to one of the most revered and influential books on entrepreneurship of all time, a book that I profoundly respect and frequently recommend to entrepreneurs, *The E-Myth Revisited: Why Most Small Businesses Don't Work and What to Do About It* by Michael E. Gerber.

In 1995, Gerber identified that entrepreneurs weren't succeeding and used several client stories to vividly illustrate his primary thesis: businesses aren't being developed and run in a "turnkey" or automated fashion (meaning that most anyone can perform just about any function in a business) and by focusing on creating systems that automate their operations, a business positions itself to succeed. I completely agree with Gerber's assessment that automating a business improves operations. I also concur on a number of his other observations about entrepreneurship and business ownership, several of which I reference in part throughout this book. But I also strongly believe that there is even more to the story about why businesses don't succeed, including two key points: (1) there are widely held, flawed assumptions about entrepreneurship; and (2) that the business environment has evolved significantly since *The E-Myth*'s publication a decade and a half ago.

Gerber discusses his client Sarah, who loved to bake and opened a pie shop. After three years, Sarah was depressed (not to mention in significant debt) and didn't know what to do. Gerber's solution was to help her create systems for her business so that her employees could run the day-to-day operations and so that she could focus on "working *on* the business, rather than *in* it."[2]

As I read Sarah's story, I felt like there were some basic assumptions that I needed to probe further. I started talking aloud to the book (yeah, I do that sometimes—at least the book didn't talk back):

"If Sarah loves baking more than anything, then why doesn't she work somewhere where she can bake all day, instead of spending most of her day marketing, doing bookkeeping, overseeing employees, or even creating procedures and systems for her business?"

"Wouldn't Sarah be happier spending more time specifically doing the work that she is passionate about?"

"Does the world really need another pie shop? I mean, you can get sweets just about anywhere, and you can get really good pies in a number of different restaurants and specialty shops."

"What kind of a return on your investment can you get from a pie shop? Does it justify all of the risks Sarah has to take?"

"Pies are pretty fattening and high in carbs, too. Aren't people trying to eat better? Pie shops aren't really consistent with current consumer trends..."

While it took me a bit of time to piece together my thoughts, I realized what had occurred to me in that very moment: *everyone was working from the wrong assumptions about entrepreneurship.* Okay, maybe not *everyone,* but certainly a whole lot of people were checking the copy machine for mechanical problems when the machine was simply turned off.

You would likely agree with me that not everyone can find success as a professional singer (especially if you have ever seen the auditions for *American Idol*); I know Simon Cowell would concur. You would probably agree that not everyone is meant to be a professional athlete, a doctor, a fireman, or an engineer. Following that line of reasoning, I firmly believe that not everyone is cut out to be an entrepreneur and that the entrepreneurship-fits-all misconception is a substantial issue affecting many new and small businesses and their owners. While the greater majority of these business owners struggle and ultimately fail, and while the approach of most advisors is to put out information on how to be successful, I personally challenge the basic assumption. You can do anything you put your mind to, but just because you *can*, doesn't mean you *should*.

> YOU CAN DO ANYTHING YOU PUT YOUR MIND TO, BUT JUST BECAUSE YOU *CAN*, DOESN'T MEAN YOU *SHOULD*.

Now, this may seem like a pretty ballsy assertion, but it is rooted in a lot of experience. I may not have gray hair (well, actually I have a ton of it; I just color it frequently), but over the past fifteen years, I have worked in various capacities with more than a thousand entrepreneurs and businesses, helping them raise more than a billion dollars in capital, performing hundreds of millions of dollars worth of mergers and acquisitions, working on business strategy, reviewing business plans and business opportunities, and sometimes, just delivering a dose of business reality.

Based on my experience with a wide variety of businesses and entrepreneurs, as well as the experience of many of my colleagues, I believe that business advisors often give success advice predicated on the basic assumption that the person receiving it should be an entrepreneur. My challenge is that a primary reason so many businesses fail is that the majority of the entrepreneurs starting, buying, and/or running these businesses shouldn't become entrepreneurs, at least at that particular point in time, and for many, not ever. The reasons affecting the "fit" of entrepreneurship vary. Perhaps the person's personality type isn't a good "fit" for starting a business, or the aspiring entrepreneur's current financial situation, responsibilities, or lack of experience make the timing inappropriate to start a business. Regardless of the specific reason, the problem is in the basic assumption. If you are not cut out to be an entrepreneur, if entrepreneurship isn't right for you, or if the timing isn't correctly aligned with the other goings-on in your life, then your business will struggle and more than likely fail, regardless of how much business advice you receive.

Is Entrepreneurship for You (and for You Now)?

The ultimate purpose of this book is to help you first understand the realities of entrepreneurship, and then use that knowledge to assess the risks and rewards associated with starting a business, based upon both your particular set of circumstances and the particular business opportunity you are evaluating.

This book will also guide you in assessing your overall fit for entrepreneurship at any point in time and if, given the highly competitive business era we are in, it is worth it for you—financially and otherwise—to launch your own business (now, or ever). It will help you:

- Dispel common notions and uncover some stark realities about entrepreneurship;
- Understand what is truly involved in running a business;
- Define what a business is (as well as a "jobbie" and a "job-business") and the risks and benefits of each;
- Evaluate your personal motivations behind your drive to start a business;
- Assess if now is the right time for you to think about starting a business based on your financial situation, experience, responsi-

bilities, priorities, and obligations—or if you would be better positioned for success by taking on entrepreneurship at another time;
- Gauge if your personality is well-suited for business ownership;
- Measure the potential risks and rewards of a particular business
  opportunity and entrepreneurship overall; and
- Decide, based on all of the above, if you should move forward with a
  particular new business endeavor, or even reconsider a current one.

You can think of this process as sort of a prequel to *The E-Myth*—a
series of assessments and evaluations that need to be reviewed before
you tackle entrepreneurship and delve into the process of systemizing
and automating your business. As bestselling business author Michael
Port said to me recently, "all of the systemizing in the world won't help
a business succeed if the business model doesn't have scalability, levera-
gability, profitability, and remarkability."

I will add that it also has to have *suitability* for the entrepreneur pursuing it, based on that entrepreneur's personal circumstances, opportunities, and goals. You will be assessing this suitability factor by using
the exercises and information in this book to build your own personal
Entrepreneur Equation.

Why I Wrote This Book:
Lucy Van Pelt and the Commitment to Excellence

I have been called a lot of things in my life—some good, some questionable, and some not fit for publication. I also have had a lot of nicknames
(again, some good and some completely obscene). One nickname that
has stuck for several decades has been Lucy, as in Lucy Van Pelt of "Pea-
nuts" fame.

Lucy was the girl who was well-spoken, self-confident (or perhaps
you'd say bossy and vain—semantics, you know), and well-known for
her various shenanigans, such as operating an advice booth. She would
hang a sign that read "The Doctor Is In" above her lemonade stand–like
booth, and for a few cents she would extend advice on a variety of topics
to Charlie Brown, Snoopy, and the rest of the gang.

In my circle I am, and have always been, Lucy Van Pelt. As far back as I can remember, friends, family, colleagues, and even strangers would turn to me for advice. No matter what, when, or where, I was the advice doctor, and the doctor was usually in. Stupid me, I didn't even think to charge five cents like Lucy did!

I think the reasons that people have always turned to me for advice include my general curiosity, my accessibility, and most of all, my authenticity: I tell it like it is; like Lucy, there is no sugar-coating here, no beating around the bush. I tell the truth in all its frank glory, with limited hand-holding, even if it is not what people want to hear. That can get interesting quickly because I hold some very unpopular opinions. If someone tells me something and then asks for my opinion, I often respond, "Do you want the real answer, or do you want me to agree with you?"

If they want the real answer, or if I feel they *need* to hear the truth, I let it rip. It's the root of my *Spinach in Your Teeth*® philosophy. If you have spinach in your teeth, a booger hanging from your nose, or toilet paper coming out of the back of your pants, I will tell you. Sure, the conversation may be awkward for a minute, but you are better off knowing the truth. Information and knowledge are power. You don't want to take advice from someone who's withholding information from you. You don't want to take advice from someone who won't tell you that you have spinach in your teeth.

The other thing that is inherently ingrained in my background is a general commitment to excellence. One of my greatest peeves is mediocrity; it is also one of my biggest fears. I want to give 100 percent to what I do so I can be proud of what I do. Likewise, I want others to do their best so they can be proud of their efforts, too. So my advice is always supercharged with excellence as a motivator.

Many business books are written by entrepreneurs who have just "lost their virginity," meaning that they have had one great success. They tell their personal story, which is perhaps compelling but often very particular to them and their situation. You should be wary of taking advice (business, sexual, or otherwise) from someone who has done something just once.

As a business strategist and advisor, I have had the benefit of seeing the trials and tribulations of more than a thousand businesses, ranging from one-man operations to major multinational, publicly traded companies, and what I can tell you is that all successes are unique—they depend on a variety of factors mixed with a sprinkle of luck and a dash of good timing. While you may be able to find some common themes, success is very difficult to replicate. Failure, on the other hand, always boils down to the same handful of issues. I have the ability to draw upon what I have seen, not just from one success or one failure, but from more than a thousand. This allows me to give advice that resonates with and can be easily followed by virtually everyone.

In addition to the breadth of my experience, I also have depth of experience and entrepreneurship empathy. I have started and been an investor in a number of new businesses. I have engaged in a few failed attempts and more recently, some great successes. Combined with my advisory experience, this gives me an unparalleled knowledge base from which I can be the Lucy Van Pelt for business and entrepreneurship advice.

So, while I don't know what Lucy's reasons were for opening her advice booth, I can tell you that it wasn't that I *wanted* to write this book, but rather that I was *compelled* to write it. Think of it as my way of setting up my booth so it's accessible to you at any time.

Who This Book Is for and What's in It for You...

While I believe just about every aspiring entrepreneur (and most active entrepreneurs) can take away something valuable from this book, I acknowledge that it may be less relevant to engineers and high-tech superstars with business models that can reach $100 million in sales within five years and are realistic candidates for venture capital funding. If you're that person, you are in a very small percentage of entrepreneurs (teeny-tiny in fact, as venture capitalists fund *a fraction of 1 percent* of all start-ups every year). However, if you fall into any of the following categories of aspiring entrepreneurs and small business owners, I think you will find this book incredibly useful:

- You are a corporate employee considering quitting your day job to launch a business.
- You have a specific skill (Michael E. Gerber calls you "technicians") and want to stop working for someone else to start your own practice (e.g., web developers, hairdressers, massage therapists, auto mechanics, etc.).
- You have been laid off and are thinking about starting a business instead of searching for a new job.
- You are an aspiring "mompreneur," seeking to run a business while you raise your kids, or after they go to school full-time.
- You are driven by the desire to create meaning for others through a service business model (e.g., a business coach, consultant, advisor, technical skills teacher, etc.).
- You are a college student considering starting a business instead of getting a job upon graduation or within the next few years.
- You are a hobbyist thinking of expanding your passion into a business.
- You are seeking or pursuing a fast track to first-time business ownership (e.g., becoming a franchisee, taking over a family business, or buying an existing business).
- You are a "solopreneur" or small business owner who is challenged by, and therefore reevaluating, your current business situation.

With the resources in this book, you can decide if you are ready for entrepreneurship and then learn how to take educated risks. If you are not meant to be an entrepreneur, you can take that knowledge and focus on excelling at something that is the perfect match for you. You will make this decision through building your own Entrepreneur Equation, which will help you:

- Save tens to hundreds of thousands of dollars of your hard-earned money;
- Avoid amassing significant debt or risking losing your most important assets (like your house or savings);

- Maximize the results of your effort and time;
- Wisely spend your savings;
- Reduce your stress and gain peace of mind;
- Gain confidence in your endeavors;
- Be empowered to make the best possible choices for yourself; and
- Exponentially increase your ability to succeed;

by helping you:

- Understand what it takes to be an entrepreneur in today's environment;
- Avoid investing in a business at the wrong time for you (or at all if your personality does not lend itself to entrepreneurship);
- Identify and evaluate the risks and rewards of a given opportunity as it pertains to your goals and circumstances;
- Evaluate whether your dreams are best served by a hobby, job, or business; and
- Gain the tools that you need to maximize your success.

I hope you find that, for less than the cost of dinner for two at a major chain restaurant, this book is a very strong value proposition for you—potentially the world's cheapest business insurance policy!

If you are involved in a small business, thinking about starting, buying, or franchising a small business, or related to someone thinking about starting a business, I hope this will be an important reference book for you for years to come. Frankly, this is all of the stuff that I wish someone would have told me about business while I was in college, or at least at the beginning of my career. It is a business reality check and evaluation unlike any out there today.

So, are you ready to get started? I'm sure you are, but before you can put together your own Entrepreneur Equation, you need a little more information. Let's start with discussing the "American Dream" and how it contributes to the widespread delusions of entrepreneurship. It will help you see whether operating your own business is really *your* dream or perhaps more like your worst nightmare.

ENDNOTES

1. Kauffman Index of Entrepreneurial Activity: http://sites.kauffman.org/kauffmanindex/.
2. Michael E. Gerber, *The E-Myth Revisited* (New York: HarperCollins, 1995), 75.

The Issue—
The Assumptions,
Myths, and Realities
of Entrepreneurship

BEFORE YOU CAN PROPERLY BEGIN to evaluate entrepreneurship, it is critical for you to understand why such an assessment is necessary. In this section, I build upon the introduction and discuss how the American Dream has contributed to delusions about entrepreneurship and how the misconceptions about entrepreneurship, coupled with the absence of a screening process, have led to staggering statistics regarding success and failures of business (hint: there are a lot more of the latter). I also introduce you to the basis of the evaluations you will be performing in this book—a two-way evaluation where you assess both your fit for entrepreneurship as well as its fit for you—as part of your Entrepreneur Equation.

1

The American Dream

UP TO 90 PERCENT of new businesses fail within a few years of inception. And yet each year more than six million people decide to become entrepreneurs. They're literally buying into the notion of "Financial Dreams Inc.," convinced that it's a magic bullet providing quick riches and a better life.

I can't think of another career or life path where a 90 percent failure rate would be acceptable. Can you imagine if 90 percent of doctors failed within a few years? How about if nine in ten policemen failed? Obviously something is way out of whack here. Why would so many people risk their time, money, and effort in a journey with such low odds of success? And why does the belief that entrepreneurship fits all persist?

It seems that people believe entrepreneurship is a virtual birthright in our country. My theory is that this belief is an extension of the concept of the "American Dream"—the ideals that shape what we do, particularly in the realm of our quest for financial prosperity.

Everyone has their own definition or connotation of what the American Dream is and means to them. Most people don't know where the term "American Dream" came from or its original context. I know that I didn't until I looked it up while writing this book.

The phrase "The American Dream" was coined by historian and writer James Truslow Adams in 1931 in his book *The Epic of America*. He said:

> The American Dream is that dream of a land in which life should be better and richer and fuller for everyone, with opportunity for each according to ability or achievement. It is a difficult dream for the European upper classes to interpret adequately, and too many of us ourselves have grown weary and mistrustful of it. It is not a dream of motor cars and high wages merely, but a dream of social order in which each man and each woman shall be able to attain to the fullest stature of which they are innately capable, and be recognized by others for what they are, regardless of the fortuitous circumstances of birth or position.

In simple terms, it is the ability to achieve prosperity (financial or otherwise) through your own actions and free will rather than your family's status.

The idea of creating your own destiny with your talents and energy, mixed with America's capitalist system, often translates the American Dream into business ownership. Everyone has heard the stories of the family from _____ (insert the name of your favorite foreign country here) that came to the United States with nothing but a dream and a few dollars (or pounds/shekels/yen/rupees) in their pockets. That family then started its own _____ business (insert the name of some local business here—dry cleaner, restaurant, barbershop, etc.). Now, decades later, this family is flourishing, financially and otherwise. The family is living its very own American Dream, complete with a fantastic house, two (or more) cars, and yearly trips to Walt Disney World. These rags-to-riches stories have shaped our collective thoughts on what the American Dream is and how to attain it. Now, this is not just an American phenomenon. Many countries have adapted the American Dream to create their own brand of reliance on business and entrepreneurship.

However, we are in a different era now. With multiple decades' worth of millions of people pursuing their own American Dream in the form of entrepreneurship, the business environment has changed significantly and rapidly.

The Game Has Changed
and Nobody Alerted the Players

When the term "American Dream" was coined in 1931, the business landscape was vastly different. In America, our economy was nothing like it is today. There was no such thing as globalization. We were a farming- and manufacturing-oriented economy that produced products and shipped them locally, regionally, and nationally. Consumers didn't own televisions (let alone computers)—think about the differences in advertising! By the end of the 1930s, about 15 percent of the college-age population attended college (around 1.5 million people).[1] Moreover, there were fewer corporate career opportunities available because billion-dollar companies (and major employers) like Walmart, McDonald's, Microsoft, Nike, and CVS didn't even exist at that time.

Since the coining of the term "the American Dream," we have had exponential progress and changes as a society. Our economy is now global, sourcing products from and selling products to every corner of the world. We have moved away from being a society based primarily on farming and manufacturing to one based in large part upon providing services and outsourcing manufactured goods. Media platforms like cable television (with its hundreds of channels) and the far-reaching internet have changed the face of business and interaction. During this changeover, there were a lot of opportunities to start business enterprises, grow rapidly and make large sums of money. Major corporations were founded and thrived, providing significant opportunities for career-seeking individuals. The U.S. Bureau of Labor Statistics suggests that today about 50 percent of the college-age population attends college, putting them on a faster track to those corporate opportunities.

This evolution has gotten us to a point where there are actually too many goods and services today (and probably too many businesses). Think of any business you can conceive of, from banking to hair salons to restaurants to gift-basket companies; the number of choices you have are staggering. There are so many businesses with goods and services competing for our attention that we are bombarded with advertising to the point of virtually ignoring most of it (if they even reach us in the first place). We are now faced with an ultra-competitive business environment where it is incredibly difficult to make a mark in the world. With so many goods and services trying to reach a fixed population that has only so much money, time, and needs, it is harder and harder for a company to make a profit, let alone a worthwhile profit that justifies the risks taken on when starting up a business.

However, in the wake of this over-competitive environment, the media darlings—the businesses that have generated great successes despite the odds and the changed landscape—are always the exceptions to the rule. Especially bad is the false light in which they are portrayed, with Hollywoodesque backstories that make for great human-interest pieces, rather than the more boring and routine reality of business.

The media touts Pierre Omidyar, the founder of eBay, as a programmer and hobbyist who, in the process of creating a small trading website for his girlfriend who collected Pez dispensers, "accidentally" created the largest trading marketplace. That story was exposed as a PR sham years ago. He knew exactly what he was doing and had a successful career as a programmer behind him.

IN THE WAKE OF THIS OVER-COMPETITIVE ENVIRONMENT, THE MEDIA DARLINGS— THE BUSINESSES THAT HAVE GENERATED GREAT SUCCESSES DESPITE THE ODDS AND THE CHANGED LANDSCAPE—ARE ALWAYS THE EXCEPTIONS TO THE RULE.

The YouTube founding myth—that Steve Chen and Chad Hurley created the company while unsuccessfully trying to upload video footage from a dinner party—has also been discredited. By the way, Chen and Hurley both cut their teeth as employees at PayPal (Hurley was one of the first and he also happens to be the son-in-law of James Clark, who founded Silicon Graphics and Netscape).

Or how about the "overnight sensation" of Midwest electronics retailer ABT, which sells more electronics out of a relatively new location than any other single location in the entire United States? That may sound amazing, but what you may not hear about is that while the current location is only a few years old, the business has in fact been around for seventy-two years.

So, armed with misinformation about the American Dream—yet ignoring how the landscape has changed and dreaming of becoming the next eBay—sharp and talented Americans who have all types of career and investment options available for them to enjoy financial prosperity without having to be born a nobleman, are instead turning to business ownership as their means of achieving the American Dream. They spend an incredible amount of time, energy, and money to launch their businesses, and yet the payoff is grim—most of these starry-eyed entrepreneurs fail altogether or just fail to succeed.

The problem, I say, with buying into the notion of the American Dream is two-fold:

1. Aspiring entrepreneurs are basing their dreams of prosperity on an approach that worked for new businesses decades ago, not today.
2. They usually start their businesses without first going through a screening process. Clearly the game of entrepreneurship has changed, and nobody has alerted the players. Being an entrepreneur today—particularly a successful entrepreneur—is more difficult than it has ever been.

Now that you have an idea of what's changed in the business playing field, it's time to address the issue of why there historically hasn't been a screening process for entrepreneurship (a process that you will undertake when you build your Entrepreneur Equation).

ENDNOTES

1. William H. Young and Nancy K. Young, *The 1930s*, (Santa Barbara, CA: Greenwood, 2008) 18.

2

Why Is There No Screening
Process for Entrepreneurship?

SCREENING PROCESSES are a very good thing. They help you ensure that you aren't marrying a bad kisser or renting a room in your
apartment to a sociopath. Most high-risk, high-reward career paths have
a screening process, too. The process identifies who has what it takes to
make it big and weeds out those who are poor matches for a lifetime in
that particular career.

For example, in the National Football League, there are a number of
steps in the screening process leading up to the "big time." You have to
be drafted on to one of the thirty-two teams' rosters. Before you can do
that, to even be considered as eligible to be drafted, you typically need
to have been an outstanding college football player, usually at a major
school. To be an outstanding college player, you have to make the college team and be given playing time by your coach. To make the college
team, you have to demonstrate outstanding athletic ability (and sometimes academic ability, too). These steps weed out the people who may
have talent but aren't suited for making a professional career in football
(and thank goodness for that, or a bunch of five-foot-six, 130-pound

guys who take twelve minutes to run a mile would all be trying out for their favorite NFL team every year).

Likewise, if you want to become a fireman, you have to endure and pass rigorous academic and physical testing. To be a lawyer, you need to graduate from law school and pass the bar examination in the state where you plan to practice law, and before you're even accepted to law school, you need to perform well on the LSAT (the standardized law school test) and produce a strong law school application, as well as have solid undergraduate grades.

Becoming a doctor is even more rigorous. You have to spend years interning in a hospital. To intern, you need to graduate from medical school. To be accepted to medical school, you have to score well on the MCAT (the standardized medical school test). The doctor path has an even earlier screen. As noted by Seth Godin in *The Dip*, "Academia doesn't want too many unmotivated people to attempt medical school, so they set up a screen. Organic chemistry is the killer class, the screen that separates the doctors from the psychologists. If you can't handle organic chemistry, well, then, you can't go to med school." These screens are a good thing, because if you need major surgery, you want the best and most committed doctor possible operating on you, not someone who throws up when she sees blood or has unsteady hands.

Yes, most careers with big risks and big financial, emotional, or achievement-oriented rewards have a screening process. Going through a screening process not only filters out those without the necessary talent or predisposition for a given career path but allows you to learn about various aspects of a profession before you make a commitment to it, which in turn helps you know that you are truly interested in that career. Spending the time and putting forth the full effort that it takes to get through the entire screen helps you demonstrate to yourself that a particular path is something worth pursuing and that it is a good "fit" for you.

However, being an entrepreneur doesn't really have a standardized and effective screening process, which is unfortunate since, unlike other career paths, to become an entrepreneur you typically have to put your own money at risk (as well as spend your time and effort). This essentially means that so long as you can get some money together, you can attempt entrepreneurship—even though you may not have any idea whether or not you are a good fit in that role or whether it is just a passing fancy that looks great on paper, but one in which you will quickly lose interest after getting your hands a bit dirty. The lack of a screening process means you won't know if perhaps the timing isn't right for you to pursue the entrepreneurial path, which will severely limit your ability to succeed.

Well, I don't want you to lose your money, time, energy, or sanity on a new business venture just because of a lack of an entrepreneurship screen. I first addressed this issue when I pioneered my proprietary five-step FIRED-UP®[1] entrepreneurship assessment as a basic test to evaluate some of the timing and mindset components that affect an aspiring entrepreneur's fit with the entrepreneurship path. Expanding on that assessment tool, this book offers a more in-depth screening process that anyone who is considering starting, buying, or franchising a business should take very seriously.

THE TWO-WAY ENTREPRENEURSHIP SCREEN
(Based on your personal circumstances)

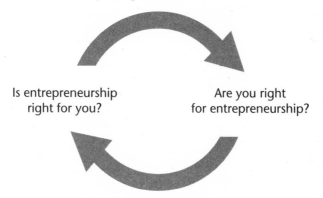

Is entrepreneurship right for you?

Are you right for entrepreneurship?

As the illustration above shows, you can think of the entrepreneurship screening process as a two-way screen: entrepreneurship evaluates you to see if your skills, strengths, and personal circumstances are consistent with running a business (for example, do you have the right mindset, motivation, and experience for it?), while you evaluate entrepreneurship to gain enough relevant knowledge to see if you have the true desire to commit to a particular opportunity and also to figure out if that opportunity is large enough to justify the risks you would take on in pursuing it.

If any part of that screening process shows a deficiency, you can then assess if it is a timing issue (whereby you can work to strengthen that area and then evaluate the opportunity again); an opportunity issue (whereby you can reevaluate other opportunities as they arise); or a personal issue (whereby you conclude that entrepreneurship will not likely ever be a match and you move on to something that is).

As you evaluate the dynamic between entrepreneurship's risks and rewards, you should ask yourself not, "*Could* I be an entrepreneur?" but "*Should* I be an entrepreneur?" As Barry Moltz says in *Bounce!*, "Many entrepreneurs risk too much... their potential return—*if* they achieve it, which most do not—is not worth the odds they accept. They are blinded by their passion."[2]

ENDNOTES

1. FIRED-UP® is my proprietary five-step screening process to assess whether aspiring entrepreneurs have what it takes to start a business (or if they should keep their day jobs). It is actually an acronym for **F**inances, **I**nspiration, **R**esponsibilities, **E**xperience, **D**edication and **U**nbridled **P**assion. It focuses on the entrepreneur, their motivation for wanting to start a business and the appropriateness of the timing (vis-à-vis what else they have going on in their lives). It focuses on the entrepreneur and does not comment on the merits of their chosen businesses.

2. Barry Moltz, *Bounce!* (Hoboken, NJ: Wiley, 2008), 142.

3

Entrepreneurship Is Not
One Size Fits All

WE'VE TALKED A BIT ABOUT the faulty entrepreneurship-fits-all assumption. Doesn't it make sense that if not everyone was meant to earn a living as a singer, race car driver, web programmer, astronaut, or chef, then not everyone was meant to run a business? Why do so many people ignore this perfectly logical conclusion? Why are there thousands of business-success books and virtually no materials (until now) on why you may not be the ideal candidate for entrepreneurship? Why hasn't there been a screening process for entrepreneurship?

My first theory is that people like to give and receive uplifting advice. Let's face it—our society is built upon blowing smoke up each others' asses (in layman's terms, giving gratuitous or insincere compliments or general good feelings). Sunshine, cupcakes, and puppy dogs create warm, fuzzy, good feelings, and more importantly, sell! Reality checks are sort of a "buzz kill," and downers don't sell nearly as well as uppers. However, our collective unwillingness to engage in a reality check has gotten us into deep doo-doo.

Our willingness to believe each others' B.S. is easily evidenced in the recent 2008–2009 U.S. national economic meltdown. This was triggered, in part, by credit card companies extending credit to people to buy things like flat-screen televisions and designer handbags that they couldn't afford. A second trigger was mortgage lenders who extended credit to a whole lot of people to buy houses that they also couldn't afford. The mortgage lenders told the homebuyers not to worry, that the value of the homes would go up as they had in prior years and that this gain in equity value would allow them to be able to afford the otherwise out-of-reach homes. Homebuyers bought into the hype and took on debt that they had no business in taking in the first place. It was one giant smoke-blowing fest. Nobody had the balls to do a reality check (i.e., step up and say *maybe you shouldn't buy crap you can't afford*), and the entire U.S. economy suffered for it.

> OUR SOCIETY IS BUILT UPON BLOWING SMOKE UP EACH OTHERS' ASSES...SUNSHINE, CUPCAKES, AND PUPPY DOGS CREATE WARM, FUZZY, GOOD FEELINGS, AND MORE IMPORTANTLY, SELL! OUR COLLECTIVE UNWILLINGNESS TO ENGAGE IN A REALITY CHECK HAS GOTTEN US INTO DEEP DOO-DOO.

Now that we have gotten into trouble from listening to the feel-good stuff, I believe we are more ready and willing to hear and accept a reality check. I don't know why so many advisors don't give reality checks; maybe because the advice is uncomfortable to give and receive, maybe because then they can't take their "37 Secrets to a Successful Business" book and supercharge it a couple of years later to be the "39 Secrets to a Successful Business—with Two All-New Groundbreaking Secrets That Are Critical to Your Success" and so on. For whatever reason, most don't deliver, like I am doing here, a reality check that says, "Hey, 90 percent of you probably shouldn't own a business."

With no screening process and hundreds of gurus focused on giving success advice, nobody has been telling you and the other aspiring entrepreneurs that there is a chance that owning your own business isn't the right path at all. If you haven't been given the tools to evaluate whether or not you have the appropriate personality, mindset, timing, or opportunity to be successful with a start-up, it is easy to understand why smart people like you continue to take the plunge at an inopportune time. You may not realize that your core competencies and experience don't match up well with entrepreneurship, or that your current circumstances make focusing on a new business today less than ideal.

Without the screening process, or the encouragement to "test drive" entrepreneurship before buying it, how would you know if you should take a risk? How can you decide if your passion is best left as a hobby instead of a business? Entrepreneurial successes are certainly glamorized by the media, so it is easy to see how it would be alluring. Not enough is done to spread the message that, just because you are passionate about something or excel at making an item or performing a service, you might not be so excellent at having it manufactured, finding customers for it, or managing the cash flow in between.

Plus, there are a lot of urban legends and general misinformation about the biggest successes. We talked a bit about eBay and YouTube's PR stories in Chapter 1. What about the widely held beliefs about Bill Gates? The story that most people believe about Bill Gates' success is that he took a huge risk, dropped out of Harvard and founded Microsoft to become one of the richest men in the world. That story misses a lot of facts. The following is a summary of Bill Gates' story, as told in *The Leap* by Rick Smith:

- Bill Gates was born to a wealthy, influential, and well-connected family.
- He went to prep school, where he was introduced at an early age to computers.
- While in school, Gates, along with Paul Allen (Microsoft's cofounder), spent a lot of time learning about computers, including hacking into security systems.
- Due to Gates and Allen's hacking abilities, the system providers offered them unlimited computer use if they would find system bugs—something that generated even more experience for Gates and Allen.

- Their experience led the prep school to offer Gates and Allen a job writing a computerized scheduling system.
- After graduation, Gates enrolled at Harvard.
- Based on an article about a new microcomputer in a magazine, Gates called the manufacturer and bluffed, saying he had written a computer program that could be used on the computer.
- The company bought the bluff and invited Gates to present the program—only then (once interest had been gauged) did he and Allen start writing it.
- Gates stayed another year at Harvard before he left to form "Micro-Soft," and he didn't drop out right away, either. He took a leave of absence as a contingency plan in case things didn't work out.
- Gates' highly influential mother created an introduction to IBM for Gates via IBM's former CEO John Opel, a crony of hers, which happened to be looking for an operating system for its computers.
- Gates was contracted to develop IBM's system, negotiating a deal where his company (Micro-Soft) would retain the rights to the software (cha-ching).
- So, Gates had around a decade of experience, limited downside risk, awareness of the huge potential of the upside, the right connections, and many other items that balanced his risks and rewards and stacked the odds in his favor.

The reality is quite a bit different from what most people know and believe about Bill Gates' entrepreneurial journey. What is clear, after reading the backstory, is that Bill Gates went through a number of screens along the path to becoming one of the world's most recognized and successful entrepreneurs.

The Entrepreneurial Match

Before we jump into the assessment, I want to talk about outcomes. I want to emphasize that it is perfectly fine not to be meant for entrepreneurship. The prevailing attitude is that anyone can do it. However, not everyone can succeed in doing it; it is hard work.

I'm here to say it is okay to be cut out for a career path that doesn't involve being an entrepreneur. As Dan Pink writes in *Free Agent Nation*, "Some discover that they lack the skills, the savvy, and the desire to make it on their own—and like it or not, they're better off inside the corporate cocoon."[1]

I liken matching someone with an entrepreneurial career path to matching two mates. Sometimes you meet a dream guy or girl who looks amazing on paper, but after you've spent time with him or her, you see that there just isn't the right connection. Or perhaps you have known two people who have been dating, and upon hearing about their breakup, your reaction was, "I could never figure out why they were together anyways." It likely wasn't that either one of them was a bad person—they just weren't a good match. If they had looked past the initial fascination with each other (and been honest that there is no "happily ever after," just reality), they would have realized that they would never make it.

That's why, outside of some instances in Vegas involving a lot of alcohol, most people date each other for a while before getting married. They want to find the right fit and partnership. The same thing goes for many careers and should apply to the owning your own business path, too. Everyone has at least one, and usually several, core strengths and skills, and running a business is not going to be a fit for everyone. In fact, given the number of different competencies required in successfully running a business, it is not a fit for most. You can't say across the board that it is better to be a country singer than a pop singer, an NBA player than an NFL player, or a consultant than a chef. Being an entrepreneur is empirically no better

> OUTSIDE OF SOME INSTANCES IN VEGAS INVOLVING A LOT OF ALCOHOL, MOST PEOPLE DATE EACH OTHER FOR A WHILE BEFORE GETTING MARRIED. THEY WANT TO FIND THE RIGHT FIT AND PARTNERSHIP. THE SAME THING GOES FOR MANY CAREERS AND SHOULD APPLY TO THE OWNING YOUR OWN BUSINESS PATH, TOO.

or worse than any other option you may be considering; it is just *different* and needs to be a solid fit for you in order for it to work. So don't feel bad if you dreamed of being an entrepreneur and that isn't your best option. You will shine more brightly when you are doing something that is a natural fit for you.

So, now you need to start assessing if you are a good fit for entrepreneurship within the area of motivation. To begin, you are going to evaluate what is driving you to want to start a new business.

ENDNOTES:

1. Daniel H. Pink, *Free Agent Nation* (New York: Business Plus, 2002), 213.

Assessing Your Fit with Entrepreneurship

TO BE ABLE TO CALCULATE your own Entrepreneur Equation, you must be able to understand what it means to be an entrepreneur and assess your fit with entrepreneurship, based in part on your personal circumstances. From your inspiration and mindset, to factors affecting timing, you can evaluate the strength of your connection with entrepreneurship.

Please take the time to give yourself thoughtful and honest feedback during these assessments. You will have your money, time, and effort on the line if and when you start a business, so you owe it to yourself to take the time to do each evaluation with care and insight. Remember that if you are not honest with yourself, you only cheat yourself in the long run.

2 A

Assessing Your Motivation

The following chapters help you explore why you want to start a business. Since there is so much misinformation about entrepreneurship, I clarify what a business is and explain what it truly means to be an entrepreneur. I also help you gain an understanding of many of the inaccurate, yet commonly held, beliefs about various aspects of business ownership. This allows you to work from a foundation of reality in regard to entrepreneurship.

Once you understand the foundation of entrepreneurship, you can evaluate your mindset. In your Entrepreneur Equation, your motivation illustrates what you hope to gain in terms of both financial and qualitative rewards from going into business. It is these rewards that have to be substantial enough to outweigh the risks in your personal equation. These chapters also help you assess if you are driven to pursue entrepreneurship based on your personal wants and needs or on a market need. If it is the former, it helps you evaluate whether entrepreneurship is the best option for you to fulfill your needs.

4

What the Heck Does an Entrepreneur Actually Do?

MANY PEOPLE, at some point in their lives, are struck with what they believe is an outstanding business idea. A portion of that number actually decide that they want to pursue that idea by starting a business. Their motivations may be influenced by their desire to solve an existing problem in their career or life, to pursue a dream, or perhaps a little of both. Common reasons that aspiring entrepreneurs and business owners give for starting a business include one or more of the following:

- Their idea will get them rich;
- Their idea will get them rich *quickly;*
- They can escape the corporate grind;
- They can do more of what they love to do;
- They can be their own boss and have the freedom to do what they want, when they want;
- They can work shorter hours and have more free time for their hobbies, families, and other passions;
- They can "do it better" if they were running the business;

- They can leave their mark on the world; and/or
- They can be in control of their career path or their own destiny.

These motivations are often based on a gross misunderstanding of what it takes to start and run a business. In fact, the words "business" and "entrepreneur" are two of the most overused and misused words in the English language.

If you don't know what game you are playing, you won't understand the rules, you won't know how to keep score, you won't know what tools to use (e.g., you can't use a baseball bat in a football game), and you won't be able to choose the appropriate uniform to wear. So, let's explore a bit about what the game of entrepreneurship means today.

In the most basic terms, an entrepreneur is someone who starts or runs a business, putting his or her resources (financial, time, emotional, or otherwise) at risk. This can be through a brand-new venture, franchising a business, or buying an existing business. These different paths to entrepreneurship come with different profiles in terms of risk, possible future financial rewards, capital requirements, experience, and other benchmarks. There are, however, characteristics that tie them all together, the most important of which is that there is actually a business involved. However, regardless of whether you are starting, buying, or franchising a business, they all require you to *run a business*.

What Is a Business, and What Is Just a Job That You Pay for the Privilege of Doing (a "Job-Business")?

In simple terms, a business is an entity that sells goods or services to customers in exchange for money. However, I would like to make a case that the definition of a business should be changed to: a business is an entity that sells goods or services to customers in exchange for money and *whose existence is not dependent upon any one person or small subset of employees.* If you take a business like Walmart, any person within that organization could leave, and the business would still exist and probably not feel any impact. The CEO could leave, the head of the marketing department could leave, the cashier at any given store could leave; yes, any of the employees could leave and Walmart would still be Walmart. It would still have value, and its shareholders would still have the opportunity to make a return on their investment.

There are a lot of entities labeled as businesses when this is really not the case. Take Tommy's Massage Therapy Inc. Tommy provides a service—massage therapy—in exchange for money. There are no other employees in this business; it's just Tommy and his clients. However, if Tommy doesn't want to do massage therapy anymore, or if he is hit by a bus, then Tommy's Massage Therapy service has absolutely no value. In fact, it ceases to exist. So, regardless of whether or not there is a corporate "business" entity around it, Tommy doesn't really have a business, Tommy has a job.

This is a job that is unlike any other. At a regular job, Tommy doesn't have much at risk. He may have to pay for a uniform or put gas in his car to get to his place of work, but basically that is all he is risking. The worst thing that can happen, the extent of the risk that Tommy bears, is that he gets fired and has to look for another job.

But at Tommy's job-business, he has to pay for the privilege of having a job (plus he has to deal with all of the other issues that come along with running a business, which we will be discussing later). He actually risks his own money to be able to have his own job-business.

In addition to spending money, time, and effort to create a job, with a job-business you are not building equity value, which I believe is the really compelling reason to create a business. In a true business, you as the owner have an entity with value that is separate from you. This is the value that you create for the business as a going concern, above and beyond the strict value of your assets minus your liabilities, which makes owning a business worthwhile. That means you can eventually leave the business (down the road, after many years of hard work) or sell the business (again, after many years of hard work) and get value for it. That is how most successful entrepreneurs make the "big bucks," by capitalizing upon the value of their business entity.

In order for you to sell your business in the future, you need to have a business that is saleable. This means that you can't do everything yourself. If you are the one-man band and the only reason the business exists is because of your relationships and your personal flair of doing things, nobody is going to buy the business down the road. How could they? Without you, the business isn't worth anything—you *are* the business, like Tommy is at Tommy's Massage Therapy service. This one-man-band thing may seem great for your ego, but it has the potential to wreak havoc upon your pocketbook, cause you a lot of stress, and may not make sense in the grand scheme of risks and rewards.

IF YOU ARE NOT CREATING EQUITY VALUE, THEN YOU ARE NOT CREATING A VALUABLE BUSINESS. IF YOU ARE JUST CREATING A JOB FOR YOURSELF, YOU NOT ONLY FORGO EQUITY VALUE, BUT YOU NOW HAVE A JOB THAT TAKES MORE TIME AND ENERGY AND RISK THAN ANY JOB YOU COULD OTHERWISE GET.

If you are not creating equity value, then you are not creating a valuable business. If you are just creating a job for yourself, you not only forgo equity value, but you now have a job that takes more time and energy and risk than any job you could otherwise get.

A whole lot of entrepreneurs don't realize this until they are deep in the middle of it. Of the approximately 28 million small businesses in the United States, it is estimated that a staggering 21.7 million of those are sole proprietorships with only one employee—the owner. Per the aforementioned statistics, many of these job-businesses are not really succeeding. Often, the entrepreneurs don't realize the difference between a job and a business (or don't realize it until it's too late). This is probably because they didn't realize what entrepreneurs actually do.

To help you understand what game you are playing (and how that impacts the risks and rewards you will be evaluating) I have created the *Job to Business Spectrum*, where equity value and upside potential increase as you move toward the right (see next page).

Now that you know what game you are playing, you have to learn about what is required to play and win the game. And now that you understand each game's respective risks and rewards, you may ultimately want to consider playing a different game altogether.

THE JOB TO BUSINESS SPECTRUM*

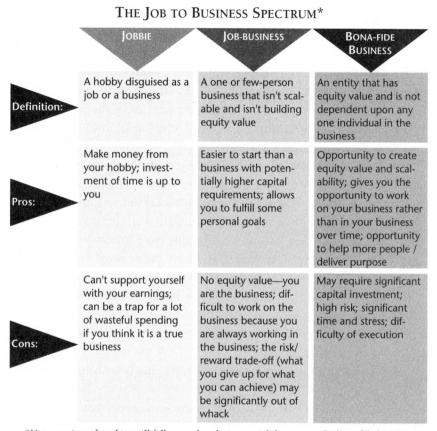

	JOBBIE	JOB-BUSINESS	BONA-FIDE BUSINESS
Definition:	A hobby disguised as a job or a business	A one or few-person business that isn't scalable and isn't building equity value	An entity that has equity value and is not dependent upon any one individual in the business
Pros:	Make money from your hobby; investment of time is up to you	Easier to start than a business with potentially higher capital requirements; allows you to fulfill some personal goals	Opportunity to create equity value and scalability; gives you the opportunity to work on your business rather than in your business over time; opportunity to help more people / deliver purpose
Cons:	Can't support yourself with your earnings; can be a trap for a lot of wasteful spending if you think it is a true business	No equity value—you are the business; difficult to work on the business because you are always working in the business; the risk/reward trade-off (what you give up for what you can achieve) may be significantly out of whack	May require significant capital investment; high risk; significant time and stress; difficulty of execution

Note, owning a franchise will fall somewhere between a job-business and a bona fide business.

So... What *Do* Entrepreneurs Do?

This seems like another silly question with an obvious answer, but it is frequently the crux of entrepreneurial misunderstanding. Most people think that entrepreneurship means that you get to spend most of your time doing what you love or want to do. Entrepreneurship is viewed as a focused endeavor; if you are interested in making custom jewelry, you should open a jewelry business. Being an entrepreneur is actually the opposite; it is very broad in its scope.

Basically, being an entrepreneur means that you have to wear lots of hats. You don't get to pick those hats, and even if you don't like those hats, or think that you look good in those hats, you still have to wear them part of the time. Being talented at making goods or performing services does not mean you will be talented at running a business that makes those same goods or performs those same services. Again referencing *The E-Myth Revisited,* Michael E. Gerber describes this as the "Fatal Assumption." This is the misconception, in Gerber's words, that "if you understand the technical work of a business, you understand a business that does technical work."

Let's start with a couple of very basic examples. Imagine you are a hairdresser and work in a nice hair salon. You love cutting, coloring, and styling hair, but you think the salon is taking too much of a cut (pun intended) out of your pay. You think that if you open your own salon, you can do what you love to do, not have to answer to anyone, keep 100 percent of what you earn, and have other people work for you that you can earn money from as well!

Or perhaps you are a copywriter for a large company. You see what your firm charges for your services, and you are not even earning half. You can just open your own copywriting business, continue to write, and make even more money.

Insert the sound of a buzzer here, because this is far from reality.

In each of the above examples, there is the same incorrect assumption. These workers believe that when they open their business, their jobs won't change—they will do what they love to do, just for themselves, and for higher pay. This is dead wrong. The reality is that if you open a business, your job is now *to run a business.*

Running a business means marketing to find paying customers, providing customer service to disgruntled clients, managing employees, overseeing payroll, managing professional service providers, dealing with vendors and suppliers, and much more. This often leads to entrepreneurs doing *less* of what they love to do.

Take Stella Inserra, a wedding and event planner and owner of Simply Dazzling Events in New York City. Over the past five years, she has been featured on the Style Network's hit shows *Whose Wedding Is It Anyway?* and *Married Away,* in addition to planning and designing events.

Despite her recognition and acclaim, she is not doing what she expected she would be doing when she started a business.

She says, "My mom was right when she warned me that the grass isn't always greener on the other side! It may be cliché, but it is true. While I am considered successful in the wedding industry, it hasn't been, nor is it, currently easy. People think that wedding planning is so glamorous, but it is not what everyone thinks it is. I spend 90 percent of my time handling administration, marketing, blogging, networking, selling, bookkeeping and other tasks. And I spend 10 percent of my time using my creative event design skills. This is the reality of operating your own business. Aspiring planners are so in love with the pretty things of the wedding industry—the linens and invitations and flowers—but the truth of the matter is that it is a 'touch' business, *business* being the key word here."

So, like Stella, the hairdresser takes on fewer clients, because she is busy marketing to find new clients for the salon, ordering supplies, hiring hairdressers to fill empty chairs, and doing everyone's favorite job, accounting (or as most people call it, "the books"). When the person assigned to open the salon gets sick or is late, she has to go in and do it herself. When a customer is unhappy, it is up to her to solve the problem. Even if she has managerial help, she needs to make sure that everything is done correctly—she can't just pass the buck and assume each job function will be taken care of. If she hires too many helpers, it eats into her profit. If she hires too few helpers, she is working longer and harder at keeping the salon open. If she wants to take a vacation, she scrambles to see if there is anyone trustworthy enough to oversee the salon in her absence. At the end of the day, the hairdresser is doing much less of what she loves (working with clients on their hair) and spending more time running a business. This is what it means to be an entrepreneur. Oh, and not to mention she may be working many more hours for similar, or even less, pay.

Stella Inserra figured she would make at least the same, or possibly even more, money having her own events business than she did when she was a catering manager for a large facility. However, she says, "That's not true; it takes a long time to get to that place. I may make more in sales, but I also have more expenses, so less is going into my pocket." While she is considered successful, she confirms that she is working more hours and making less money now as an entrepreneur than when she was employed.

What about the copywriter? The story is much the same. He has to spend a lot of time marketing to find clients (who may be less willing to hire a one-person copywriter than a big fancy firm, even if the same person is doing the job at the end of the day). And when I say a lot of time marketing, I mean a whole lot of time marketing, because without clients, he doesn't make money. If he hires a salesperson, it eats into his profit. And he has to update his website frequently, do the books in a timely fashion, submit quarterly tax filings, design and assemble brochures, and manage any additional personnel he has hired. So again, less time is devoted to copywriting and much more time to running the business. If he goes solo for a while, he won't have paid time off like he did at his old job. If he wants to go on "vacay", while he is sipping margaritas at the beach, nobody is doing the work, and therefore there isn't any money coming in. Did I mention the stress and difficulty of setting up benefits (health care, etc.)? This is no cakewalk, folks.

So, the bottom line is that if you love doing something (cutting hair, writing, fixing cars, etc.), you will likely maximize your happiness (and potentially, your wallet) by spending the most amount of time actually doing that something. If you love the idea of running a business entity, that is the job of the entrepreneur. It is not to cut hair, sell shoes, write copy or anything else—an entrepreneur's job is, again, to run a business.

So, back to your fantastic business idea. The way you are going to really make money from this idea is to create an entity and create systems and procedures so that it can be run by anyone. But the creation is all on you, which is not easy to do (have you ever tried to teach someone how to do something that you are good at in the same way you do it?). And in doing this, you are not necessarily doing what you love— you are doing everything else you can think of and hundreds of things you have never imagined.

Is starting, buying, or franchising a business the answer to your problems, or does it create a set of new ones? Only you will be able to answer that for yourself.

EXERCISE 1

TARGET FOCUS—MOTIVATIONS:
Defining Your Baseline Motivations List (Part 1)

Begin to think about your reasons for wanting to start a business using the chart directly below for guidance.

1. As you read the columns, circle the reasons that are most consistent with why you want to start a business.

COLUMN A	COLUMN B
I want to get rich quickly	The risk/reward potential makes sense for me. Even with what I am risking, I have the opportunity to make significantly more (100%, 200%, 300%+) each year
I am bored at my current job and feel unfulfilled	There is a gap in the market that customers are desperate for a solution to and willing to pay for
I will get to do even more of what I love to do each day	I love to wear multiple hats and the idea of managing all aspects of a business is a good fit for my skills and experience
I have always wanted to do "x"	I have unparalleled industry experience, knowledge and/or contacts that make me the ultimate candidate to make a difference in this market
I want more free time	I want to do whatever it takes to make this endeavor succeed
I want to be known for something great	I want to make a positive impact on and for others
I can be my own boss	I will enjoy servicing my customers; I want to provide outstanding service to my customers to make their lives better and create loyalty to my business
I want to grab a piece of this hot new area where everyone is making money	I want to compete in an area in which I have a unique competitive advantage
I have an amazing idea	I have a very solid business model that can generate a significant return on my investment
Everyone tells me that I would be a great business owner	People that have lots of relevant business experience have evaluated my business plan and are investing their money because of their belief in my ability to execute

2. Looking back at the motivations you circled, ask yourself:
   • Are your reasons for wanting to start a business mostly in Column A of the chart or Column B?
   • Do you think your desire is driven by a market need or by something lacking in your life?

Column A represents suspect motivations to start a business, while Column B represents good reasons to start a business. The more circles you have in Column A, the higher the likelihood that you are driven by unrealistic assumptions and setting yourself up for failure.

3. Take any remaining realistic motivations and write them, plus any others that you come up with on a piece of paper. This will be the beginning of your baseline motivations list.

Keep this list handy, and as you read on, continue to evaluate whether your assumptions are realistic, and if your new business is the best way to achieve your objectives, crossing out any motivations that you find unrealistic along the way.

5

Why the HBIC and the BMOC
Have Very Little Control

ASK ASPIRING ENTREPRENEURS why they want to start a business, and you are likely to find one of the most popular motivations is to "be my own boss." The ability to work for yourself might actually be another definition of the American Dream, especially for people working in small to midsize companies across the United States. If you have seen actor Steve Carell's character Michael Scott in the television show *The Office*, this is not a hard dream to understand. In *The Office*, Michael is the regional manager of the Scranton branch of a paper distribution company called Dunder Mifflin. He represents an amalgamation of all of those stereotypical reasons people are frustrated with their superiors. In particular, he illustrates the frustration that you may be smarter than your boss and that your boss may be generally incompetent.

There is actually a name for the phenomenon of incompetent superiors: the Peter Principle. Introduced in 1968 by Dr. Laurence J. Peter and Raymond Hull in *The Peter Principle*, the principle says in part that, "In a hierarchy every employee tends to rise to his level of incompetence." This principle also states that in a typical corporate structure (think corporate ladder) employees are promoted for doing well or at least for performing competent work. Eventually, each employee is promoted to a position where he can no longer do well (their "level of incompetence"), and they remain stuck there in perpetuity, unable to be promoted ever again. It further states that, "In time, every post tends to be occupied by an employee who is incompetent to carry out his duties" and "work is accomplished by those employees who have not yet reached their level of incompetence."

So, when you work for a company, at some point up that company's corporate ladder are a bunch of bosses incapable of being good managers and superiors. No wonder there is so much frustration.

It is never fun to work with someone incompetent, especially if that person is your superior. You may think that the way of escaping this scenario is through getting rid of your so-called bosses by working for yourself. You dream of running around with a T-shirt that says HBIC or BMOC ("Head Bitch in Charge" or "Big Man on Campus," respectively). You envision yourself wielding some light-saber–esque type of wand that gives you the power to have everyone answer to you. You tell everyone what to do, when to do it, and how to look while doing it. You are now the boss, and you are in control. You say, "Jump!" and they say, "How high?" Right? Wrong.

The GAGOOS of Being the Boss

In a company, even with some incredibly incompetent people working above and around you, there are very few people who have a direct or permanent effect on what you earn. Outside of the outlier situations, like having a saboteur in the office, mostly there are a couple of people that have a real tangible impact on you, your career, and your paycheck. This probably includes your direct supervisor and may include, depending on the size of the company, a compensation committee, a group head, and/or the company or divisional president. These people hold the power to decide your schedule, your pay, who you work with, what projects you work on, and whether or not you remain employed with that company. That's it. That is the full extent of their control over you, and if things don't work out, you can cut bait and go to work somewhere else, with the only risk being the downtime it takes for you to find another company to work for.

However, employees tend to get the GAGOOS syndrome (otherwise known as the "grass is always greener on the other side" syndrome) and spend time daydreaming (and I do mean dreaming, because it is *far* from reality) about how great it would be to be the boss. Then, you wouldn't have to work with stupid people, right? Then, you could set your own agenda and work with the best and the brightest minds around. Then, an incompetent fool wouldn't be in charge of your destiny, and you would be the master of your domain, right? Survey says... (insert buzzer sound here) wrong—again.

The problem with the GAGOOS syndrome is that the grass is only greener in your head. When you get to the other side, you see that the light was reflecting on the grass in a certain way that made it seem much greener from far away, but up close, it is the same damn shade of green, or worse—the grass is actually brown and dying.

So, the premise that if you start your own business, you get to be your own boss and not have to answer to anyone is total GAGOOS. The reality check on this one is not pretty. When you start your own business, you actually have *more* people you work for. Yes—that's right—more people to answer to, and more people who affect your future and your pay. These people have even more of an effect on you than any boss possibly could at any job.

> WHEN YOU START YOUR OWN BUSINESS, YOU ACTUALLY HAVE *MORE* PEOPLE YOU WORK FOR. YES—THAT'S RIGHT—MORE PEOPLE TO ANSWER TO, AND MORE PEOPLE WHO AFFECT YOUR FUTURE AND YOUR PAY. THESE PEOPLE HAVE EVEN MORE OF AN EFFECT ON YOU THAN ANY BOSS POSSIBLY COULD AT ANY JOB.

How can that be, you ask? Let's talk about some of the people that you, as a new business owner, work for, and how they can affect you.

Your Customers Are Your Bosses

I always say that the most important asset of a company is its customers, and I will reiterate that again here. If you have no customers—or more accurately, no paying customers—you have no business. It is impossible to have a business without any customers. This gives your customers unbelievable power—they own you. So, if you believe owning a business means you get to be the boss, forget it; the customer is the number one boss, bar none.

If you think that you have worked for some of the most incompetent, god-awful, foolish, horrible superiors before, they may pale in comparison to your new bosses—your customers. This is exacerbated if you work in a business that services end-customers (rather than a business-to-business scenario, which isn't a picnic either). I have worked for nearly a decade and a half with businesses that sell products and services to the consumer; let me tell you that customers as a group can be beyond anything you have imagined.

Have you ever spoken to someone who works in customer service? If you don't work directly with customers in your current job, then I suggest you speak with someone who does before going to work serving customers. Some customers will blatantly try to scam you or steal from you. I have spoken to numerous customer service representatives that have recounted stories about people wanting refunds because their dog chewed up a product and now believe it is "defective." There are the representatives who work for a major bath and home retailer who explained that every year, right after Christmas, customers would return dozens upon dozens of *used* holiday tablecloths. One customer even had alterations made to the tablecloth to fit her unusually shaped table. The reasons for those returns—it "just didn't work for me."

There will be customers that will try to not pay you, there will be ones that try to nickel-and-dime you, customers who return products as damaged that they actually broke themselves, and customers who will take the product out of the box, replace it with something that you don't even sell, and try to return it for a full refund. There will be customers who will dispute your charge on their credit card because they didn't like the way they were treated or who will complain that the meal you served them was too cold and needs to be "comped" or discounted. Then, there will be customers who are so lonely that they will want to keep you on the phone, tied-up in person, or engaged in an email dialogue about all of their personal problems (none of which relate to your business).

You will send promotional emails to customers with a 50 percent discount on one item from May 1–6, and dozens will email back asking when the offer is good through, how much is it good for, and whether they can use it when they get paid on May 10. Guess what? All of these people are your new bosses. Lucky you—as a business owner, these are the people for whom you now work!

One of my favorite essays of all time is a perfect example of what you could face. It is called "Reservations of an Airline Agent," written by Jonathan Lee and originally published in the *Washington Post* in the mid-1990s. Lee recounts his experience as an airline reservations agent who worked with customers to book flights. Here is one example of what he endured:

> "...the woman who wanted to know why she had to change clothes on our flight between Chicago and Washington (she was told she'd have to make a change between the two cities)...asking a woman from New York what city she wanted to go to in Arizona, she asked 'Oh...is it a big place?'...and a direct hit from a woman who wanted to fly to Hippopotamus, New York. After assuring her that there was no such city, she became irate and said it was a big city with a big airport. I asked if Hippopotamus was near Albany or Syracuse. It wasn't. Then I asked if it was near Buffalo. 'Buffalo!' she said. 'I knew it was a big animal!'"

I highly recommend you look up this piece online (it doesn't have an official URL, but it's all over the web; just Google it) and read it in full, as it is truly a gem and a great example of what you may have to look forward to in working with customers.

You have undoubtedly heard the saying that the customer is always right. The reason for that saying is that the customer *believes* that he is always right and if you don't take care of that customer (right or not) he will soon become an ex-customer. He will also badmouth you to every person he knows, including other existing customers and potential new customers. So, now you have a bunch of different bosses that each think that he is always right, regardless of whether it is true or not.

This may seem but a small annoyance in the grand scheme of things, but let me reiterate why your customers are your number one boss. Unlike your boss at your current job or previous employers who may be able to exercise influence over you if you remain employed, your pay, and possibly who you work with, your customers have much more control and influence. Being fired from a job risks your salary, but if you are fired, you can quickly regroup and seek other employment. If your customers fire you, meaning that they don't patronize your business anymore, you can't quickly find replacements, and more than just your salary is at risk. If customers don't patronize your business, in addition to having your salary on the line, you are risking the entire investment you have put into the business, and all of the collateral you have put up to secure any financing for the business. The customer has much more control and a firmer grasp on you than any boss at any job ever could.

Obviously, you do have some control over whom you choose to serve as a customer or client, as established by Michael Port's "Red Velvet Rope Policy" in *Book Yourself Solid*. However, while you can choose to cut loose some potential or existing customers, you still need to have a paying customer base to have a business. And these customers will still dictate how you run your business because if it is not to their liking, they won't patronize it. Therefore, the customer is still in charge of, or at least has a strong degree of control over, your business's future. This is the case regardless of whether your client is a consumer or another business.

If you don't like your boss, you can ask for a transfer or quit and find another job. If you don't like your customers, you cannot just quit. You are tied down and committed financially and hopefully, emotionally as well. So, think about trading one, two, or a handful of bosses for dozens, hundreds, thousands, or millions of bosses, each with their own agenda.

Your Employees Are Your Bosses

If you have children, you may have realized that even though you as a parent and head of a household should control your household, you really don't; the kids do. What you do is dictated by the kids, and you usually have to attend to the kids' needs before you can even think about your own.

Your employees in a business are analogous in many ways to your kids at home. Technically, you are the boss, and you have the ultimate say about their employment with your company. But in many ways, you have to attend to their needs before you can worry about your own. To be productive, you need to set forth procedures for them to follow. If they screw up, you need to fix their mess. If they don't show up, you need to cover for them. Sometimes, you need to be their personal psychologist and shoulder to cry on, too. And if your employees are not happy, they can wreak havoc upon your business (through sabotage, sheer laziness, or otherwise).

Yes, you control their employment, but they control whether your business is going to be successful and profitable through their performance. Oh, and they get paid before you do. So, who really works for whom?

Your Capital Partners Are Your Bosses

Many entrepreneurs can't afford to fund their business entirely on their own. They require some sort of outside capital to start the business and to continue operating the business. In fact, even large-scale businesses use outside money (such as lines of credit from the bank) to manage the ongoing functions of their businesses. If you are not funding and supporting your business 100 percent on your own, but rather taking in outside capital of some form, those investors and lenders are also your bosses.

There are two types of investors who invest in new companies. One group is the unsophisticated investors. These are friends, family members, and acquaintances that either know you or know someone who knows you. These people probably don't really understand your business—

in fact they may not really understand business at all—but invest either because they believe in you, have some infatuation with your business idea or model, or because of peer pressure (someone else is investing, and they invest alongside them).

As investors, these people become co-owners of your business. Because they don't work with you on a daily basis and yet you are using their money, they now want to get updates on a regular basis. They may want to put in their two cents worth of ideas, like telling you, "Don't you think the store would look so much better with a singing plastic fish on the wall?" Or worse, they may want to come and hang out at your office or place of business. They bring their friends by to show off the business they invested in or demand free or discounted products and services. You will have to answer to these folks, because they are now co-owners of your business and therefore people you can't ignore. These people, based on their lack of business sophistication, will at best, take up a lot of your time, and at worst, will make crazy demands on you and the business.

Then there are the sophisticated investors. These can come in the form of angel investors or venture capital funds. These are the glitzy investors that are hyped in the media and grace countless magazine articles and news programs. Sophisticated investors fund a tiny minority of all new businesses; for example, venture capital firms finance only a fraction of 1 percent of businesses each year. However, they often fund some of the biggest successes (although, in general, most of the companies in a sophisticated investor's portfolio will not be successes at all). These investors look at two main things—the strength of the management team (and their belief that the entrepreneur has what it takes to make the businesses successful) and the size of the opportunity. They only invest in businesses that they believe have a business model that has the potential to be a huge winner, knowing that in their portfolios, one big winner will make up for all of the other losers.

Now, sophisticated investors are supposed to be, by definition, sophisticated, so they keep a close eye on the businesses that they invest in, and those businesses need to supply them with a lot of information. Sophisticated investors don't manage businesses—that is not their job—but they do take their job as investors very seriously. The moment that the business is offtrack, and that means anything from not growing as quickly as you had originally hoped, to having greater expenses than projected—the types of issues that plague most businesses on a day-to-day basis—the sophisticated investors are going to make you answer to them. They are going to give their input and tell you what you need to do to manage the business better. If the business doesn't improve, or improves but not quite to the magnitude that they want, they are going to take action.

Most sophisticated investors won't invest in a company without substantial rights (these can come in terms of rights of the boards of directors, voting rights, or otherwise) to protect their interests and the interests of the investors that they represent. These rights nearly always include the ability to remove or replace the management of the company at its discretion. So, if you hit some bumps in the road, your sophisticated investors can actually fire you from your own company! This presents a serious Catch-22 for you, as the cachet, involvement, and capital of a sophisticated investor provides a lot of rewards, but certainly not without risks. Clearly, sophisticated investors, to the extent you take them on, are your boss; you answer to them. In fact, they can even fire you, an option they often give themselves in their investment contract if the business isn't meeting its financial projections, or make significant operational demands on you, just like a boss at any other job can.

> IF YOU HIT SOME BUMPS IN THE ROAD, YOUR SOPHISTICATED INVESTORS CAN ACTUALLY FIRE YOU FROM YOUR OWN COMPANY!

If you take out any type of a loan for your business, then your lender will also be your boss. Lenders provide money to the business based, in part, on staking claim to the business's (or business owner's) assets. That means that the bank or other lending institution will give you a loan, but in the agreement it says that if the business goes south, it has first dibs on the assets. Most new businesses don't have a lot of assets or history, so many lenders require that the new business owner personally guarantee the loan.

A personal guarantee is exactly what it sounds like. It means that you agree that if you fall behind on payments, or if the business is struggling in certain areas and you aren't complying with the specifics of your lending agreement (called covenants), in addition to handing over the assets of the business if there is any shortfall in value, you will guarantee that the lenders get their money back. This usually requires you to put up some other substantial personal assets, like your house, as collateral. So, if the business is in trouble, you risk not only your paycheck, but all of your business assets, the money you put into the business, and any major loan collateral, such as your home.

Your lender is also clearly your boss, and you have to answer to this boss properly or risk potentially losing everything.

Your Franchisor Is Your Boss

I am a big advocate of having people explore the entrepreneurship angle slowly and methodically. And by this I do not mean that you should spend all of your time strategizing and none of your timing *doing*. You need to take action, but sometimes in a series of steps that give you appropriate feedback and evaluation points along your journey. Franchising can provide a lot of guidance to new entrepreneurs to help them navigate the new business process (assuming that you are franchising from a well-established, successful franchisor). It helps to minimize, although not eliminate, some of the downside risk, or failure. However, it does this by limiting the franchisee's choices and decisions in the business process, as well as upside potential.

What this means is that you are "sort of" your own boss. Actually, you really are not your own boss at all. You are what can best be described as halfway between an employee and a business owner, which means that if being your own boss is the motivation behind your wanting to start a business, you are not achieving that fully through franchising. On the *Job to Business Spectrum*, becoming a franchisee falls somewhere between a job-business and a business.

As a franchisee, you have to follow a number of parameters set by the parent franchisor. This is done to standardize the brand, goods, services, and customer experience at every franchise, so that whether a customer patronizes a franchise in Albuquerque, New Mexico; Camden, New Jersey; or Seattle, Washington, that customer has the same experience.

Franchisors also remove the decision making from you in many areas so you can focus on the blocking and tackling of running the day-to-day business.

Some of the areas that a franchisor may mandate are store location and size, signage, number of employees hired, product suppliers, uniforms, pricing, procedures, marketing practices, hours of operations, training, and ongoing improvements to the business. Franchisors will often audit or inspect franchisees and have secret shoppers patronize their franchisees' businesses to ensure that they are up to par. They will communicate their vision and ask you to carry it out, while they share in your revenues or profits. They likely have the ability to terminate your franchise if you don't follow their rules and standards. They may also be able to influence or limit how and if you are able to sell your franchise in the future. So, if you wanted to be the big cheese and not have to answer to anyone, then franchising isn't going to quite cut it for you.

Everyone Else Is Your Boss, Too

If you thought that customers, employees, capital partners, and franchisors ended the list of who you really work for when you own your own business—just wait—there's more! The complete list of everyone that you will have answer to when you are your own boss continues to grow. If you have office or retail space, your landlord will give you lists of rules and regulations you must follow (in the case of the latter, perhaps even telling you what hours you need to be open for business and what goods you can carry). Of course, landlords also want to get paid, and if you don't pay them on time, they will kick you out. Your vendors also act as a boss. Vendors tell you when you have to pay them, what you can order and then, why they can't meet your deadline, even when they originally promised that they would. Regulatory bodies tell you to file paperwork, apply for permits, and follow other rules and regulations, not to mention require you to pay part of your earnings as taxes.

So, what did you learn? As your own boss, there is a limitless number of people telling you what to do, day in and day out. This is probably not the vision you had in mind when you first thought about becoming the HBIC or the BMOC.

Stella Inserra, whom I mentioned in the previous chapter, thought she would be her own boss when she started Simply Dazzling Events. She said, "Most people think that wedding planning is about designing pretty things, but I have to do what the client wants, based on their aesthetic and taste. I am at their beck and call and at the end of the day we do what they want, not what I want. The customer is the boss, which did not occur to me before I started my business. I thought I would be the boss, but to generate income I have to accept the reality that my clients are my boss."

In starting a business, you want to be in control of your own destiny. But the reality is that you are at the mercy of a wide variety of entities that you depend on for your business. Sure, they may not set the rules on what hours you need to work, or how to dress the way a typical employer would, but if customers don't like your brand message or you aren't working hard enough for them, they won't patronize your business. You can set your schedule, as long as your customers are available and want access to your business during those hours. You can pick your uniforms, as long as your customers think those uniforms present an appealing and appropriate image to them. When you start a business, you can have employees answer to you, but if they don't pull their weight, they can bring down your business. You can pick your vendors, but they can affect whether or not you have goods to sell to your customers in a timely fashion. In reality, as a business owner, you have less control now than you ever did before as someone else's employee.

There is not as much freedom in the "freedom to be your own boss" as you might believe. Please be realistic about what being your own boss means, and the additional responsibilities and costs required to be in charge. The reality is that being your own boss is probably not a good reason to want to start a business.

EXERCISE 2:

TARGET FOCUS—MOTIVATIONS:
Evaluating Control Factors

Think about the people in the organization at your current job (or a job you may be applying for).

1. Write down the names and titles of the people who have control over your career and future. Call this the "job control" list.

2. Next to each name, write down what function(s) these people have control over, including:
   - your schedule
   - your salary and bonus
   - your location (whether you work at home, in the office, etc.)
   - your ability to be promoted within the organization
   - which people in the organization you work with
   - any other areas that are important to you

3. Go back to that list and cross out any names that don't *truly* have the full power and influence to make a decision. When you are finished, this should be a fairly short list.

4. Next to each remaining name, write down how you can control these relationships to have more influence over your career path. Feel free to use new sheets of paper if needed.

5. Review the list and evaluate if the issues are specific to your particular company, or if would they improve by finding another job.

6. Now, create a second list of every person who may have control over your success in your own business. Call this the "business control" list. This list may include:

- your customers
- your employees
- your investors
- your landlord
- your vendors
- your franchise parent company
- anyone else who may have some control over the success of your business

7. Write down what functions each of these people or groups has control over, including:
    - your schedule
    - your ability to make a salary or profit
    - your location
    - your ability to grow the organization
    - your ability to make choices about the business's focus
    - any other areas of influence

Compare the job control list and the business control list. Do the lists surprise you? Do they justify your motivations? Use these two lists to further evaluate your motivations and make any necessary changes or notes to your baseline motivations list.

An Illustration:
Control, Mobility, and Freedom at a Job and When You Own Your Own Company

At Your Current Job

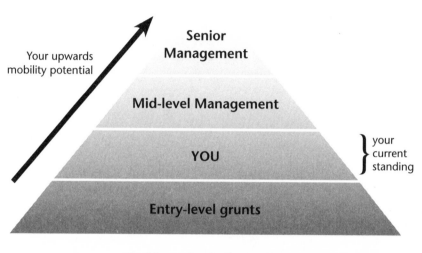

Get the picture?

6

Your Ego Made You Do It

NOW, JUST LIKE MY NICKNAME-SAKE Lucy Van Pelt, I often give advice, but I am not in any way a psychiatrist, so I don't know all of the fancy technical background information on the term *ego*. What I do know is that unlike its frequent connotation, ego isn't always a bad thing. Your ego is, in part, your self-esteem, based upon your perception and reflection of yourself built through interaction with others. Sometimes your ego is trying to help protect you from getting hurt, and at other times it is meant to help you express yourself to others. While your ego is usually trying its best to help you, it is usually not good for business.

Control of Your Own Destiny or Fear of Rejection?

One way your ego interferes in a career path is by convincing you that running your own business gives you control of your own destiny. This feeling is, as with many ego-driven feelings, a bit misguided. The desire to control your destiny may actually be your ego trying to protect you from rejection. It tells you that if you aren't working for someone else, or applying to work for someone else, they can't fire you, and they can't prevent you from getting hired or getting a raise. They can't reject your work (i.e. have control over you) if you aren't working for them in the first place.

As discussed in the last chapter, this ignores the reality that if you own your own business, you are controlled not by a few people, but rather by many; these people being *customers*. It is much worse to get rejected by everyone in the United States—306 million potential customers that don't want to buy your products or services—than a few prospective employers that don't want to hire you. The ego doesn't understand that it is much easier to reach and sell yourself as a prospective employee to potential employers a few times in your life, than reach your target customers and keep selling your goods and services to them each and every day.

Your ego doesn't understand this because the potential rejection with employers is direct, versus indirect rejection with customers. If you reach out to an employer to be hired or to your boss for a raise, or if you get fired, you take it personally. If you are rejected by potential customers, at least some of the time, you don't even know that you are being rejected—you have never made a true initial connection to be able to be really offended by the indirect rejection in the first place. If you are directly rejected by a customer or potential customer, you can hide behind the corporate entity so that you don't take it personally (or at least your ego leads you to believe you won't).

IT IS MUCH EASIER TO REACH AND SELL YOURSELF AS A PROSPECTIVE EMPLOYEE TO POTENTIAL EMPLOYERS A FEW TIMES IN YOUR LIFE, THAN REACH YOUR TARGET CUSTOMERS AND KEEP SELLING YOUR GOODS AND SERVICES TO THEM EACH AND EVERY DAY.

Let's be honest, if you can't woo your boss into a raise, or woo a prospective employer to hire you, how can you woo your employees to perform at top levels or woo customers to patronize your business? If you don't have those skills in one arena, you aren't going to have them in the other. Whatever rejection you are running from will be exacerbated by a factor of at least a hundred when you are on your own and your money is on the line.

The Glamorous Life

Another thing that your ego does is guide you to try to impress other people. They call it "keeping up with the Joneses," or more accurately these days, "outdoing the Joneses." Your ego tells you that if you are feeling down about your career or other things, starting your own business can give you a spark or even the beginnings of an exciting life. You may think it sounds sexy and gives you stature to be a CEO, owner, and entrepreneur of "Youco." You can tell everyone that you are the HBIC or the BMOC, and that makes you feel good and powerful.

Starting a business to give you an ego trip or to give you a fancy story to tell at cocktail parties are terrible reasons to start a business. It is that exact false sense of reality that will actually decrease your chances of being successful (and then your *failure* will be the topic of neighborhood party conversations).

I never understood those people who do things to impress people they can't stand. People take expensive trips, buy cars they can't afford, move into neighborhoods beyond their means, and sometimes, even change their career path to show off to people they really don't like. If you live for the story, just tell the truth in a fancy and clever way. It is a lot cheaper and easier with a hell of a lot less risk. Buy a government savings bond for fifty dollars and tell your neighbors that you are an investor in the long-term government securities business. Or bring back your recyclable glass bottles to collect the five cents each and tell everyone you have a side business in recycling. Most of the people won't know what you are talking about, and it will sound sexy without your having to take on the risk of a real business.

I'll Show Them!

A more severe case of showing off for the Joneses is proving other people wrong. You want to seek revenge on the doubters. Sally broke up with you because she never thought you had the drive to accomplish anything. Your mom never praised you enough. The people at work never respect your ideas. Now, you'll show them how great you are by running your own business!

I am not saying that you can't get inspired by trying to prove someone wrong, but don't use that as your sole inspiration to start a business. Business is much more complicated than that and needs to be inspired from an actual market need, not a personal need to prove someone wrong. Proving your worth to others is a nice stroke to the ego, but it's not enough of a reason to launch a business.

Everyone Tells You That You Should Do It

The other way the ego gets involved is when other people start fueling it. "You are so smart," you are told by everyone, "Why are you working for someone else?" You think you have a great idea, and everyone who hears about it tells you that you will make millions of dollars. You deserve to be a big success, and everyone else agrees.

The first question you need to ask yourself is, "Who are these 'everyones?'" Is it Bill Gates, Warren Buffett, or Richard Branson giving you this advice? Or is it your sister, whose total business experience amounts to helping her kids run a lemonade stand? You need to do a reality check separate from your ego, and when you hear advice or feedback from someone, ask yourself, "Does this person know anything about business; in particular, the type of business that I am thinking of buying or starting?" If they don't, their advice is probably worthless. It is like the students at a school for the blind complimenting your fashion sense. It seems nice on the surface, but it is actually throwaway commentary; it doesn't hold much practical value.

Please note that I am not saying that you shouldn't seek out moral support. Many champions of self-employment, including Pam Slim in *Escape from Cubicle Nation*, advocate having a group that will cheer you on when things get tough, and I believe that everyone needs that kind of support. However, there is a huge difference between receiving moral support to help you endure a difficult challenge and receiving useful feedback to help you evaluate business risk. You need to understand and respect that difference.

Even if the person hyping you up is credible, ask yourself, "What does this person know about me, and what do they have at stake?" Is he someone that will tell you that you have spinach in your teeth, or is he a "yes man" who will tell you what you want to hear because he wants to be friendly? Unless this person is really digging into your business model, your financial position, your marketing strategy, and other critical components that will make your business a success, and is so engaged with it that he is willing to put his own money at risk, then don't rely on this fluffiness either. Without a lot of in-depth knowledge backing it up, and particularly, without any quantifiable risk behind it, his advice is worth about as much as the paper on which it is written.

Don't let your ego force you into something in a misguided way to try to protect you or pump you up, or worse—make an impression on someone who you shouldn't care about and who doesn't have a stake in the future of your business. Business and ego do not mix. Keep your day job and opt for the clever storytelling instead.

EXERCISE 3

TARGET FOCUS—MOTIVATIONS:
Defining Your Baseline Motivations List (Part 2)

For this exercise, you need to take out your baseline motivations list generated in Exercise 1.

1. Revise your list to include additional reasons that you have thought of regarding why you want to start a business, crossing out any that you believe are based on unrealistic and/or unachievable assumptions as addressed in chapters 4 and 5.
2. Cross out any motivations that you believe are influenced by:
   - fear of rejection
   - seeking others' approval
   - proving a point to a third party
   - feedback primarily from one or more third parties that have little experience and/or no risk in your venture

This pared-down list should start to show you your true motivations. You will use this list to help create the "rewards" side of your Entrepreneur Equation later in the book.

7

Business Ideas—
Worth Almost as Much
as the Paper They Are Written On

ONE OF THE BIGGEST misconceptions in business revolves around the value of business ideas. You may know someone who came up with a great idea—or maybe you came up with it yourself—and someone else pursued it and made a mint. If you could just find a way to get paid for thinking of the next big business idea, you would be set for life. The problem is, you can't.

A Penny for Your Thoughts ... If You're Lucky

The biggest bummer about business is that the ideas behind them aren't worth anything. Ideas may have had some value back in the day when there were very few businesses in any given sector. Now that almost everything has already been thought of, not only is it hard to be innovative, but extracting value comes not from thinking of an idea for a business, but from turning it from idea to reality through work.

I really wish that ideas were valuable. If they were, I could have retired years ago. When I was a youngster, I was always coming up with what I believed to be outstanding business ideas—ones certain to make lots of money. One early business idea that I had was disguised as a game that I played with my younger sister, called Store. I was about eight when I created Store, and my sister was just a little tike. Store went as follows: I would find inventory in my sister's bedroom, basically her favorite items—stuffed animals, stickers, toys, etc. I would then take those items and set them up in my bedroom, arranging them in a way that replicated a fun and friendly retail environment. Then, she would come into my bedroom as a customer and shop the store. I would, of course, provide unparalleled customer service, and then my sister would use her allowance money to purchase items from the store. On days when my selling skills were really sharp, she would buy everything in the store. Since they were her items to begin with, I had no inventory risk and 100 percent gross profit margins! Best of all, I was selling out of my bedroom, meaning that my parents were paying the "rent" on the store. It was the ideal business until my mom shut it down (and grounded me) before I could expand it throughout the neighborhood.

My early ideas for business success ranged from the standard lemonade stand and door-to-door cookie sales to designing custom T-shirts (if you saw my artistic abilities, this one would really frighten you), and more. Early on, I attempted each of these businesses and got bored pretty quickly. As I got older, the business ideas became more varied and I became lazier—I just wanted to think of the business ideas and not really do much else. By college, these business ideas ranged from products like a set of NFL-based action figures that you could "draft" to create your own dream team, complete with custom football jerseys that you sent away for with your team colors and the players' names on the back, to a line of purses that you could change the look of by putting a new cover over it, to a whole slew of theme restaurants.[1]

I had notebooks filled with business ideas, any one of which could have been successful if I had taken the time to seriously pursue it.

Many of my business ideas were executed at a later date by someone else. No, not someone I told or helped, just someone else in the universe with the same or a similar idea that actually took on the risk and put in the time, money, and effort to make it happen (sometimes they were successful, sometimes not). At first this agitated me, but now that I understand what it takes to make a business successful, I have made peace with that reality.

The reason why I am no longer bitter about someone else making money when I had conceived of the same business idea first is that I now understand that business ideas by themselves have no value. The value is in the business *execution*. I have said it a thousand times if I have said it once: good ideas can fail, and bad ideas can succeed. The difference is the risk, time, commitment, and perseverance to take an idea, decipher if there is a market need for it, create a way to reach potential customers with that need in a cost-effective manner, and make the product or service at a cost that it will be desired by the customer and still leave enough money left over for you to profit from it. Not to mention working at it every day indefinitely, constantly innovating and providing outstanding service and value to your customer so that someone doesn't steal your customers and business away from you.

If you aren't convinced that ideas have very little value, let me give you some different examples which all, in different ways, illustrate that business ideas have very little to do with business successes.

Online Grocery Shopping: Same Idea, Many Different Outcomes

If you believe that business ideas have value, then how much is the business idea for starting an online grocery service worth? There were many who came up with this idea, tried it, and failed. The most high-profile disaster was Webvan. Founded in 1999, the online grocer went from an idea to national expansion faster than a Ferrari goes from zero to sixty. Webvan went public, and at its peak was worth thirty dollars per share, or $1.2 billion.[2] By July 2001, only eighteen months after its inception, it went out of business, putting two thousand employees out of work.

Others had similar business ideas—starting online grocery services—some went well, some didn't. A company called Peapod also had the idea to become an online grocery service. It was the same business idea, but with a drastically different outcome. Even though Peapod had its struggles as well, it was purchased by Dutch Supermarket company Royal Ahold, where today it remains an operating subsidiary.[3] While Royal Ahold doesn't break out the specific financial performance of Peapod in its annual report, Peapod continues to expand to service new markets. While we can only speculate that its expansion indicates that it is doing well, at least it is still in existence.

So, if there were value in a business idea alone, how would you attribute value to just the idea of starting an online grocery company? How can you define that value, particularly when you have one major online grocery company that went from zero value to $1.2 billion and back to zero in eighteen short months, while another remains in business to this day? The answer: there is no value to the business idea—it is in the execution. The same business idea can be executed brilliantly, poorly, or somewhere in the middle.

The UFC: A Business Idea That Went to the Brink of Bankruptcy with One Owner and Became a Huge Success with a Different Set of Entrepreneurs

One of the fastest growing sports in America is Mixed Martial Arts (MMA). The premier league for MMA is the Ultimate Fighting Championship or UFC. What made the UFC such a successful league?

Was it the business idea of creating a Mixed Martial Arts league? I am going to give that a big "no." The UFC was founded in 1993 by a company called Semaphore Entertainment Group. It was splashy and unique, yet the company almost went bankrupt.[4] As the company explored options before completely going out of business, Dana White (current president of the UFC) and his business partners, casino moguls Frank and Lorenzo Fertitta, offered to buy the UFC. Under this new ownership, the UFC has prospered, with *Forbes* valuing it today, less than a decade after its purchase, at about $1 billion.[5]

Was it the business idea that had changed? No, in fact it was not only the same business idea, it was the same damn company. What did change was the way the company was run, managed, and particularly, the way it was marketed. So, was it the business idea that created value? Obviously not, unless you are prepared to argue that the same business idea can be both worthless and worth $1 billion. It was the execution, and the people executing the idea, that created the value.

Businesses That Were Successful without a Great Business Idea

If you need further convincing that the business idea itself has no value (or that it has no influence on the success of the business), let me quickly give you a few businesses that were very successful without a novel business idea.

- McDonald's certainly wasn't the first, or last, hamburger joint, so clearly that business idea—"Let's open a restaurant selling hamburgers!"—wasn't what made McDonald's successful.
- Starbucks wasn't the first coffee retailer, nor the only means to get coffee. In fact, when Starbucks was founded, you could get coffee at nearly every convenience store, Dunkin' Donuts, or even at home if you preferred. The business idea of opening coffee stores on every corner certainly wasn't the reason why Starbucks was successful.
- Then, there is the Snuggie—the blanket with arms that's basically just a bathrobe that you put on backward. This wasn't a new idea— bathrobes have been around for a long time— and Snuggies aren't even attractive (you look like a monk when you wear one), but they are marketed brilliantly and more than $100 million worth of Snuggies have been sold in a year's time.[6] It may be more of a product than a business, but whatever you want to call it, the basic idea is not what made Snuggie successful.

As you can see from the aforementioned examples, the business ideas had very little influence on the outcomes of the various businesses. Basically, the ideas are just a starting point to help you get focused. It is what you do afterward that creates the value.

Ideas versus Execution, Continued

Nobody whose head is screwed on straight will buy a business idea from you, or anyone else, because any value related to a business idea is in its implementation. Maybe if you give someone a business ideas, they will one day send you a coupon for a free product, but that is about it. The further something gets away from an idea, the more value that exists. Things like customers, profits, and competitive barriers to entry create value.

The reality of the lack of value in business ideas is a shock and a disappointment to many people who want to get compensated for thinking of "the next big thing." If I haven't persuaded you yet, then the best way that I can illustrate to you why, in the grand scheme of business, the idea has such little value is through the chart on the next page. I have taken some, but certainly not all, of the facets required to run a business and broken them down. A few of the tasks are specific to certain types of businesses, but most are required by all businesses.

What this chart is meant to demonstrate is that there are so many tasks required in running a business; thinking of the initial idea is just one of many (this list isn't even all-inclusive, but I figured you would get the point after thirty-something examples of business tasks). Sure, the idea kicks off setting the business in motion, but coming up with an idea is a one-time thing that isn't particularly difficult, doesn't require much risk, and doesn't take a lot of work. Even if you were lying in bed fine-tuning the idea every night before you went to sleep for six months, this pales in comparison to the amount of work required to get the business started and make it successful. The other facets of starting and running the business, of which there are many, are quite difficult to do. They require a lot of risk to do, and to do well. They aren't done once but have to be attended to on a pretty much daily basis. They take a lot of hard work.

So, in looking at this whole thing we call a business, would you place a lot of value on a one-time idea that took no risk to produce, or on the other thirty-plus tasks that have to be done indefinitely, day in and day out, that take a ton of risk and hard work? Hopefully, that answer is crystal clear, and my breakdown gives you more insight on why busi-

Task	One Time or Ongoing	Difficulty	Risk	Work Required
Conceiving Original Business Idea	Once	Low	Low	Little
Conceiving Business Model	Once	Low	Low	Little
Creating Initial Business Plan	Once	Low	Low	Little
Fine Tuning Business Model	Ongoing	High	High	Lots
Creating Updated Business Plans	Ongoing	High	High	Lots
Hiring Employees	Ongoing	High	High	Lots
Managing Employees	Ongoing	High	High	Lots
Training Employees	Ongoing	High	High	Lots
Investing Money	Ongoing	High	High	Lots
Taking on Risk & Opportunity Cost	Ongoing	High	High	Lots
Designing Products/Services	Ongoing	High	High	Lots
Setting Pricing	Ongoing	High	High	Lots
Finding Vendor Partners	Ongoing	High	High	Lots
Manufacturing Products	Ongoing	High	High	Lots
Finding Retailers or Resellers	Ongoing	High	High	Lots
Building Out Your Store	Once/Ongoing	High	High	Lots
Performing Services	Ongoing	High	High	Lots
Identifying Customers	Ongoing	High	High	Lots
Marketing to Customers	Ongoing	High	High	Lots
Servicing Customers	Ongoing	High	High	Lots
Performing Customer Service	Ongoing	High	High	Lots
Automating Your Systems	Ongoing	High	High	Lots
Managing Technology	Ongoing	High	High	Lots
Managing Logistics	Ongoing	High	High	Lots
Following the Competition	Ongoing	High	High	Lots
Outmaneuvering the Competition	Ongoing	High	High	Lots
Creating New Innovations	Ongoing	High	High	Lots
Managing Your Brand	Ongoing	High	High	Lots
Protecting Intellectual Property	Ongoing	High	High	Lots
Decreasing Operating Costs	Ongoing	High	High	Lots
Managing Your Service Providers	Ongoing	High	High	Lots
Administrative Work	Ongoing	High	High	Lots
Growing the Business	Ongoing	High	High	Lots

ness concept ideas have no value so that you, like me, can also make peace with not getting compensated for them.

Why the Word "Scheme" Usually Follows the Phrase "Get Rich Quick"

Many people who want to get compensated for their business ideas are basically get-rich-quick type of people (otherwise known as lazy and/ or delusional). There is no getting rich quickly in business. Businesses require work. Here is my final attempt to demonstrate why you can't depend on ideas to get rich quickly.

There is a young man who calls me every six to nine months. He was pawned off on me—I mean "referred" to me—by one of the lawyers I do a lot of business with. Sometimes referrals are great, and sometimes referrals are someone's way of passing the buck. This particular situation is the latter, and I have never forgiven my lawyer friend for this "referral." I will call this young man Chad. Chad is desperate to make money from ideas, but doesn't have much else to offer.

Chad first contacted me because he knew of a great niche food manufacturing and marketing business that he wanted to buy. He had a contact (I use that word very loosely, as it was his word, not mine) who was a part of said company's board of directors. This contact apparently told Chad that the company's shareholders would consider selling the company for the right price. He wanted to see if I could help him raise the money to purchase the business.

I will keep a long story very short. When asked how much money he was going to contribute, Chad had none. Not $10,000, not $1,000; he literally didn't have a penny to contribute toward the potentially multimillion-dollar purchase price. When I asked Chad what his previous experience was in the food business that he was going to bring to the table ostensibly to help grow the business and create more value from it, he said he had none. Invariably, I told him with no money and no experience, he wasn't going to make a great partner for any investors who might consider helping purchase that food company. He was expecting to earn ownership and even a management position in the company, but what was his added value to the business going forward?

His answer; "It was my idea to buy it." I quickly explained that it wasn't a very novel idea and that without anything else to contribute, he wasn't going to be able to make that happen. I thought he understood, and Chad dropped that idea.

Chad and I had many similar conversations relating to other "ideas." My most recent contact with Chad was a few months ago. I felt a bit of dread when I heard his voice on the other end of the phone, but I always do try to provide a few words of encouragement (or a quick reality check, as the case may be) when possible. This time, Chad informed me that he knew of a business that was struggling that he again wanted to buy, but his "financing" (again, his words, not mine) had fallen through, and he wanted to see if I could help him find new financing. I was shocked to hear that he had financing in place for an acquisition, so I was compelled to learn more.

I shouldn't have been. He told me that his intended acquisition target was a publicly traded company. At the time, it had investment bankers representing it as it explored the possibility of a sale. As for his "financing," it was as follows: the business had certain valuable assets that exceeded the value of the business, in his opinion. He knew a second company that would pay more for those certain assets than the public value of the target company. He was—in his mind—going to finance the purchase of the business by selling the assets of the company off to this second company, then use the proceeds to buy the original business and keep the leftover cash. Clearly, the investment banker explained to him that he didn't own the assets of the company and so it wasn't an option for him to sell them in advance of actually buying the business.

Once again, Chad had no money and wanted financing to buy the business. I tried to explain that if the certain assets had value that could be extracted by selling them to another company, the company would just pursue that strategy itself because its shareholders would want to receive that value. Above and beyond that issue, was again, how was he going to get a financing partner if he wasn't contributing any money?

Again, it was his "idea." You can now visualize me pounding my head against the wall. Chad, like many other potential entrepreneurs, is enamored by his ideas. They think they are valuable. They are not.

Chad is constantly looking for get-rich-quick opportunities. There is a reason that the word "scheme" usually follows the words "get," "rich," and "quick." It is because in reality, that doesn't exist. With the über-rare lottery-type exception, real riches follow hard work. It follows risk, dedication, and a bit of luck and fortune. There is no real trade for new business ideas. Even if you are an inventor, you have to do more than conceptualize your idea—you need to show that it works. Work is required in terms of patenting, prototyping, and more, to turn an idea into something with monetary value. If Chad stopped thinking of schemes and actually did some work, he might eventually have something to offer in terms of money and experience. Think of what he could potentially bring to the table in ten years if he focused and made an actual effort to create real value in a business? It could be quite a lot, but I have a bad feeling that ten years from now, Chad and I will still be talking about his "ideas."

Nobody's Buying Just an Idea

As noted in a previous chapter, the number one attribute that professional investors look for when they invest in a business is the entrepreneur(s) behind the business. If they believe you can take a business from an idea to a valuable entity, then you and your idea are investment-worthy. If you are in love with your ideas and think that is where the big value lies, then you are not investment-worthy. Basically, if you are too lazy to do anything other than think of ideas, stay far away from the business path. In fact, if any of the following apply to you, you should just forget it; it isn't going to happen:

- You have an idea that you want to sell.
- You have an idea that you want someone else to execute without you being centrally involved in making it happen.
- You think your idea is going to allow you to get rich quickly.

- The more work you do to implement your business idea, the more value you will receive, because the value is all in the implementation.

Obsessed with Your Idea

Before I move on, here is one other quick issue with business ideas. Sometimes you get a great business idea that you become obsessed with it. As opposed to the lazy, get-rich-quick dreamers, you are actually totally willing to do the work to make the idea happen. In fact, it is all you want to do; you will do anything it takes to get it done, and the reason is that you are in love with your business idea.

Now, it is great to have a passion for a business—that is a helpful element if you want to be successful—but I have met countless entrepreneurs who want to make their business idea a reality so badly that they don't do much research beyond thinking about the business idea. Their obsessions are rooted in a handful of reasons. They want to leave their mark on society, they "know" it will make them money, or some other non-reality-based reason.

The problem is that the business idea is where they stop working. They never really get to the business model or to the customer need with any real research or thought. They just extrapolate that if they think it is a great idea or that everyone will want it, then everyone will, right? Wrong.

There are a lot of business ideas that would serve a customer need but don't have a means to make money. For example, there was an online delivery service back in the big dot-com boom called Kozmo.com. You could go to its website and the company would deliver snacks, movies, and other small goodies to your location for free in under an hour. When I lived in San Francisco in the late 1990s, I used Kozmo. com to bring cartons of ice cream to my office when I had to pull all-nighters at work. It was a very popular service among my friends and colleagues. Kozmo.com addressed a customer need—access to snacks and sundries on demand—but couldn't make money from it. It wasn't making enough money to justify the costs of delivery and running the business—including paying the delivery driver and order taker, or paying for gas, marketing, etc. Kozmo.com started to charge a minimum fee, but that changed the customer demand. The customer wanted access, but only if it was free with no minimum charge. Even though the company had raised a lot of money, had a high-profile business partner in Starbucks, and had a business model that satisfied the customer, the business couldn't make money. Kozmo.com went out of business in just a couple of years.

Then, there are the people who think there is a major customer need when there isn't one. In my review of more than a thousand business plans, I have seen all kinds of plans that offer goods and services that ultimately aren't needed, let alone desired, by customers. This is particularly an issue with people who want to be creative and just hope that there will be someone who likes what they put out, rather than working backward from the needs of the target customers.

If you are going to obsess over a business idea, it better be because you are satisfying an actual customer need or want in a way that can make some money. If not, then you should probably keep your day job.

ENDNOTES:

1. Giving a shout out to my friend Dave who assisted in the creation and brainstorming of many of these useless ideas!
2. Kent German, "Top 10 Dot-Com Flops," CNET, http://www.cnet.com/1990-11136_1-6278387-1.html.
3. Claire Saliba, "With Webvan Gone, Where Will Online Shoppers Turn?" *E-Commerce Times*, July 10, 2001, http://www.ecommercetimes.com/story/11884.html.
4. http://www.entrepreneur.com/startingabusiness/successstories/article180692.html.
5. David Sweet, "How Upstart UFC Crushed Its Competition," MSNBC, Nov. 5, 2008, http://www.msnbc.msn.com/id/27562254/.
6. CNBC, *As Seen on TV* documentary.

PERSONAL BRAINSTORM

TARGET FOCUS—MOTIVATIONS:
Assessing How Your Idea Influences Your Motivation

Note: You can choose to write down your answers to your personal brainstorms or just reflect upon them.

Check your baseline motivation list to see if one of your motivations is that you have a great business idea. If so, ask yourself if you are motivated to start a new idea because you believe your idea is valuable.

Now, assign your business idea a value of zero dollars. Now ask yourself if you are still interested in starting the business. If your answer is no, then cross the "I have a great idea" reason off of your baseline motivations list. If you are still interested, think about what else you have at this time that may be of value. This could include:

- Achieving milestones, such as building a working prototype, landing paying customers or filing defensible patents; or
- Bringing unparalleled experience, knowledge and/or relationships to the table.

Think about what value you have created to date and can bring to bear in a new business. Is this enough to keep you motivated to succeed and for how long? When you evaluate your Entrepreneur Equation, you will want to think about these types of items and what they can do to decrease the risk and/or increase the rewards of owning your own business. Creating value helps you to stack the odds of success in your favor.

8

There Is a Reason
That You Enjoy Your Hobby
(Hint: It's Not Work)

I N THE MANY DISCUSSIONS I have had with entrepreneurs over the past fifteen years, one of the top ten reasons entrepreneurs give for wanting to start a certain business is that they dream of doing their hobby full time. They love playing golf, collecting figurines, dancing—you name it—and because they enjoy it, they think that their key to career happiness is to pursue something related to their hobby full time.

There are two sides to this issue. First, I am a huge supporter of the theory that you need to be passionate about what you do in order to maximize your success. I do believe that businesses that have upper management and owners who are in the same demographic as their target customer, and who use and enjoy the type of goods or services produced by their company, are better at understanding the customer perspective. This makes for more successful businesses.

On the other hand, part of the reason that we enjoy our hobbies is because they are done in our free time. They are—by definition, leisure—

not work. We enjoy our hobbies because we do them at our discretion and control. We don't have to worry about them producing a paycheck. We can relax when we pursue our hobbies.

Unmasking the "Wizard"

What is your favorite food? Maybe it's ice cream, pizza, chocolate, or steak? Whatever it is, think of that favorite food that brings you joy to eat. Now, what if someone made you eat that food and only that food every day? Pizza for breakfast, lunch, and dinner. Pizza for snacks and for dessert. Pizza when you were sick or healthy, home or out to dinner. That is it, you are 100 percent committed to pizza. Most of you would get sick of pizza after a while. While it may be your favorite food amongst other choices, if you were forced to eat it every day, it would probably lose much of its appeal. This is the same with hobbies. They are great because you aren't compelled to pursue them. Once a hobby crosses the line to become something you must do to earn a living, your relationship with the hobby changes.

This happened to me when I used to collect toys. I was a very avid collector, and since I pursue everything I do with ridiculous zeal, I amassed several extremely rare collections featuring prototypes and hard-to-find exotic toys. Several years into my "addiction," I took on my first toy industry client. At first I was thrilled, as now I had a role in the inner workings of something about which I was truly passionate. However, as I got more involved with the client and had access to anything I wanted, the thrill of the hunt (a critical part of the collecting hobby) died down. I learned about how the toys were conceived, and some of the intrigue was lost. The whole experience was sort of like Dorothy and her friends peering behind the curtain to find that the Wizard of Oz was not an awesome, powerful stud but rather some regular little guy. It killed the fantasy and the magic: the mystique of the wizard was gone. This was the same feeling I had as I peered behind the curtain of the magical world of toys. It wasn't so magical anymore. This was great for my bank account, but not great for my hobby.

Passion Doesn't Guarantee a Living

My experience with my toy client also gave me additional insight into some other issues relating to the hobby-as-a-business phenomenon. Many hobbyists believe that because they understand a particular hobby (and some know everything there is to know about their hobby from the hobbyist perspective), it would be easy for them to transition into a business focused on the hobby. There is an incredible amount of naïveté regarding how difficult it is to run a business. Just because you understand the product or service of a business doesn't mean that you can effectively run a business in that industry.

With my various clients, I have seen hobbyist customers who will openly blog or post online about issues such as the companies' prices being too high. Customers have suggested that the retail price of certain items be revised to a price that is actually lower than my clients' costs of manufacturing those goods. Also, many of the hobbyists aren't realistic about the businesses' ongoing costs and expenses. Sometimes, they don't grasp the need for companies' employees to be paid actual competitive wages. They don't seem to realize that just because it is a hobby to them doesn't mean that everyone involved wants to work for a reduced rate (or for free). They also believe that if they were in charge, they could circumvent things that are completely outside of a company's control, such as shipping delays due to containers being caught up in U.S. customs.

Another issue I have seen with hobbyists that want to start hobby-based businesses is that many hobby niches aren't large enough to support a full business. As Pam Slim notes in *Escape from Cubicle Nation*, "intense passion for something and a viable business model to turn this passion into a decent living are two totally different things."

It may be great that you love to knit holders for the heads of your golf clubs in the shapes of cute animals, but that doesn't mean there is a bona fide business that can be based around it. Using the 10 percent profit proxy for healthy products companies (which will be discussed in further in chapter 25), if you want to make $50,000 a year, you would have to sell about $500,000 worth of knit animal toppers every year. If you sell them for ten dollars wholesale, that is 50,000 pieces that you would have to sell each and every year (which is around 200 each day, assuming a typical business workweek) to make that $50,000 salary. In many hobby niches, this is completely unattainable or at least highly challenging (as I imagine it might be with knit animal toppers for golf clubs).

Another problem is that hobbies are all about *your* likes and wants, and businesses are all about your customers' likes and wants. This is an especially hard transition for a lot of creative hobbyists to make. You may love designing classy fashion and are appalled at tacky outfits. As a hobbyist, if someone wants you to make a pair of orange and purple polka-dotted, bell-bottom jeans, you can easily say no. But if you are a business owner, passing on the job may cost you a customer, which you may not be able to afford. As a business owner, what matters most is what your customers want because they are the ones paying you.

As mentioned in previous chapters, when you start a business, you actually spend a small portion of the time doing what it is you love to do. If you love teaching dance and want to open a dance studio, you don't get to teach dance all day. You have to find customers, collect payment, find other employees, manage paperwork, take daily phone calls from Joey's mom during which you continually explain that her son is not the next Mikhail Baryshnikov, keep the studio clean, do your accounting, and a whole host of other things. If you are really convinced that you love your hobby and want to do something related to it each and every day, you may be better served getting a job in the same industry. This way, you can entertain your passion without the risk of having to create a sustainable business yourself.

The "Jobbie" Phenomenon

When hobbyists want to make money from their hobby, often they end up with what I call a "jobbie." A jobbie is a hobby disguised as a business or a career. This happens because, as noted, someone decides to make a product or offer a service associated with a hobby. Or, they have a pursuit in an area that they love that doesn't really make them a full salary. My litmus test is that if you are pursuing the endeavor full time and are not making in profit—not sales—the minimum wage (currently $7.25 per hour at the federal level, higher in some states) on an hourly basis and have no real, credible plans to do so, you have a jobbie. Additionally, if you are not pursuing your endeavor on a full-time basis, and are rather dabbling and making some cash on the side, you also have a jobbie.

Jobbies tend to disproportionately affect certain groups, such as stay-at-home moms, creative types, recent college graduates, and good-old dreamers. There is nothing wrong with a jobbie inherently. It is actually *great* if you can make a bit of extra money from your hobby or can support your hobby, instead of having a hobby that just sucks up your money with nothing to show for it except for some fond memories. Just be realistic about it and know what it is. Make sure that you are not dependent on the jobbie as a source of income. You are not going to do yourself any favors by pretending that you are starting a business that ultimately goes nowhere because it didn't have the foundation to be a business. Also, when you have a jobbie, you can sucker yourself into buying crazy amounts of inventory, spending an outrageous sum on a high-end website, and costing yourself a lot of money with delusions about your jobbie's potential. Jobbyists sometimes dream that they will make huge sums of money from their side business. If you think that you are going to make a ton of money, create a real business plan, complete with financial statements and reasonable assumptions, and then evaluate whether it is a bona fide business opportunity or a jobbie.

You can also delay making real money by kidding yourself that this jobbie is actually going to become a full-blown business. Sometimes that is the point of a jobbie—a crutch to fall on so that you don't have to get a real job. Just be honest with yourself, even if you aren't with those around you.

That being said, a jobbie may actually be a perfect alternative to starting a real business. If you can pursue your passion and make a bit of side money, you may be able to satisfy your personal wants and needs without taking on an inordinate amount of risk (again, assuming you are cognizant that you are starting a jobbie and not investing at the same levels that you would for a bona fide business).

A jobbie can also be a good stepping stone for you if you are evaluating a business down the road. It will allow you to test out interest in your products and services on a small scale and see if you can maintain your passion for the opportunity (and your customers) before you quit your day job. You just need to make sure that if you are going to move your jobbie into a bona fide business, that you evaluate the scope of that undertaking with a thorough and honest assessment.

> A JOBBIE CAN ALSO BE A GOOD STEPPING STONE FOR YOU IF YOU ARE EVALUATING A BUSINESS DOWN THE ROAD. IT WILL ALLOW YOU TO TEST OUT INTEREST IN YOUR PRODUCTS AND SERVICES ON A SMALL SCALE AND SEE IF YOU CAN MAINTAIN YOUR PASSION FOR THE OPPORTUNITY (AND YOUR CUSTOMERS) BEFORE YOU QUIT YOUR DAY JOB.

I urge you to be very cautious about assuming that you can turn your leisure-time passion into a true business that will provide an ample reward to be worth the risk. In most cases, the risk/reward balance won't be there. If it isn't, don't quit your day job; just look forward to your free time where you can pursue your hobby and feel fortunate that you have the balance in your life to have free time to pursue a passion. If you can make a jobbie out of your hobby, then more power to you, but don't get delusions of grandeur and think that a windfall is around the corner without some additional in-depth evaluation.

EXERCISE 4

TARGET FOCUS—MOTIVATIONS:
Should You Have a Hobby or a Jobbie?

If wanting to pursue one of your hobbies for a living is one of your motivating factors, write down the answers to the following questions:

1. What are the benefits of separating your hobby from your job?

2. How would you feel if you were no longer able to pursue your hobby in your free time?

3. In relation to your hobby, are you willing to put your customers' needs before your own?

4. Can you create a jobbie?
   - If so, what is the maximum investment you want to risk to make some money on the side from your hobby?
   - How might this serve you better than creating a job-business or business?
   - Could a jobbie serve as a starting point to evaluate whether there is a legitimate and robust business model in the area of your hobby? If so, how?

Evaluate these answers to decide: (a) if you want to pursue any money-making strategy from your hobby at all and (b) if yes, whether you would be better served with a jobbie than a true business?

9

You Will Still Have to
Work with People

SOMETIMES, WANTING TO LEAVE YOUR JOB and start a business stems not just from escaping a particular boss or set of co-workers or even from fantasies of being in charge. Sometimes—and this happens more frequently than you might imagine—it is that you don't like to work with other people in general. You are a loner, or prefer to be a solo artist, but businesses don't work when only one person is involved.

I can truly appreciate that it is difficult to work with other people. People, especially ones that you are compelled to work with day in and day out, can be really annoying. They can smell funky, talk too loudly, do poor work or hang around your office when you are busy. However, people are part of life, and if you want to earn a living, whether at someone else's company or your own, people are going to be involved in some way, shape, or form.

I hope that one of the lessons that this book has already impressed upon you is that customers are the single-most-important asset of your business. If you have no paying customers, you cannot have a business. If you have customers, even if you don't have anything to sell, you can find a way to make money; you can beg for or borrow someone else's goods and services to sell if you have customers. Having no customers, however, is the worst fate possible. You may have the best services or goods, a great place of business, snappy marketing materials, smart employees, and more, but if you have no paying customers, it makes no difference; you will not make any money, and your business will fail.

The last time I checked, those with the ability to pay for goods and services are classified as people. Even if you work with animals or plants, their humans are the real customers who pay you in the end. Until cats, dogs, and trees step up and get jobs so that they can become paying customers, I see no way around having your customers be people.

Since your customers are people, you by definition as an entrepreneur need to work with people. You need to work with them closely, possibly more closely than you did when you worked in your previous job, because these customers decide whether or not you make money and cash a paycheck. You need to sell these people your goods and services, you need to convince them to hire your firm or continue to patronize your place of business, and lucky you—you have to make sure they pay in full and on time. There is definitely a lot of people contact in the customer realm. Even if the product or service that your business sells isn't people-oriented (such as writing computer code), someone needs to hire you and your company, and someone needs to pay you; if not, you don't have a business. Those "someones" are people, and important people at that.

The same goes for other aspects of the business. If you take money from investors, banks, or other lending institutions, those are staffed by people. You will need to work with them to make sure the business is growing and succeeding, and if it isn't, you are going to be seeing and hearing a lot from those people.

You will likely need employees at some point if you are going to grow, and while there have been some promising developments in robot technology, it isn't quite optimized yet, so you are going to have to hire—gasp—people!

You will require professional services for your business. You will have a person as your lawyer, another person as your accountant, and you will have to hire people for any other services you require, from technology to marketing to janitorial services. Your landlord is going to be a person.

If you sell a product, your vendors or suppliers are going to be people that have people working for them.

So actually, you have probably increased the number of people you have to work with daily exponentially just by making the decision to start your own business. If your main motivation to start a business is to not work with people, or at least minimize the number of people you work with, you are looking in the wrong direction. As I recently told an entrepreneur for whom I performed a FIRED-UP entrepreneur assessment, if you don't like people that much, there is probably a much easier, more cost-efficient solution to your problem. Go to your current boss and ask for an office with a door you can close to keep people from bothering you at work. Or, see if you can negotiate to telecommute from home one or more days a week so that you have some physical separation from the people. Those quick fixes will be more effective for your problem, with a lot less risk, than going the entrepreneurial route.

> IF YOUR MAIN MOTIVATION TO START A BUSINESS IS TO NOT WORK WITH PEOPLE, OR AT LEAST MINIMIZE THE NUMBER OF PEOPLE YOU WORK WITH, YOU ARE LOOKING IN THE WRONG DIRECTION.

Okay, maybe you misspoke. You can handle working with people, but you don't like to work in teams. If you can't work in a team, how are you going to manage employees (and foster teamwork amongst them)? Maybe you can work with people if you pick the best employees. Well, you can only pick your employees from amongst those who apply, and if you aren't paying a primo salary, the best employees are probably not going to apply.

If you do find someone you can tolerate, there is no guarantee that they will like you or your company, or want to work for you for an extended period of time. Whatever people-issue you have in your job, it will become worse and more intense when you're the boss. Plus, these employees will have a hand in deciding your business's success or failure, something on which you have a whole lot riding. To minimize the people interaction, go with a job over a business any day.

EXERCISE 5

TARGET FOCUS—MOTIVATIONS:
Working with (or without) Others

Think about what it is you don't like about your current interactions at work. Write down:

1. The names of the people who cause you issues, and

2. What those specific issues are.

Looking at this list, would these issues improve or be removed if:

- you took on another role at your existing company?
- you took a job at another company?
- you started a business?

Now evaluate:
- if each issue is related specifically to a person or if there really is another issue that is causing your stress or unhappiness;
- if there is a way for you to improve that issue without taking on a lot of risk; and
- if you need to start a business to solve your issue—and if so, evaluate if the risk of starting a business is worth solving that issue.

You may want to ask a trusted source if you need objective feedback.

Oh, and be sure to cross the "I don't want to work with people" reason off your baseline motivation list if it is there!

2 B

Assessing Your Timing

Sometimes, the issue of entrepreneurship compatibility is not so much that it is not right for you but rather that it is not right for you *right now*. Timing is a key ingredient to success, and several of the areas in my five-step FIRED-UP entrepreneurship assessment deal specifically with timing. Some people who would otherwise be great at running their own business shouldn't open a business today because the timing is off for them.

While there is probably never the perfect time to start a business, there are quite clearly some less-than-ideal times. There are also many things you can do to stack the odds in your favor. While you will still have to successfully execute your business plan, and it doesn't 100 percent guarantee success, being *prepared* will certainly improve your chances exponentially.

Factors such as experience, skills, and personal responsibilities are all very dynamic. So is the ability to learn functional areas of business that you may be less familiar with. Your learning curve and your personal circumstances will change over time, so the purpose of the following chapters is to help you evaluate if now is a good time for you to pursue a business endeavor or if there are things that you can do to shift the risk/reward proposition toward a direction that is more favorable in your Entrepreneur Equation.

10

Your Personal Responsibilities: a.k.a. You Can't Make Two Things Your Number One Priority

ONE OF THE MOST DYNAMIC FACTORS in your life is who and what you are responsible for at different points in time. That's why the "R" in FIRED-UP stands for *Responsibilities*, meaning your timing as it relates to your current priorities. Responsibilities are something that entrepreneurs often don't give enough weight to when making the decision to start a business. It is also an area where you really need to be honest with yourself. No blowing smoke up your own behind, okay?

Following are a couple of questions that you should answer honestly, or else you will be doing yourself (and those around you) a disservice. As you respond to these questions, including the subquestions underneath each, it will help you evaluate your responsibilities. In doing so, remember that two things can't simultaneously be your number one priority.

Two Questions to Ask Yourself

1. Am I ready and prepared for, and wanting the responsibility of owning a business?

Having a business is like having a child (one that never fully grows up). You are the one responsible for it, no matter what happens. This is something that is going to take a lot of your money, time, and "blood, sweat, and tears." When something goes wrong, you need to fix it. When the security system is tripped at 3 a.m., you have to go to the store and attend to it. When a customer has an issue, you need to deal with it. If responsibility isn't something you are great with (think: consistently forgetting to water the plants, take out the garbage, or pay your bills on time, multiplied by a factor of a hundred), then business ownership is realistically not a good fit for you.

To make your business grow, you need to nurture it. You need to dedicate a whole truckload of time, money, and effort to it. Out of all the things you have going on in your life—including your family and friends, hobbies, and other pursuits—is your business going to be the most important to you? Are you ready to be responsible and make your business a top priority in your life?

2. Who am I responsible for?

It is hard to answer these questions on priorities without taking a look at who you are responsible for. Often you aren't alone, so you need to determine who else feels the impact of your decisions, such as your partner, spouse, and kids. Not only are they affected by your monetary decisions, these individuals are competing for your time and attention. If you have a family, you need to figure out what happens financially if you can't provide for their needs (or more likely their wants) because your money is tied up trying to make the business a success. You are not only risking your assets and future, you are also risking theirs. You may be willing to sacrifice now for a potential payoff later, but are they?

There is often more on the line than just your salary, which brings up a lot of important questions that relate not just to you, but to your family as well, such as:

- What if you lose your entire initial investment?
- What if you use your house as collateral or to guarantee a loan and then lose your house?
- Will starting your business mean you have to use your child's education fund? If so, is that fair to your child?
- What happens to your family in the worst-case scenario?

We all want to think that we are going to win, but what happens if you lose? You need to be as realistic about the downside as you are optimistic about the upside, especially pertaining to how that downside impacts those you are responsible for.

Sometimes starting and growing a business doesn't jeopardize your entire savings, but rather it requires smaller sacrifices and change from your family. A lot of people don't like change, especially when it is preventable. Your family may be accustomed to a certain lifestyle—new clothes, yearly trips, trading in their cars every few years for an upgrade—that you will no longer be able to afford. If things go awry, the financial impact could have an emotional impact on your family.

What if you have to tell your child that he can't go on his class trip because you need the money to buy a new computer for your business? How will that make you feel? How will that make him feel? What importance do you place on that impact? Or perhaps your wife now has to drive a station wagon with wood paneling circa *The Brady Bunch* instead of a shiny new Lexus SUV. Is she going to be happy about that, and if not, how does that affect the whole family? Can you be happy if your family isn't?

There are other effects on you and your stakeholders that happen when you have to prioritize your business. When you have to take care of your business, even if the driving force behind it is to provide for your family, it usually means more time spent away from family. Is your significant other strong and supportive enough to be able to run the household—without resentment—while you focus on your business? How will your kid feel when you miss every one of his baseball games, or can't attend her ballet recital because you are focusing on this business? Time is a more precious resource than money, and while money can accumulate over time, our available time just keeps decreasing; there is no way around this.

You need to ask yourself honestly if now is the right time to start a business given your other responsibilities, priorities, and stakeholders in your life. While I am not suggesting that you let anyone hold you back, you do need to know who else is a stakeholder. And I am not suggesting fake responsibilities like the mom who wants her son to be a doctor instead of a Jani-King franchisee. That is just your mom putting her dreams on you; you are not responsible for that. I am talking about your partner, spouse, and children. Or maybe an ill parent that needs you to care for her. These are real stakeholders.

Not Right Now versus Never

Realizing that your current responsibilities and priorities make starting a business ill-advised right now does not necessarily mean that entrepreneurship is never right for you. It may simply mean that it's not right for you right now. It is a whole lot easier to bet the farm when you are the only person who owns the farm, or if the farm isn't required to pay for your child's education or your mother's chemotherapy. When you evaluate your timing for entrepreneurship, think of what is at stake for the other stakeholders in your life and evaluate the risk and reward from their perspective as well as yours. As bad as you will feel if you lose the farm, you will feel even worse if your child hates you or your wife divorces you for screwing up their futures.

PERSONAL BRAINSTORM

TARGET FOCUS—TIMING:
Evaluating Your Stakeholders

Do you have family members who are stakeholders in your decision to start a business? If so, reflect on what lifestyle changes and other sacrifices your family will have to make if you start a business. Once you have identified those areas, you should talk to them openly and candidly to find out how they feel about those possibilities. Use this information to evaluate if now is a good time for you to start the business, or if putting it off by several years can create a positive impact and/or alleviate some downside risk for you.

11

Wanting to Run
before You Walk

THE PHILOSOPHER Friedrich Nietzsche said, "He who would learn to fly one day must first learn to stand and walk and run and climb and dance; one cannot fly into flying."

Not that I read Nietzsche. I actually heard it quoted by Eddie Murphy's character in the 1980s cult classic *Coming to America* (a great source for philosophy, I know). Regardless of where I initially heard it, it makes a valid point that applies to many attitudes on business.

Most people want to go right to flying or, at least, from walking to flying. They see what someone else is doing, and they do not process the amount of experience they have. They don't think about all of the time and dedication it took to perfect the craft.

Getting to the "Big Leagues" Takes Practice

If you know anything about me, you probably know how much I love the National Football League, in part because of the mastery required by its players. The world-class NFL players don't just become stars overnight. Many started playing in Pop Warner leagues while in elementary school. The majority of them played high school and/or college football or some equivalent foreign league. Each of them practiced for hours on end to improve their skills.

Then, even after they make the NFL, the best players continue to hone their craft. They still practice multiple times a week. They review their competition by watching game films, come up with strategies for future games, and complete drills on blocking and tackling, all of which they have done for years.

They have experience gained from years of practice, and which they continue to refine. People can't just wake up one day, decide to play in the NFL, and suit up the following Sunday. They would get creamed.

The same goes for business. You can't just wake up one day and fall into an industry or a business in which you have no experience and expect to be an immediate star. You will get creamed.

I am sure NFL players would have loved skipping the hours on the practice gridiron doing high-knee drills through tires, running laps, lifting weights, and pushing blocking sleds. However, that is part of the foundation required to get to the next level. You need to do the same in the realm of business. This means learning both the industry and the aspects of business you may not be as familiar with, such as financial statements and accounting, before you are ready for the big leagues—starting a business on your own.

Experience Is Different From Business Experience

When you gain experience, you need to learn it from the business perspective. Just because you are familiar with widgets doesn't mean you would know how to run a widget business. If you collect model cars, you may know every model that was produced in the last ten years, but that doesn't mean you know how to manufacture them. That doesn't mean you could negotiate with vendors, manage retail accounts, and build a sales force to sell them. You may have gotten your hair cut every two months for your entire life, but that doesn't mean you know how to run a beauty salon. When you are familiar with something, you may have a perspective on it, but that does not equate to business experience.

Experience is not about age; it is about relatable skills, practice, and relevant knowledge. I have known college graduates that had been working in a given industry since they were legally able to do so, and I also know forty year olds that have as much experience in their industry of choice as a goldfish. That is okay. The great thing about experience is that you can always build it; you just need to put in the time and effort.

Take, for example, New York–based fashion designer Jason Wu, a client and friend of mine. Jason gained national recognition in 2009 when the new First Lady, Michelle Obama, chose one of his stunning one-of-a-kind gowns to wear to a slew of inaugural balls. He was only twenty-six at the time. You may look at this twenty-six-year-old who designed a white chiffon dress that now resides in the Smithsonian Institution and label him an overnight sensation. However, he is far from it.

Jason has been working in the fashion industry since he was sixteen. He started out designing miniature couture for fashion dolls, which caught the eye of collectible fashion doll manufacturer Integrity Toys. Jason was first brought on board to design for a specific line of dolls, and his talent was immediately evident. Jason proactively sought exposure to the other aspects of the business. He learned more about the business, and in short order, was promoted to the position of company creative director, a post he still holds today.

Knowing that he eventually wanted to design people-sized fashion, for women in particular, Jason enrolled in Parsons The New School for Design (which as any *Project Runway* fan knows, is the prestigious fashion school in New York where Tim Gunn was on staff). He knew that, in addition to honing his design skills, he needed to learn more about the business. To accomplish that, Jason pursued an internship with Narciso Rodriguez. About his internship experience, Jason said, "It was a small environment and I was with one other intern...and I got to see a little bit more of the industry at work. I learned how a design company ran, which I had never seen before."

This experience gave him the reality check about what it meant to be a designer. "I wanted to design," he said. "I didn't know until I interned how much went into producing a show and selling to fashion buyers. That was very important for me to see and understand." It is also interesting to note that the other intern with Jason at Narciso Rodriguez decided after seeing the business side that he just wanted to focus on design, and so rather than starting a business, he went to work in the industry.

By the age of twenty-three, Jason was ready to become an entrepreneur. He took his experience in both the industry and business and started his eponymous clothing line for women. He won the Fashion Group International's Rising Star Award and was a finalist for the 2008 Vogue/CFDA Fashion Fund. So, while it is easy to see why some who don't know him view Jason at age twenty-six as an overnight sensation, that "overnight sensation" actually had ten years of focused business experience behind him.

BY SEEING THE INNER WORKINGS OF A BUSINESS, YOU CAN GET MORE INFORMATION ON WHETHER YOU WOULD EVEN WANT TO OWN A BUSINESS. YOU WILL WORK WITH MANAGERS YOU WILL WANT TO EMULATE, AS WELL AS OTHER CO-WORKERS WHOSE BUSINESS STYLE YOU WILL WANT TO MAKE SURE YOU NEVER FOLLOW.

Many college students study entrepreneurship with the hopes of starting a company. However, most college graduates don't have the business experience, as Jason Wu did, to successfully be able to do so. That is why even though financially your risks may be at an all-time low, it is still sometimes advisable to take your first steps in the real world with a job where you can learn on someone else's dime. Jason Wu started with a collectible fashion doll company and then interned for a well-known women's fashion house. Think of it as the continuation of your college education, but this time, instead of you paying for it, they pay you. (It's much better that way, don't you think?)

Every experience you encounter, positive and negative, will give you a richer toolbox from which to work. By seeing the inner workings of a business, you can get more information on whether you would even want to own a business. You will work with managers you will want to emulate, as well as other co-workers whose business style you will want to make sure you never follow.

Sometimes You Have to Be Willing to Go Backward to Move Forward

In addition to business experience, you also need to garner industry experience. I always advocate that if you want to start a business and you haven't had significant experience in that industry, you need to learn that industry before you are qualified to start a business in that field. If you have been working in a different industry, this can be especially difficult because ego gets in the way. Why should you, the MBA-holding Mensa member, take a job as a busboy in a restaurant alongside people who haven't attended college and may not even speak English? Because you don't know anything about restaurants and you are about to invest hundreds of thousands of dollars to start one, that's why!

You are not taking a low-paying restaurant job as a means to earn a wage. You don't intend to stay in that position; however, you need the relevant experience. You need to learn the business, and it is great that you can have an opportunity to learn while actually getting paid.

This may be hard to swallow after spending six figures on an advanced degree, or working many years in another industry, but you need to be willing to take two steps backward today to find out if you will be able to take twenty-five steps forward tomorrow. While you are at the restaurant, you can evaluate if you even like the industry (you will likely find it is more fun to eat spaghetti than to serve it every day). See if you can get yourself promoted to manager and do a good job at that position. If you can't make manager, or do a lousy job as manager in someone else's restaurant, why would you think you should invest in starting a restaurant business of your own?

Not to mention that if you do start your own restaurant, you need to know how to perform every job, because if someone doesn't show up one day and you are short on staff, guess who is going to have to fill in? You guessed it—you. It is also easier to manage your employees if you understand their jobs from their perspective, which you can only do if you have performed those jobs. That is why many major restaurant chains mandate that their managers work in each job function in the restaurant for a few weeks as part of the management-training program.

The Training Wheels Come Off *after* You Practice

If you really want to lay the most solid foundation and take on additional risk, I advocate getting help and going the training wheels route. When you first learn to ride a bike, you use training wheels to get the feel of the bike and to boost your confidence. After you practice and gain experience, then off they come.

Potential entrepreneurs don't like this; they always want to run before they walk. They want to ride without the training wheels. What happens then? They crash to the ground (and if they aren't wearing a helmet, smash their heads open). This is because they were too stubborn or had too big of an ego (or perhaps were just too stupid or lazy) to try training wheels first. In a similar vein, it just makes good sense to take golf lessons and practice your swings, drives, and putts before you get out onto the green; or to try out the bunny hill the first time you ski and then practice on more and more difficult terrain before you head over to the black diamond trail. Remember the Bill Gates story from chapter 3? He focused on milestones along his path; he didn't just "try to fly" on day one.

If you are serious about starting a business and you are going to sacrifice for it, investing your own capital, time, and effort, then you want to have the best chances for success. So, get the relevant experience first so that you have the building blocks to make your business successful. Don't tell yourself that you are too old or too powerful to learn. The school of life is about nonstop learning. Even in business, there is continuing education as you grow, so stop looking for the shortcuts. If you are looking for a shortcut, look elsewhere because there are none in entrepreneurship.

EXERCISE 6

TARGET FOCUS—TIMING:
Evaluating Your Experience

For each new business venture you consider, complete the following exercise.

1. Divide a piece of paper into two columns.

2. In the left column, write all of your relevant experience related to (a) your potential new business venture, as well as (b) business ownership in general.

3. In the right column, write down all of the ways you could enhance your relevant experience. Some suggestions include:
   - Interviewing potential customers
   - Shadowing a business owner in your industry
   - Taking on an internship at a direct or indirect competitor
   - Taking on one or more jobs at a similar company and seeing if you do them well
   - Building prototypes
   - Getting tutored in functional areas like accounting, marketing, and contracts

4. Think about how pursuing each of the items on the right side could add to your experience.

5. If you completed each item in your right-hand column, would that give you a new item for your left-hand column?

6. How would pursuing any or all of the items in the right column materially enhance your prospects for success?

You will use this evaluation to further assess your Entrepreneur Equation and decide whether you should start the given business now or if you would be better served by stacking the odds further in your favor by gaining additional experience. This is especially critical if you do not have experience in the industry you are considering, or if you have limited experience and understanding of all of the areas you will be responsible for in your business.

12

When the Heck Are You Going to Have Time to Start a Business?

THE ENTREPRENEURSHIP BUG hits a lot of people while they are at work. We have already touched on the issues of incompetent co-workers and unpleasant office surroundings, as well as actually having to perform something called *work*—all of which make people daydream for a way out. However, never forget that starting or buying a business also requires work. *A lot* of work.

There is a metric ton of work involved in exploring a business model and laying the foundation of a business. You have to research your target customers and the need for your products or services. You have to put together business plans and other materials. You have to do more research on vendors or office locations. You have to build prototypes, write initial code, or achieve early milestones. You have to raise capital. You have to put together a marketing plan. You have to create a corporate structure and much, much more. When you have a job and are working eight- to nine-hour days, and add in commuting, lunch and potty breaks, having dinner, saying a few words to your significant other (and possibly kids), watching *American Idol* and getting some sleep, there isn't a whole lot of free time to spend on starting a business.

If you are working while trying to start a business in your free time, you will either take years to get all the work done (which, by the time you get it done, half the research will be out-of-date) or do a crappy job (i.e., take shortcuts and not do the work), both of which will set you up for failure.

On the other hand, quitting your job and forgoing your weekly paycheck to explore entrepreneurship takes nerve, risk tolerance, and financial security. Many aspiring entrepreneurs can't fathom doing that either (another red flag is waving here, folks…if you are too risk-averse to go without a paycheck for several months, quitting your day job is not advisable).

The (Legal) Problem with Double-Dipping

Some people try to get clever and figure out a way to double-dip and do both endeavors at the same time. In plain language, that means that some people try to lay all of the groundwork for their new business while they are employed. I love this idea in theory; however, there may be a couple of issues with this master plan.

First are the moral issues. Your employer is paying you to spend your work day thinking and working for them. A lot of people feel entitled at their jobs. "I have worked here for years," they say. "They owe it to me." No, your company actually pays you cash, and perhaps gives you benefits, in exchange for your work. That is all they owe you. It is a fair trade, and you can leave if you aren't satisfied with it. It isn't appropriate to use their time, resources, and assets to work on anything other than what it is they are paying you to work on. And if you do it on your lunch break or after hours, you shouldn't be using their resources; their resources should be used to create value for their shareholders, not you.

Some people don't care about the ethics. If the moral argument doesn't sway you, then you may be more persuaded by the legal argument. If you are working for another company, there are actual legal reasons why you can't be working on your new business. First is that pesky paperwork that you may have been given when you first started your job. You may not have read the paperwork, but often it says something along the lines of anything that you create while working for the company, using their resources or otherwise, belongs to the company. That means *anything*. Even if you haven't signed that type of paperwork, companies can make a strong legal claim that if you wrote a business plan using their computers and printed it out with their paper, ink, and printers, made phone calls to potential suppliers using their phones and phone service, or researched the idea using their resources, while they were paying you, they own it.

There is a great high-profile legal case that perfectly illustrates this issue. Carter Bryant was employed by the toymaker, Mattel, in the company's collector Barbie doll division. He was a well-known designer who designed many of Mattel's high-profile collectibles. During his lunch breaks, he started developing and sketching the foundation for a new doll line. These dolls were very different from Barbie; they had an exaggerated, cartoonish appearance. Their clothing had an urban street vibe and reflected more of what modern girls were wearing.

Mr. Bryant presented his concept to the Mattel team, which wasn't interested. For whatever reason, it wasn't a fit for Mattel at that time, and so the team chose not to pursue it. Carter was unfazed by Mattel's rejection and decided he would create a prototype of the dolls on his own time. After hours, he used some of the people he knew in the firm to create some basic mock-ups of what the dolls would look like. When he was satisfied that he had enough groundwork laid, he took the doll concept to a smaller toy company named MGA.

He told MGA that he had designed the dolls in his free time and on his own accord. MGA agreed to partner with him to make and distribute the dolls. The Bratz line was born.

Within a couple of years, the Bratz had become a billion-plus-dollar business. It was one of the greatest successes in the toy industry's history. After Bratz saturated the market and ate into Barbie's profits, Mattel filed a lawsuit against Carter Bryant and MGA saying that it owned the Bratz dolls because they were developed when Carter was working at Mattel. Carter and MGA rejected that notion because the dolls were developed in his free time.

The case went to trial and the courts agreed with Mattel. Mattel owned the Bratz doll line. Despite the fact that the entire commercial development of the line—including the manufacturing, branding, sales, distribution, etc.—happened after Carter Bryant left Mattel and on MGA's dime, and the line was merely in concept form before he left the firm, he had conceived of the idea and the base of the prototypes while he was still employed there, giving Mattel ownership.

While parts of this ruling were overturned on appeal, and ultimately the verdict was overturned during a retrial, giving the line back to MGA, it is estimated that several hundred million dollars in legal fees were spent litigating this case. It has also been reported that Carter Bryant himself personally settled with Mattel privately out of court and MGA contends that the legal battle damaged the Bratz brand.

So, if you start a business which in any way was conceived during your employment elsewhere and/or used any of that employer's resources, even just to lay the foundation, it may not belong to you. If you enjoy any success, you may be risking a major lawsuit. Mattel waited until the Bratz line had become very successful to file its claim. The more success you have, the more likely someone will come searching for pay dirt.

It is always better to test out a business before you take a full leap, but you must be careful. If you can't work on the business while you are at work and you have limited free time, when will you have time to start your business?

PERSONAL BRAINSTORM

TARGET FOCUS—TIMING:
Starting a Business While You Are Employed

If you are currently employed, or have recently left a position, ask yourself the following questions:

- Do you have paperwork that you signed with your current employer preventing you from competing with the business and/or soliciting customers?
- Does your company have a policy that everything developed during your tenure belongs to the company?
- Have you used any of your employer's resources in any way to research or lay the groundwork for your business?
- Are you planning to solicit any existing customers of your employer? How about any prospects of your employer?

If your answer to any of the above questions is "yes," you may have some serious legal restrictions on starting a new business.

Also ask yourself if you are better off leaving your position before you start your business. You may be able to take a part-time job with fewer restrictions in an unrelated industry to make some money while you evaluate your business opportunity. You should consult a lawyer on both points for guidance on your specific set of circumstances to find out what risks there are in starting your business on the side while employed.

13

Often It Is Who You Know versus What You Know

WHEN YOU WERE GROWING UP, were you ever roped into doing fund-raisers under the guise that it was entrepreneurial? Maybe you sold Girl Scout cookies or candy bars for your basketball team. Or perhaps you were tapped to peddle wrapping paper for the student council or pizzas to help build a new school library. It seemed like every organization had some fund-raising product for us to peddle.

The fund-raising groups tried to sweeten the deal by offering prizes. Whoever sold the most of the given product got something coveted by kids like a new bike or an AM/FM radio (today I guess it would be an iPod, but, hey, that was what they gave when I was a kid).

If you considered yourself entrepreneurial, you were probably excited to flex your selling muscles. You traipsed all over the neighborhood selling your fund-raising wares, sure you were going to sell the most and get a new bike.

After a couple of weeks of working every relative and neighbor you knew (and several you didn't), you had sold an impressive several hundred boxes of said product—cookies, frozen pizzas, candy bars, sheets of wrapping paper—whatever. Your win was as good as gold.

115

Then, you got to school and found out that Susie sold five times the amount you did, not because she was a great salesperson with an entre-preneurial spirit, but because she had a wealthy family and her dad was the managing partner at a several-hundred-person law firm and forced each of his underlings to buy twenty boxes of cookies. The dad basically bought the win, the bragging rights, and the bike (which Susie didn't even need because she already had two).

Business is often like that. It is sometimes not what you know, but who you know.

If you don't know Jack, Bo, or anyone else that matters, you may very well be screwed, or at least start with a major disadvantage. The first place that you lose out is in trying to fund your business. If you are an entrepreneur that needs capital, not knowing people with capital is go-ing to make it very difficult for you to get your hands on some.

Investors often invest in a business because they know you or be-cause their friends are doing it. So, if nobody who knows you has the ability to throw some funding your way, there aren't going to be a bunch of others following their lead. This reality becomes a frustrating aspect of starting a business.

If you have a more ambitious business plan, you will be seeking pro-fessional capital. Without the endorsement of someone who has con-nections, you will not likely make it through the sea of business plans that the investors receive each year. They, too, invest in management, and one of their first screens is to see if anyone they trust and respect can vouch for the entrepreneur (or entrepreneurs) involved. That screening process, coupled with the sheer number of inquiries that they receive each year, puts you at an immediate disadvantage in trying to obtain significant financing.

Who *Do* You Know?

The connections (or lack of connections) issue continues to rear its ugly head as you progress in establishing your business. You can often get better deals with everyone from suppliers to professional services firms with a solid introduction. Plus, you want to have some reference checks before you partner with a stranger as an important vendor or legal consultant. Not knowing anyone can cause you to pay more for products and services, receive unfavorable business terms, or make it hard to negotiate a deal at all.

Securing customers is predicated on who you know. If you are in the services business or in another business-to-business industry, landing new customers is often dependent upon getting referrals. I have been on both sides of this. I have received many clients through referrals. I have also lost many engagements because the potential client had a board member with a buddy to whom he wanted to give the business.

My personal worst example of this happened with a company I was courting for a couple of years. I had provided advice and guidance to the company to help prepare them for raising growth capital down the road. As part of the company's preparation for its capital-raising process, it wanted to beef up its board of directors. The management team had a few people in mind, and one of them was a former colleague of mine who was an expert in this particular industry, and who I respected and had previously worked with very closely. I made a personal introduction and provided a formal recommendation to the company to add this person to its board.

My colleague was given a position on the board, and a few months later, when the company was about to engage me and my firm to raise capital for them, this former colleague, who I had recommended formally for his current position with the company, sold me out. He talked the company out of hiring me and my firm in favor of another investment banking firm where his best friend worked.

So, even though I had put forth a ton of effort, built a relationship with this company for more than a year, and knew (and even recommended) the director, I lost the deal (and a $750,000 fee) because someone else was *better* friends with the director.

Connections: When More Is More

The "who you know" thing comes into play all the time. They didn't come up with the "old boys' club" phrase out of thin air. Even if you are in a consumer-oriented business, getting retailers to sell your product, or getting people to recommend your business in the beginning is much more difficult if you don't have a lot of connections, or aren't that keen on using them.

It is the early stages of the business that are the hardest. It is much more difficult to get to the first million in sales than it is to get to the second. It is the first several years and early stages where most businesses struggle and ultimately fail. So, this is the critical time for you to depend on others for assistance.

I know it sucks and creates an unfair disadvantage for the little guy, but it is reality. So, think about what kinds of connections you will need in terms of capital, vendors, professional service providers, customers, and in other aspects of your business. If you don't have any, you may want to make some more friends—preferably wealthy, well-connected ones—before you think about leaving behind your day job.

EXERCISE 7

TARGET FOCUS—TIMING:
Evaluating Your Network

1. Make a list of everyone you know that you think could help you with an aspect of your new business.

2. Put each person into one of three teams:
   - The "A" team being those who would do anything for you.
   - The "B" team being those whom you have a good relationship with but aren't necessarily in your inner circle.
   - The "C" team being those you shook hands with a few times.

3. Next to each name write down each functional area of your business that person could help you with, such as:
   - Raising capital
   - Introductions to potential customers
   - Introductions to vendors

- Technical skills
- Introductions to relevant service providers or performing services as a service provider
- Any other specific areas where you may need help (be sure to list the specific area)

4. Put a star next to anyone you would feel uncomfortable approaching for assistance today.

5. Add to your list any areas/functions where you don't have any contacts and circle those.

6. If you have a number of stars, assess whether having more time (three months, six months, a year) would help you improve the relationships with any "starred" individuals so that you would feel comfortable asking that person for assistance.

7. If you have a number of circles, these represent holes in your current network. If you had more time, where could you work to supplement your network and fill in those gaps? Would you be able to seek out and build relationships with people to help you with the "circled" areas?

Evaluate whether having extra time to build these additional relationships would make a difference in improving the potential for the success of your business, particularly as you evaluate your Entrepreneur Equation at the end of the book.

14

Money Sicknesses Make for an Unhealthy Business

FOR THIS BOOK to be fully effective, it requires you to have a lot of honest conversations with yourself. Now is time for another one of those honest conversations. You need to ask yourself, "What is my relationship with money?" (This exercise only works if you provide a truthful answer.)

A lot of us—myself included—have really messed-up relationships with money. Understanding our relationship with money is critical because it takes money to start or buy a business and to continue to finance the operation of the business. While you are involved with your new business, you need to be able to support yourself and take care of your responsibilities, and that requires money too. Whoever said that "money makes the world go 'round" wasn't kidding.

Sometimes when you are in a relationship, it is hard for you to be objective about that relationship. The same goes for your relationship with money. So try to take a step back, or even get some insight from those who know you well, so that you aren't B.S.–ing yourself when you evaluate your tie to your money, or lack thereof. If you have any of the following issues with money, it is going to be very difficult for you to maximize any new business endeavor.

No Money

This is the easiest money relationship to evaluate. Starting a bona fide business costs money. If you are clever and can barter, borrow, and beg your way into covering a lot of your start-up costs, and have persuaded someone like your parents or a friend to let you live in their basement, or your spouse to support you while you pursue your dream, you may be better off than most, but not having money is an immediate roadblock to entrepreneurship. Even if you consider franchising, most franchisors require an upfront franchise fee and for you to be able to finance the start-up costs. Additionally, many established franchisors (I recommend working with an established franchisor to get the most out of the franchise route) require a minimum net worth from potential franchisees.

THE MORE MONEY AN OUTSIDE INVESTOR CONTRIBUTES, THE MORE OWNERSHIP OF THE BUSINESS THEY WILL REQUIRE. IF YOU START GIVING AWAY OWNERSHIP, YOUR BUSINESS BECOMES MORE AND MORE OF A JOB.

The less money you have, the less able you are to start a business. Businesses are risky, and part of the risk is putting your money on the line. Even if you find investors, they will be less likely to put in money unless you are sharing a substantial part of the risk. Moreover, the more money an outside investor contributes, the more ownership of the business they will require. If you start giving away ownership, your business becomes more and more of a job as you have more people to answer to and less personal participation in the upside of the business.

If you have limited cash, bootstrapping (scrappily starting your business without external capital) may be an option for you. You may also be able to raise capital with a working prototype. However, this is going to favor certain industries and types of business. The entrepreneurs behind a new tech business may be able to raise capital with just a working prototype of its new application. The entrepreneur behind a new retail store may have a much more difficult time under these circumstances. You may decide to scale back and start a smaller business because you don't have much money. But if you go too small, ask yourself how much money you can make from the business and if you can take what you have done and scale it into a larger business opportunity. Based on your answers to those questions, is it worth it?

If you don't have money, you should consider making and saving as much as you can before starting a business. The opportunity will still be there once you have saved up the start-up capital (and if it is not, then it was a fad, not a business, and you dodged a bullet).

Lack of Financial Responsibility

If you can't manage your own finances, then you shouldn't be an entrepreneur trying to manage a business (and implicitly, the business's finances).

Many Americans have lots of debt. If you have debt from credit cards and loans, especially where you are paying a high interest rate, you need to pay that debt down first.

Getting rid of your credit card debt is a no-brainer. You may be paying up to 18 percent per year or more on your credit card balance. You would be thrilled to have an investment that gained 18 percent a year. Another way of looking at this is if you wouldn't take out a major business loan that required you pay 18 percent a year in interest on that loan, then don't do the same on your credit cards. Paying your credit cards off is your best "investment" and should be required before you invest in your own business.

But being responsible with your finances goes much deeper. Financial responsibility is about making good decisions and only buying things when you can afford to do so. If this is not a strong suit for you in your personal life, and if you tend to make bad judgments about your personal expenditures, these issues will be amplified even more for your business. If you can't evaluate what you should and shouldn't spend your capital on without getting into debt, and if you seek immediate gratification from making purchases, you will get yourself into big trouble in your business.

When you start a business, you have to sacrifice. If you are used to having your every whim fulfilled, you will eventually resent the business. Or worse, you will get yourself into a bad debt situation from which you can't escape. Sometimes, it takes years before you can even pull a reasonable salary out of the business while you are funding the business's inception and early growth. Are you going to be able to pass up the newest iPhone or a luxury vacation because you need to spend your money on the business?

If managing your money is something that you are not good at, that you feel you don't understand, or something that you don't want to deal with, don't start a business, period.

Being "El Cheapo" (a.k.a. Ultra-conservative with Your Money)

The last messed-up relationship with money that I will talk about is one that I suffered from for many years (and relative to what I am worth, maybe still suffer from). To understand it, you have to understand my family. My father was a union electrician, and for most of my life my mother was a stay-at-home mom (before she got a jobbie and before my parents got divorced). My parents moved to an up-and-coming area in the northern Chicago suburbs when I was two years old. My father had gotten married later in life (at least it was considered later in life at that time in the early 1970s; he was 36) and had lived with his mother prior to marrying, so he had saved up a lot of money. My parents were able to buy a nice house in what was then an emerging area called Deerfield.

Fortuitously, Deerfield became one of the most prestigious suburbs in the Chicagoland area. It had—and has—one of the best and most competitive public school systems in the country. My family was surrounded by professionals like lawyers, doctors, accountants, and commodity traders. Since my father had gotten in early, he was able to afford the house, but it was a stretch. He was not, however, able to afford the entire lifestyle of my neighbors.

Worried about the influence of our neighbors, our father set out to teach my sister and me the value of a dollar. However, he went a bit overboard and made us completely afraid of spending a dime. There was always the requirement to save for fear that if we spent our money, we wouldn't have any later in life and we would be destined to live in a box in downtown Chicago under Lower Wacker Drive (Chicago's version of "living in a van down by the river," as Chris Farley made famous in his *Saturday Night Live* "Matt Foley" sketches).

This fear followed me through college (where it intensified when I racked up $40,000 in college loan debt) to my first job out of college in investment banking. When I graduated, I took the cheapest apartment I could find in a nice neighborhood in San Francisco; a studio apartment that was only about four hundred square feet. I was fortunate to have landed a lucrative job and was able to pay my college loans off within my first full year after school.

My savings were starting to accumulate, and after several years, I had a very healthy bank account. However, I was cautious about every single purchase. I didn't have any concept of balancing saving money with actually enjoying it. I went to dinner and would never order anything expensive off the menu. Ordering alcohol at a restaurant or a bar was a no-no because it was way too costly. While my colleagues were shopping at Saks Fifth Avenue, I was still trekking over to T.J. Maxx (which, frankly I still do, because I love getting the "Maxx for the Minimum").

It took me years, and lots of dollars in the bank, to relax to the point where I could actually enjoy a nice dinner out without forgoing the appetizer or dessert because it was too expensive, or buy a pair of shoes that cost more than $39.99. With this kind of money sickness, it was hard for me to invest in a meaningful way in anything early on in my career. Even though I had the financial capability to take the risk, I simply didn't have the stomach for it.

I have managed to get better control of my money sickness over time. As I evaluated starting businesses and investing in other people's businesses, I became more comfortable with certain types of investment risk.

My risk taking is typically based on very calculated, educated decisions vetted over long periods of due diligence, which I think is a sound strategy and one I am very comfortable with. It is the Warren Buffett way. In fact, when the 2008 financial crisis hit, I was not affected as much as many of my peers because of my more calculated financial approach.

That being said, if you can relate to having a similar type of money sickness, or if you have any other financial dysfunctions, you need to take extra time to evaluate the long-term implications of any investment you are going to make (as well as the reality that you may not make much, if any, money for a while) and decide if you can emotionally handle the financial relationship you will be required to have as a business owner. If not, well, you probably know how this sentence should end.

PERSONAL BRAINSTORM

TARGET FOCUS—TIMING:
Creating Value Before You Take On Risk (No Money)

What can you bootstrap, barter, or otherwise finagle in starting up your business to get to a point where you have begun to create some significant value? The more value you create through achieving milestones, the more that value will help you to minimize some of the business risks.

EXERCISE 8

TARGET FOCUS—TIMING:

Assessing Your Financial Situation and Responsibility (or Lack of Financial Responsibility)

Write down the answers to the following questions:

1. Do you have debt?

2. If you have debt, how much debt do you have?

3. If you have debt, is it from investing activities (such as buying a house or getting an education) or spending activities (such as credit card purchases, car loans, etc.)?

   If you have a large amount of debt—other than in your mortgage, assuming you can still pay the mortgage while you invest in your business—seriously consider paying off the debt before taking on an investment in a business.

4. Do you consider yourself financially responsible?

5. Do you want to sacrifice your lifestyle to invest in the business?

If your answers to four and/or five are "no," I hope you don't need me to tell you not to start a business right now.

EXERCISE 9

TARGET FOCUS—TIMING:
Assessing Your Financial Risk Tolerance (El Cheapo)

Write down your answers to the following questions:

1. How do you feel about financial risk?

2. How much of a dollar or percentage return will you require to risk your salary and/or savings (or to take out a loan) to start a business? (For example, would you trade a $50,000 salary each year for a chance to make $55,000 (a 10 percent return) or even $75,000 (a 50 percent return) per year? Would you require more?)

3. Are there alternate investments you are considering instead of investing in a business?

4. Would you be able to meet your financial investment targets with less risk by keeping your salary and investing your savings elsewhere?

If you are stressed by financial risk, that creates an issue for the risk side of your Entrepreneur Equation. The opportunity cost of giving up an alternative investment is also a risk. Your return requirements will help you evaluate the other side of the equation, which shows the rewards of the opportunity. Your answers above will help you evaluate both sides of your Entrepreneur Equation in more detail.

2 C

Assessing Your Personality

While the timing section helped you evaluate issues that are dynamic and may change over time, the personality assessment goes to the core of who you are. There are some people who, regardless of any enhancements in skills and experience or shifts in their priorities, will still be happier and shine more brightly without taking on the responsibilities, stress, and risks of business ownership.

In this section, you will evaluate whether several of the core factors of business ownership are consistent with your strengths, preferences, and personal disposition. Regardless of the strength of the other variables in your Entrepreneur Equation, if your personality is not a fit for entrepreneurship, you should not start a business.

15

Business Is a Roller Coaster, Not a Merry-Go-Round

WHEN YOU GO to the amusement park, do you prefer the roller coaster or merry-go-round? The experiences could not be more different.

The roller coaster can be really scary, with highs and lows, thrills and chills, and unexpected happenings at every turn. While you are waiting in line, the excitement of the unexpected is intense—sometimes good, sometimes bad. With the roller coaster, there is quite a bit of risk and reward involved. If you love the ride, you will have the time of your life. If you hate it, you may be dizzy or puking for the rest of the afternoon.

The merry-go-round on the other hand is, well, pleasant. Heck, it is called a *merry*-go-round! It may bring you some enjoyment but certainly not excitement (unless you are two years old). The merry-go-round is predictable—you know exactly what is going to happen on the nice little ride around in a circle. It may be enjoyable, but it doesn't send the adrenaline pumping through your body like a roller coaster. The merry-go-round is a low-risk ride. There is no surprise in the outcome; you know what you are going to get beforehand.

131

It doesn't matter which you like—it is your personal preference. (I prefer a third option, which I call the "food ride." This is when you stand in line at the amusement park and get to a counter where you can order an ice cream cone or a slice of pizza, both generally low-risk options.) But let's say you're one of the people who *loves* roller coasters. Does this mean you want roller coasters 24/7? What if you had to ride the roller coaster every day, from the time the park opened to the time the park closed, with just a few times a day that you could take a break on the merry-go-round? If that doesn't sound like the time of your life, you may want to reevaluate starting a business.

Entrepreneurship is the ultimate roller coaster, unlike any you have ever seen before. First, you have to use your own money to build or buy the roller coaster, and even though you are helping to build it, you can't fully see what it looks like before you get to ride it. You don't know where the turns, loops, and drops are, or how many there will be. Then, you have to wait in a really long line to get on the roller coaster. Once you are on, you have to buckle up for a crazy ride. There is exhilaration, and there is fear. There are places when nothing is happening and places that induce sheer panic. No matter how well it is built, it will likely break down somewhere along the ride, leaving you stuck and hoping that it will get fixed and you will get out unscathed. Not to mention that this is the world's longest ride and that once you get on, you can't just climb off halfway through.

High Highs and Low Lows

Many new businesses have what is called a "honeymoon period." As you can guess, this is the beginning of the business's history when everything goes well. The honeymoon period typically lasts for the first several months (and sometimes a full year or longer) after opening, when, because it is the new thing, the company gets a lot of business. The honeymoon period is common in the restaurant industry. This is because when a new restaurant comes to town, everyone wants to check it out. A new restaurant opens and is often immediately packed. However, once those people who only wanted to check out the new restaurant have gotten their "shiny new thing" fix, they don't come back. Then, the restaurant's patronage levels off to a normalized state of business.

A couple of years ago, there was a new restaurant built less than a mile from my home that had everyone buzzing for months. From the first day it opened, it had two-and-a-half-hour waits. Even if you made a reservation (which you needed to make two weeks in advance) it could take thirty minutes to get seated. Every person within a ten-mile radius of the restaurant wanted to be among the first to try it out. However, the food was mediocre, the prices were high, and the service was average at best, so a lot of people never went back. After the first six months, the restaurant had quieted down. (That's not to say that the business won't revise its concept at some point and build its client base again; the point is that it started like gangbusters due to the honeymoon period and then leveled off.)

This is why most large restaurant chains won't include a new restaurant in their "same-store sales" calculation (which calculates the growth or decline in the average sales at all restaurants on a yearly basis) until at least twelve to eighteen months after a restaurant opens and the restaurant patronage returns to a normal, more predictable level. They know the brisk sales—the honeymoon period—made after the opening of a restaurant skew the reality of the normal average sales at that unit.

The honeymoon period can cause some crazy highs and lows for you and your business. Take, for example, Marty and Joe (names changed), who were colleagues at a prestigious advertising firm. They were getting sick of corporate office politics, and because they were both client relationship managers, they felt that, hey, since *they* had brought in the clients, *they* shouldn't have to give up so much of the fees. If they had their own firm, they could capture all of the client fees and be the BMOCs.

They had been courting a few potential clients who were evaluating new advertising firms for new media business. I am not commenting on the ethics of this, but Joe and Marty tested the waters to see if these clients would sign with them if they left their existing firm to start a new company. Either they didn't have non-compete agreements with their old employer, or they were too dumb or ballsy to worry about getting sued; I didn't ask. Either way, what happened was that a few prospects agreed that if Joe and Marty started a new company (let's call it "New-co") then they would give some of their advertising work to Newco.

That was all the juice Marty and Joe needed. They didn't want to leave their high-paying advertising jobs until they were sure that they would have clients for Newco. Those potential clients made good on their promises, and Marty and Joe booked almost $600,000 worth of business during that first year. After expenses, they took home a tidy profit for the year and felt they had a great base upon which to grow the business. They were on cloud nine. They had a great honeymoon period with an initial push of great clients.

Marty and Joe were flying high; they were the best of friends, were doing well, and believed that the world was their oyster. However, they didn't realize that what they had experienced in year one was that honeymoon period. When year two came, the honeymoon was over.

To say that year two wasn't what they expected would be a bit of an understatement. They started to call on new client prospects in an effort to build their business. However, the prospects weren't as impressed with their client list as Marty and Joe had expected. Then, the worst-case scenario occurred. Within a three-week period, their two biggest clients (which had accounted for most of Newco's revenue in year one) had management changes. One client brought a new CEO on board who decided the company should bring their new media division in-house and terminated the relationship with Newco. The second brought on a new director of marketing who decided that he preferred to have the prestige of a big-name firm as an advertising partner and also pulled the business from Newco. Without their biggest clients, Marty and Joe struggled to find projects for their second year.

The roller coaster went up, then down, and then hit a corkscrew. Marty and Joe began to fight constantly. They each blamed the other for the drop-off in business. Things were tense at the office. They terminated their one other employee, whom they could no longer afford to pay. At the end of year two, they had only made $70,000 in revenue for the entire year. After expenses, including rent, marketing, travel, and administrative costs, among others, they basically had no profits to show for their second year and nothing to take home in their pockets.

Joe decided he couldn't take the ups and downs of running a business and left a few months into year three to go back to work at a larger agency. Marty kept going and a couple months into year three, he received a referral from a former colleague that ended up paying off in spades. The roller coaster was going back up again and by the end of year three, Marty had reinvigorated Newco (or so he thought) and had made about $265,000 in revenue. It was not as much as Newco made in year one, but since Marty no longer had a partner, he felt he was again on the upswing. He was once again in a good mood, enjoying the success of being out on his own.

However, roller coasters don't go up indefinitely, and Marty's roller coaster was no exception. In year four, Newco's sales contracted again to less than $100,000 for the year. After expenses, Marty's profit didn't justify the risks or the hours he was working. After all of the ups and downs, Marty could no longer take the instability and closed Newco. Marty tried to return to a large advertising firm, and it took him about nine months to find employment because potential employers were

JOE & MARTY'S ROLLER COASTER RIDE

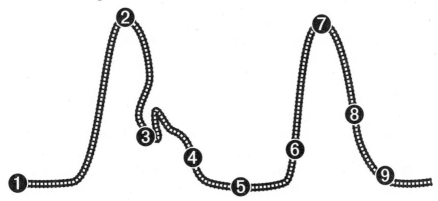

1. The ride begins...Marty and Joe start Newco.
2. Going up...year one ends with $600,000 in revenue.
3. Corkscrew...two major clients pull their accounts.
4. Going down...year two ends with $70,000 in revenue and almost no profits.
5. Hitting bottom...Joe leaves Newco.
6. Back up again...Marty gets a new client referral.
7. On a peak...Marty has a healthy year three with more than $250,000 in revenue.
8. Going down again...year four again is a down year, only $100,000 in revenue.
9. Marty gets off the ride.

worried that he was used to being the BMOC and wouldn't be able or willing to work in the corporate hierarchy anymore.

The Reverse Honeymoon

While some businesses benefit from a honeymoon period, other businesses endure a reverse honeymoon period. Nobody knows that the new business exists, so it takes a good deal of time to build the business. The business may go through months of virtual nothingness. It may take months and months to get through a sales cycle and gain momentum. This can be emotionally devastating, as the business is so slow in the beginning that you wonder if you will ever gain any real traction.

While a honeymoon or reverse honeymoon period can create ups and downs, a variety of other factors can also create a roller-coaster ride for businesses. This includes factors ranging from having a novelty product, to making a bad acquisition, to competition moving very quickly. This means that even if you execute very well for a period of time and you are worth a bunch of money on paper, you still may not benefit from the upside or reap any of the financial benefits of your business by the time you are able to extract money from the business.

I have seen this happen many times. For example, take the five-year-old consumer products company that one of my colleagues worked with that was worth $100 million a year ago and, due to mismanagement, has no equity value today. The entrepreneurs behind it thought they had hit the big time, but given that all of the money generated by the business has been used to grow it, they probably won't see a penny from their investment or hard work.

There is another hybrid product and service company that I have done some work with that has been in business for nearly ten years but is now losing money (and the bank is requiring a personal guarantee from the entrepreneur to keep the business afloat). Unfortunately, this is not an uncommon situation; I could name two dozen other similar examples without much thought.

Even when an opportunity is significant, because of the amount of capital required to be reinvested in the business to help it grow or the requirements of the other investors in the business, sometimes the business isn't worth much by the time an entrepreneur would realistically be able to liquidate some or all of his equity. With increasing competition, this situation will likely become even more prevalent over the next several decades.

Financial ups and downs are not the only rollercoaster-esque aspects of business. There are all kinds of other fun things that happen which create drama and highs and lows during running the business. From your warehouse being destroyed (this almost put Build-A-Bear Workshop out of business early in the company's history), to hiring employees that quit unexpectedly, to having your computer systems crash and losing valuable data, there are many issues that pop up that will make you sad, angry, or frantic. Sometimes, problems follow something great. For example, you get a huge order from a major retail chain (a major high), only to find out your suppliers can't help you fulfill it in time and you blew your big chance (a major low). Highs and lows are just part of the rollercoaster ride.

IF YOU ARE A PERSON WHO APPRECIATES HAVING CONTROL—WHICH IRONICALLY IS WHAT MANY ASPIRING ENTREPRENEURS CITE AS A MAIN REASON TO START A BUSINESS—THE ROLLER-COASTER RIDE OF A NEW BUSINESS MAY MAKE YOU INSANE OR AT LEAST EMOTIONALLY AND MENTALLY EXHAUSTED.

The aforementioned are just a few of the many examples of the various surprises, highs and lows that you will face. While you will enjoy the good ones, the bad ones will seem even worse given all you have at stake. It also creates a system of questionable balance as you swing from the highest high to the lowest low. If you are a person who appreciates having control—which ironically is what many aspiring entrepreneurs cite as a main reason to start a business—the roller-coaster ride of a new business may make you insane, or at least emotionally and mentally exhausted.

Achieving balance and finding time for work, friends, family, health, exercise, and leisure time is hard. Remember that balance and the roller coaster are often not compatible.

PERSONAL BRAINSTORM

TARGET FOCUS—PERSONALITY
Understanding the Highs and Lows of Business

Think about if any of the following apply to you and how that may make you feel or react to the ups and downs of business:

- You don't like surprises or the unexpected;
- You lose your cool when things don't go as planned or stress out easily;
- You prefer when things are predictable; and/or
- You can't quickly adapt to changes.

As you think about the risks and rewards of starting a business, make sure to factor in the ups and downs of the business roller coaster. If you want the merry-go-round, I wouldn't advise quitting your day job.

16

The Shiny New Thing Syndrome: When It's Fun for a Day and Okay for a Week... But Sucks for a Lifetime

NEW THINGS ARE FUN. I personally love shiny new things and am easily amused by them. Whether it is a new food product, television show, restaurant, or shoe style, I am intrigued because "new" is fun.

I am clearly not the only one that shares this sentiment. A large part of the U.S. economy is built upon selling us things that we don't need, but that we really want, mostly because they are new. Moreover, new is exciting. Think about those advertising pitches that talk about "new" (usually with a big yellow sunburst around the proclamation of its newness). Now with *new* extra-stain removal power! Now with a *new* removable pouch! Now in a *new*, leak-proof container! *New* colors now available! We consumers love new, new, new!

It is fun to turn your attention to something new. Think of what a great feeling it is to get a new car. If you get a new house, have a new baby, or join a new religion, you may even throw yourself a party. You love to tell your friends about your latest new phone-computer-bike-television-toy-whatever. New things prevent you from having to rehash the same old stories over and over.

New versus Commitment

Liking new things isn't bad except when you are trying to make a commitment. There are people who take commitment very seriously, and then there is someone like Larry King, who has been married eight times to seven different women. I am not judging; you can feel whatever way you want about commitment. I personally hate commitment in a lot of areas in my life. I currently don't have a pet or child—or even a plant—because I don't want to make the commitment to take care of something living. However, I am personally committed to making good when I give my word on something. If I am putting my own money and time at risk, you can be sure that I am committed 100 percent. If you aren't so good about professional- or work-related commitments in your life, you're going to want to think long and hard about an entrepreneurship commitment, as it is a costly commitment to abandon.

> LIKING NEW THINGS ISN'T BAD EXCEPT WHEN YOU ARE TRYING TO MAKE A COMMITMENT. THERE ARE PEOPLE WHO TAKE COMMITMENT VERY SERIOUSLY, AND THEN THERE IS SOMEONE LIKE LARRY KING, WHO HAS BEEN MARRIED EIGHT TIMES TO SEVEN DIFFERENT WOMEN.

Have you ever watched someone do something that he is really good at and thought that it looked easy? It was new and intriguing. Maybe you saw two dancers perform a tango, a golf pro play a round of golf, or a pastry chef make an elaborate dessert? You got so excited by it that you wanted to do it, too! Then, you tried it out and instead of it being exciting because it was new, it frustrated you because you couldn't do it at all.

You thought it was going to be easy. You invested in dance shoes, golf clubs, or a set of All-Clad cookware to pursue this new endeavor. However, it wasn't easy and now you are pissed off because you just wasted money on new shoes, clubs, or pots and pans. The problem was that you hadn't given one iota of thought to the fact that the reason it looked easy for the others is that they had the experience; they spent a lifetime (or a good part of their lifetime) perfecting their skill and then continually using it, practicing it, and refining it. Maybe instead of putting in the time to improve, you decided that this new thing was stupid and turned your attention to another new thing. If you quit, your risk was pretty low—the cost of the clubs or the cookware wasn't going to send you into bankruptcy. However, if that "something" you tried had been a new business, quitting would have a very high price tag.

If you are someone who is easily intoxicated by a new idea, business concept, or business model, but you have the attention span of a fly, then you are going to have a hard time following through and making your business a success. Sometimes a new business model seems exhilarating. It is new, shiny, and fun, and you are pumped about it. You tell a few people about it and you are really convinced that you are going to have the best business ever. So, you do some research and as you are learning more about the industry, you start thinking about all of the work that is required to make this cool new thing a reality. Then it becomes less exciting. It is still cool and still new, but it isn't quite as cool as it was when it was brand-new. As more time goes by and you think about spending your life (or even the next five years) focused on this one thing—and I do mean focused, as all of your efforts are going to be focused on this business—then the once-shiny fun thing starts to look like torture.

The business model may go from brilliant to stupid in your mind, and you are wrestling with what to do when—ta da!—another new business concept is presented to you. This one is even better than the last (of course it is—it is *new*), and therefore business idea number one is abandoned for business idea number two.

I spoke to one aspiring entrepreneur recently who was interested in opening a Subway restaurant franchise. She didn't have any expertise in the restaurant industry, but she was really jazzed to sell $5 foot-longs to every hungry customer in her city. I encouraged her (as I do with many entrepreneurs without industry experience) to take a job on nights and weekends at a Subway to see what it was like to be in that environment as a workplace. I can tell you that after a few months when the idea was no longer shiny and new, submarine sandwiches weren't so appealing anymore and she was thrilled that she didn't spend the more than a hundred grand in expenses of starting a franchise before taking the time to check it out. She saved herself a whole lot of money and has refocused her thinking about her career.

If you are the type of person who is always looking to the next new thing, entrepreneurship is not for you. I am not talking about being intrigued and focused on "new" in terms of producing new ideas for an existing business, such as new approaches to customer service, new features for existing products, or improvements to your existing technology. I am talking about "Business Attention Deficit Disorder" (which could be called BADD, as it is definitely bad for business), a condition in which you can't commit to one business when presented with the newness of something else.

Business success requires focus and dedication on a single path for a long period of time. The excitement factor should increase as you achieve milestones, not decrease as the newness wears off. If you don't like commitments, or if you are hyperactive and easily distracted by the possibility of "something better"—beware! It is perfectly okay for you to be obsessed with the new, just not if you intend to run a business, because you will always be wondering what else is out there.

EXERCISE 10

TARGET FOCUS—PERSONALITY:
Are You in It for the Long Haul?

1. Write down on a piece of paper any projects that you have started in the past five years that you have stopped, quit, or abandoned before finishing.

2. For each project, ask yourself why you stopped and write down that reason. Some potential reasons could be because:
   - It was too hard.
   - You got bored or lost interest.
   - Other things became bigger priorities.

3. Now, add to the list any skills, learning processes, or activities you have tried that you thought were going to be easy but were much harder than you expected.

4. For each of those, write what you did once you encountered the difficulty (continued on, gave up, cried for three months straight, etc.).

5. Under your list, write down whether you relate a lot, a little, or not at all with the following statements:
   - I often don't follow through on promises.
   - I get bored with projects easily.
   - I am always seeking the next big challenge.
   - I like learning something new more than doing something repetitively.
   - I love shiny new things.
   - Old things don't hold my interest.

Use your answers to items one through four, plus any "a lot" or "a little" answers to item five to assess whether you have a pattern of discontinuing projects or have difficulty making commitments. If so, it's no big deal (unless, of course, you invest in a business that you abandon part of the way through). Reflect on whether, given your reasons for stopping other projects, you may likely be in the same situation with a business. If so, you should either reconsider the business route altogether or initiate a jobbie on a very small scale to see if you can maintain interest. Think about whether there is a way that you can make a commitment to small milestones in starting your business before investing heavily in it. If so, what can you do to make sure that you will be in it for the long haul?

17

Businesses Don't Happen Overnight

I AM REALLY SHOWING OFF my range of sophisticated cultural references here, but one of my favorite books (and related movies) is *Charlie and the Chocolate Factory* (also known as *Willy Wonka and the Chocolate Factory*), which had a great character named Veruca Salt. Veruca was the stereotypical spoiled brat that had no patience and wanted anything and everything at her whim. In the original movie version, she sang a song called, "I Want it Now," which reflected that not only did she want a bright shiny new thing, but she didn't want to have to wait around for it.

"I want it now" is not an uncommon philosophy in our society, as we have become a society of immediate gratification. Almost anything in the universe that we desire is just a quick mouse click away. We no longer place a lot of value on that whole "patience is a virtue" saying. In the business arena, the media intensifies this sentiment by talking about overnight sensations, leaving out the part that the overnight sensation actually was working hard for decades before becoming an overnight sensation!

One way that our impatience rears its head is by tricking us into thinking that we have experience. We have already talked about how often we don't want to take the time to prepare to do something; we just want to start doing it (sometimes known as "Ready. Fire. Aim!"). Another way impatience asserts itself is when we believe that the business will run smoothly and be immediately successful.

If you are like me, you like to complete tasks and check them off the list. Impatience in a business can stem from that desire to see tangible progress. However, that progress is not always up to you and will therefore not be completed in your timeframe. Financial success aside, everything else in a new business is going to take two to three times as long (maybe longer) than you think it should (and than it probably should) take.

Your lawyer will take too long to set up the corporate structure and any other documents you need. Your web developer will take at least double the time quoted to develop your website. Your store will take longer than you had anticipated to build out (setting your opening date back a few months). Your new employees will take twice as long as anticipated to train (and then still won't fully understand what they are supposed to be doing). Your vendors will send you products after the date they had promised. When your office equipment breaks, it will take longer than necessary to fix (especially if it is something important, like your computer with all of your data).

If you cannot deal with the stress of inefficiency, or you are impatient and likely to blow up at every issue, get your high blood pressure medication ready when you start your new business.

While it isn't good to be so relaxed that no real progress is ever made, impatience and unrealistic expectations are not qualities that play well in the entrepreneurial arena. While I mentioned that some businesses have a honeymoon period, some don't, and the ones that do eventually wear off. The bottom line is that you have to be mentally, operationally, and financially prepared for your business to take a while to gain (or regain) momentum.

On the mental front, it can be quite an emotional defeat when your business realities don't match up to the dream you had in your head.

I can't tell you how many times I have met entrepreneurs that have opened _____ (fill in the blank with your favorite small business model—retail store, online store, services firm, etc.) that fell short of their expectations. Each time, the entrepreneurs had visions that once they did the "up front work"—such as creating or sourcing products, putting together the website, building out the store, setting up the credit card processing and PayPal accounts and putting together some flyers and other marketing materials—they were ready to go, and the money would start pouring in. They had visions of the phone ringing off the hook with orders, boxes stacked high by the door waiting for the post office to pick up and deliver to all of their new customers, and, of course, themselves laughing all the way to the bank. They opened their business and that didn't happen. In fact, not much of anything happened.

Consumer businesses can take a while to build momentum, and business-to-business products and services often have a long sales cycle. These factors are consistently not processed or severely underestimated by new entrepreneurs. When the business opens and dollars don't start flowing, discouragement sets in. This doesn't mean that you should sit around and do nothing (conversely, you have to work extra hard to reach and convert customers), but it doesn't mean you should give up either.

Sometimes building your business becomes very painful and happens slower than you have ever imagined. Let's say you have a new rock band and in order for you to get paid, selling CDs, playing concerts, selling merchandise, etc., you need to have fans. So, you figure that the best way to build your fan base would be to take a low-paying gig at a smaller club to get some exposure and credibility. So, you submit your music to the slacker in charge of bookings, and he never calls you back. You follow up several times, and by the twelfth time he is sick of listening to your voicemail messages, so he calls you back. Before he discusses anything else, he wants to know how many fans you can bring to his club for a show.

You are confused. You are a new band, so you don't have many fans other than your friends and family members who come out to support you. This is why you are agreeing to the gig at the low-end club in the first place! He sees it differently. He explains that he is also trying to run a business and that he needs people in the club to pay a cover charge and/or buy lots of alcoholic beverages. If you don't have enough fans who you can guarantee will show up at the club, he can't book you. Or, if he is very generous, he may say that at a minimum he can't pay you unless you have at least "X" number of fans who show up. Oh, and if you take the unpaid gig, your time slot will be at 5:30 p.m., when there is sure to be nobody at the club. So, you try to build your fan base, but you can't do that without having some fans (or at least forgoing payment). You realize it is going to be a very slow and painful process for you to build that fan base.

You May "Want It Now," but You Don't Get to Have It Now

If you have delusions that your business is going to take off on day one and that you are going to soar to success, you are in for a heck of a surprise. If you require immediate gratification or consistent recognition for your achievements, you are going to have a hissy fit when your business doesn't provide that. It is going to be a long and bumpy road, so don't delude yourself into thinking anything different.

The other problem with immediate gratification is that you need to move on to get your next gratification fix. For a business to build real value takes a long-term commitment. Not just a commitment to getting things humming but a commitment to keep things going day in and day out, where a lot of the days there may not be that tangible gratification you seek. In fact, you may not realize value for decades. Do you have what it takes to commit not just for now, not just five years from now, but for decades? Imagine yourself ten years in the future. Do you see yourself working in this business? If not, then don't put yourself on a path to do just that.

PERSONAL BRAINSTORM

TARGET FOCUS—PERSONALITY
The Patience Factor

Ask yourself the following questions:

1. How long can I dedicate to building a business?
2. Can I commit one-and-a-half to two years to assess whether the business will work?
3. What will I do if I do not make any profits in the first six months? What about the first year? What about for two years?
4. Can I see myself running this business in five years? Ten years?

Use these answers to evaluate whether you have the patience required to nurture the ups and downs of a business over a long period (especially if that period has lots of downs).

18

Do You Have the
Core Competencies
to Be a Santa or an Elf?

PEOPLE WHO ARE SUCCESSFUL and happy professionally usually are because they are good at what they are doing. Most people have a few skills and strengths that stand out above all others in a professional environment. The problem is that when you are an entrepreneur, you really need to wear a lot of hats, and this requires you to excel at each skill that each hat represents.

This is a major reason why many people aren't suited to be entrepreneurs from the get-go. They need to have a well-rounded skill set to be able to manage a business. They also need to be strategic visionaries for their organizations.

Making Christmas Happen Takes One Santa Claus... and a Whole Lot of Elves

To make a business successful, just like Christmas, it takes one Santa Claus and a lot of elves. Santa has the vision and keeps the big picture in mind, and the elves assist with the execution. The elves don't do anything without Santa's direction. And if the presents don't get delivered on Christmas, the elves don't get blamed, Santa does.

If you look at most hierarchies, they are shaped like a pyramid with a few people at the top setting the vision and strategy and lots of people underneath making that strategy a reality. This structure is seen in all kinds of groups. On the reservation, there are few chiefs yet lots of Indians, and on the sports field there are few coaches and lots of players (and for professional sports, just one principal owner). The structure works because it is hard for groups of people to make effective decisions; have you ever heard the phrase "too many cooks spoil the broth"? This structure also works in terms of core competencies, because most people aren't visionary strategists, they are "doers." In the Santa context, that means most people are elves.

In keeping focused on core competencies, if you are a doer, then you should do a doer's work. There is no shame in being a doer. In fact, not much progress would be made in this world if there weren't doers. The doers get things done! They lay the bricks that build the buildings, they prepare the food that customers enjoy, and they teach the children that are the world's future. The doers may not get to fully participate in the upside of any endeavor; however, the doer's life is typically a lot less stressful because doers wait to be told what to do (and don't have a big risk if the doing doesn't get done!).

Are You Santa or an Elf?

I had one particular friend that desperately wanted to start her own business a few years ago. I was baffled when she told me this because in her previous jobs she had always complained when there was a lack of direction. When she was told what to do, this woman was a superstar. She was unstoppable. She could do anything and do it well. However, if you didn't tell her what to do, then she did virtually nothing. She didn't have the innate drive to "pick up the ball and run with it" unless someone specifically told her to do so.

Fortunately, after a few conversations covering this issue, she acknowledged that she did better work when she had specific guidance and decided against the entrepreneurial route (and is now in a fantastic job where she has been promoted twice).

Basically, you can't run a business when you are waiting for directions. There is no goddess of entrepreneurism that will appear in a vision or pop out of the cash register and give you guidance and suggested next steps. Not only is it up to you as an entrepreneur to set the direction, strategy and work process for yourself, but you need to do that for every person in your organization. If you are a doer, not only will this task be daunting, it will be nearly impossible.

Core competencies are all about maximizing what you are best at— your innate skills and the areas in which you shine. If you are going to leave your comfort zone and try something new that is not aligned with your competencies, you may not want to test it out by starting a new business, where you have thousands of your own dollars on the line.

EXERCISE 11

TARGET FOCUS—PERSONALITY:
Assessing Your Strengths in Terms of Role

Write down the answers to the following questions:

1. When you interact in groups, what role do you typically play (and like to play)? The leader? The heavy lifter? The free rider?
2. Have you managed groups of people before now? If yes, what did you like and dislike about the managerial role?
3. How would you feel about managing employees, customers, and/or the direction of an organization?
4. Do you like to take on responsibility? Why or why not?
5. Do you like to take the ball and run with it or prefer to wait to be given specific instructions to follow?
6. Do you like to look at the big picture or focus on details?

If you aren't sure about any of the above, ask some friends or colleagues to give you some feedback (make sure these people are "spinach in your teeth" people and not smoke-blowers).

Review your answers and write down next to each whether that preference or strength is more consistent with being a "Santa" or an "elf." If you are trending more toward elfdom, you will want to avoid running a business, which puts you squarely in the Santa position. Instead, consider taking your entrepreneurial spirit and put it toward your work in someone else's organization.

19

The "Secret" Is *Hard Work*

WHEN YOU WERE LITTLE, did your parents, or perhaps a teacher or some other authority figure, tell you that you could be or have anything you wanted, that you were only limited by your dreams? Mine didn't, so maybe not... However, you are undoubtedly, like me, familiar with that concept. We love dreams. In the United States, we even have our very own American Dream. We go to movies with fairy tale, dream-inspired endings. If you wish it and you dream it, they say, it is all possible.

Hoping and Dreaming Aren't *Doing*

People who wish and hope and dream for things are not so good with business. They spend more time hoping than doing. Have you ever met someone who spent so much time telling you about their dreams, that if they spent half the time they spent talking actually doing something, they would have accomplished whatever it was they were dreaming about in the first place? I know lots of people like that. Wishing never translates well into becoming an entrepreneur.

Chip Bell and John R. Patterson, authors of *Take Their Breath Away*, perfectly illustrated this in a guest post they wrote for my blog, *Unsolicited Business Advice*:

> Three turtles sat on a log in the edge of the swamp. One decided to jump in. How many are now on the log? Nope, there are still three. Deciding and doing is not the same thing. Until you execute, all decisions are just plain-old intentions. Execution—putting skin in the game—is the true test of commitment. "I believe, I support, I approve" are all just weasel words unless they are coupled with visible demonstration.

This sage insight applies to starting a business, too. As Chip and John noted later in the piece, the road to hell is paved with good intentions. Wishing, intending, and dreaming are not the same as doing.

> AS CHIP BELL AND JOHN R. PATTERSON NOTE IN OF *TAKE THEIR BREATH AWAY*, THE ROAD TO HELL IS PAVED WITH GOOD INTENTIONS. WISHING, INTENDING, AND DREAMING ARE NOT THE SAME AS DOING.

Now, I have never personally read the new age self-help book, *The Secret*, that was a sensation a couple of years back, but my general knowledge of popular culture—from my late-night viewings of *Oprah* to my frequent visits to various pop culture websites—coupled with my discussions in social circles gives me the gist. *The Secret* touts the law of attraction, saying that if you think positively about something, that positive thinking will help you attract whatever it is you want. From what I understand, it suggests that if you create some kind of picture collage of your goal and use it as a visual aid to inspire you to keep thinking about that goal, that goal will be fulfilled. I think of it as sort of a perverted version of a book written decades ago by Napoleon Hill called *Think and Grow Rich* but without one key element: *hard work*.

Oh Yeah, That "Hard Work" Thing

This is where the difference comes into play between the wisher and hoper, and those with real desire. The wisher and hoper read the book literally. They want to make a million dollars, so they cut out pictures of money and all of the things they will buy with the money and tack it up on the wall. They look at it every day, think about it, dream about it, and wait for the good fortune to fall in their lap.

If you have desire, you let the money (or whatever may be on your vision board) be the goal and the fuel to pursue your dream. Then, you come up with a credible plan of action to achieve that goal. You use the positive attraction to help continue with your plan and keep you going when the times are tough, but you actually *do the work*. You don't believe that your thoughts alone will bring you riches; you understand that by having a goal and a positive attitude you can have a path to achieve those riches if you stay focused and do the work. This is probably what *The Secret* was intended to convey, but not everyone got that message.

Do you *wish* you had a successful business, or do you desire *to start* a successful business? Do you hope you can be successful, or do you know that your desire for success will ensure its outcome? If you fall into the wishing and hoping camp, you probably don't have what it takes to start and run a business. Businesses sometimes are fortunate enough to have some luck, but a good portion of that luck is made out of shrewd business decisions, dedication to the tasks at hand, and plain-old rolling-up the sleeves. Businesses are not successful because of miracles, vision boards, and good old wishing and hoping.

So, do you wish you had your own business, do you dream of having your own business, or do you have the true desire to be an entrepreneur and won't let anything stop you from achieving that goal? Only one of those is the right answer if you want to start or buy a business.

RECOMMENDATION

There is no assessment here. If you want to take your dreams and create an action plan to move from thinking to doing, I recommend reading Barbara Sher's *Wishcraft*. As of presstime, it is available free for download on her website, www.wishcraft.com.

SECTION THREE

Assessing the Business's Fit for You

NOW THAT YOU HAVE ASSESSED your fit for entrepreneurship, you must evaluate each opportunity, as well as the prospects of business ownership to assess their risks, issues, and rewards, and then evaluate those risks and rewards in terms of your personal circumstances.

3 A

Assessing the Opportunity

This section allows you to think critically about a particular new business opportunity to see if it is worth pursuing in the current environment. This section concludes with two specialty chapters for those who are thinking of buying a business (instead of building one) and also those who are in a position to inherit a family business.

20

It Takes Money to Make Money

THE FINANCIAL ASPECTS of starting and running a business are often underestimated, but they are arguably the most critical areas (and the areas that usually cause the most trouble) in your new business. In my FIRED-UP entrepreneur assessment, the very first step is the "F," which deals with your finances. This is not a coincidence, because when you are considering becoming an entrepreneur, it is paramount that you have (or have access to) enough money to (1) start up or purchase the business; (2) operate the business, including the ongoing working capital and investment needs of the business; and (3) also live on (you still have to pay your bills, right?).

When you start or buy a business, you need to translate your business plan from written ideas about your business concept into a set of numbers called a pro forma financial model or financial projections. These financial models will do three very important things for you:

1. Help you evaluate if the opportunity makes financial sense (i.e., if it has the potential to produce an attractive return for you on your investment) and is worth you pursuing;

2. Help you identify how much money you need to start or buy the business, as well as have enough cushion to be able to fund business operations for the first two years; and
3. Provide a benchmark for the valuation of the company and how much ownership you will give up to investors if you need to raise equity capital.

IF YOU DO NOT (OR CANNOT) EVALUATE WHETHER YOU WILL BE MAKING AN APPROPRIATE RETURN ON YOUR INVESTMENT, AND WHETHER THE FINANCIAL TRADE-OFF OF THE BUSINESS IS WORTH THE RISK FROM A FINANCIAL PERSPECTIVE, STOP, DROP, AND ABSOLUTELY DO *NOT* QUIT YOUR DAY JOB.

I want to particularly emphasize number one above, because I have seen business plans that have no financial projections, limited financial models, or unrealistic financial models. You cannot (I repeat, *cannot*) evaluate whether you have a good business opportunity that is worth investing your money, time, and effort in from just a written plan and qualitative ideas. If you do not (or cannot) evaluate whether you will be making an appropriate return on your investment, and whether the financial trade-off of the business is worth the risk from a financial perspective, stop, drop, and absolutely do *not* quit your day job.

Garbage In, Garbage Out

Creating a financial model is a daunting task for many entrepreneurs, most of whom have about as much experience with Microsoft Excel and building financial statements as they do with Celtic dancing (the latter probably being less intimidating to attempt). In addition to being unfamiliar with the programs most often used to make the model work, many entrepreneurs are not well-versed in financial accounting. They don't know revenue from profit, they can't tell you what EBITDA stands for, and they certainly don't know what a good gross margin for their product or service is.

Like anything you don't have experience with, understanding and operating within the financial world is hard at first. In fact, financial modeling has a steep learning curve, which is why people who build and evaluate financial statements for a living usually get paid quite handsomely.

While you can find someone to help you with the mechanics of financial statements and assist you with putting them together, the financials of your business are its lifeblood. The financial model is built upon your assumptions for every aspect of the business, from the number of customers you will have, to the pricing of your goods and services, to the margin you will receive on your product based upon anticipated vendor costs. You will have to detail your growth assumptions, your expense assumptions, your ongoing working capital assumptions, and your anticipated start-up costs.

Even if you have someone who can build the model, the usefulness of the model is predicated upon the quality of the information you input. There is a concept that applies here—garbage in, garbage out. If you put garbage in (i.e., non-thoughtful numbers that are not backed by realistic assumptions), you will get garbage out (i.e., a model that won't help you to evaluate the opportunity and the business's financial needs and will put you in a pickle of a situation down the road). Norm Brodsky, an *Inc.* magazine columnist, makes an excellent suggestion in *The Knack* that you do your numbers by hand instead of with a computer program. He says "….to be successful in any business you need to develop a feel for the numbers…tracking the numbers by hand is the best way I know of to learn the language."[1] This suggestion can be used both to develop your financial model and to practice on an ongoing basis in your business.

Now, there will be people who say that projected financial statements are just guesstimates, and, to some extent, they are absolutely correct; you will never know exactly what will happen with your business, and there is a 99.99 percent chance that you will have to revise them frequently as your business evolves. However, your financial statements should be educated guesses based on a set of logical assumptions (e.g., if you need to capture 90 percent of a market to break even, you probably don't want to be in that business). While you may not be able to predict everything that will happen with your business, you need to have a base set of realistic assumptions that show, under conditions that are considered achievable, you will make a worthwhile return on the investment. The more milestones you have hit, the more realistic those benchmarks should be.

Once you have your financial statements together and have established through numerical data that the upside financial reward of your business is worth pursuing, as well as how much money is required for you to start or buy and run the business, then you need to figure out if you need or want to raise capital. If so, you need to decide if you are going to do it through taking on partners who have ownership in the business (raising equity) or through getting a loan that you are ultimately responsible for (raising debt).

Whose Money Are You Using?

If you have the financial capability to do so, you may choose to use only your own money for the business. There are three good things about using solely your own money: (1) not having to give up ownership in your business; (2) not having to worry about the capital-raising process; and (3) not having to work with investors who may drive you crazy.

However, there are downsides to going solo. The first is that all the risk rests with you, and if you are using the majority of your net worth to fund the business, this means you have the added risk of having all of your eggs in one basket and potentially not being able to support yourself (and anyone else who needs supporting, like a family) for a couple of years while you ride out the ups and downs of the business's early years.

Secondly, you may not have enough money invested in the business if you're only relying on your means. Statistics show that most entrepreneurs don't take on outside investors or lenders; however, most businesses are also severely undercapitalized, and this is a leading cause of their eventual failure.

A third disadvantage of footing the bill yourself is that if you start to run out of money, you aren't going to have a partner with deep pockets to turn toward to help with the tough times (and trust me, you aren't going to be able to raise new money during the tough times—struggling businesses are not desirable investments for the guys with the money).

If you don't have enough money to fund the business, or you want to share part of the risk, you need a lender or one or more investors. Then you get the fun of raising capital. In a very unscientific poll that I continually take among entrepreneurs, backed up by a decade and a half of anecdotal evidence, 99 out of 100 entrepreneurs rate raising capital as one of the worst aspects of starting and running a business.

IN A VERY UNSCIENTIFIC POLL THAT I CONTINUALLY TAKE AMONG ENTREPRENEURS, BACKED UP BY A DECADE AND A HALF OF ANECDOTAL EVIDENCE, 99 OUT OF 100 ENTREPRENEURS RATE RAISING CAPITAL AS ONE OF THE WORST ASPECTS OF STARTING AND RUNNING A BUSINESS.

I know quite a bit about raising capital. Both by myself and as part of teams, I have helped companies of all sizes, ranging from a single entrepreneur with a business plan to large public companies, raise collectively more than a billion dollars for their businesses. What I know firsthand is that the smaller your business is and the more you need the money, the harder it is to raise the necessary capital. The earlier stage the business is in (i.e., a start-up) and the less money the business produces in terms of profits (and if you haven't started, there are no profits), the fewer the number of organized entities devoted to investing in the business. It makes sense from a risk perspective, as the further along a business is in its development and business cycle and the more profits the business is producing, the less risk there is in the investment. Therefore, the more profits you have, the more investors that will want to jump on board.

In addition to knowing that there are few places for you to turn to for your capital needs, I also know one additional consistent truth about entrepreneurs and raising capital: *early-stage and new business owners under-*

estimate the cost of starting and running the business 99.99 percent of the time. In every early-stage business I have seen, the entrepreneurs say that their financial projections are conservative in terms of revenue and expenses. They also always claim that they are raising more money than they need and that they have a cushion. Every time, I have told them that their projections—as is the case with all entrepreneurs' financial projections—are too aggressive. And every time, the entrepreneurs lecture me about why they are the "exception to the rule." Then, a year later, after their revenue estimates have fallen short and their expenses are greater than expected, they give me the reasons why they have missed their projections. There has yet to be an exception to this in my personal experience.

Investors know this, and it is why seasoned investors always take a "haircut" to the projections when they evaluate the investments; they assume that they are overstated on the revenue line and understated on the expense line.

Wade Beavers, CEO, and Joe Sriver, founder and president of the mobile technology company DoApp, know this all too well. They said that the biggest surprise of a new business comes because the entrepreneurs "expect to generate revenue immediately" from the get-go. If you are not in business already, Wade says it is "hard to realize the complexity of getting a product to market and selling to people...it will probably take up to three times longer to generate any revenue than you expect."

So, do yourself a favor when you build your financial statements. After you make your assumptions on your business and do your financial projections to find out how much money you need, go back and revise them so that the amount of money you actually need is one-and-a-half to two times the amount you originally thought you needed. I believe that is usually the scope of underestimation by entrepreneurs. This means that if you think you need $100,000, you really need $150,000 to $200,000. If you think you need $3 million, you really need probably around $4.5 million, maybe more. You get the idea.

If you need more of a cash outlay in the beginning, then you know what that means? Yes, it means that you need to put more of your own money at risk, find more investors, or have each investor you've already found write you a larger check.

Skin in the Game versus Sweat Equity versus Other People's Money

Once you know how much you need (and have increased that figure because you underestimated it on the first pass through), you have to figure out how you are going to get the capital. The biggest surprise to you may be that you need to invest a meaningful amount of your own money. This is called having "skin in the game." Nobody wants to invest when you are only contributing your ideas and time (also known as "sweat equity"). You will get partial credit for your time, but if you believe in what you are doing, you need to be financially invested as well.

If you decide to go the investor route—that is, to find other people to be your financial partners and give away ownership of the business—you have another set of headaches to deal with. First off, where will you find your investors? Most business models aren't big enough in their scope to attract the attention of sophisticated investors like angels (individual or groups of high-net-worth investors) or venture capitalists. These investors want to invest in businesses that have the ability to give them a 30–50 percent return (or sometimes higher) on their capital on average for every year they hold the investment. They use this benchmark because they know a large percentage of their investments are going to fail (as most new businesses do) or be limited in the scope of their success, so they need the one that really succeeds to make up for the nine others that flop. These investors also need a way to get their initial investment (and hopefully a return as well) out of the business, so they expect that in some realistic time frame, usually five to seven years, the business will be big enough to sell or to take public in an IPO (Initial Public Offering). This set of criteria means that your business may not be a fit for an angel or venture capital investment.

So, if you are not fundable by seasoned angels or venture capitalists, you have to go to who you know—friends, family, and acquaintances who may consider investing in your business (sometimes called "DDLs," an acronym for those doctors, dentists, and lawyers that your friends and family know who are expected to have some extra cash lying around). This is a tough task. It is hard to ask people you care about to give you money. Once you accept it, you make a deal with the devil of sorts, because now your relationship with this person has gone from its existing form to also being business partners. Sometimes you will have to make decisions for the sake of the business that will not make your friends and family happy. This makes for some seriously uncomfortable future interactions.

Even if your friends, family, and acquaintances happen to have enough money to help you fund your business, they may be a liability rather than an asset. They may want you to employ your lazy cousin Nick. They may demand free goods and services. They may ask you for a million favors in return. They may be so worried about their investment that they call you for reports every day (I hear about this one a lot). Think about this carefully before taking an investment from a friend, family member, or acquaintance.

If you are one of the few that does have a business that meets the potential criteria of venture capitalists, it is just as hard to get funded. Venture capitalists receive hundreds to thousands of business plans for review every year. They dismiss many that are received over the transom; that is, plans that aren't introduced by someone that they know and that can vouch for them. So, if you are not in the inner circle of the venture capital community (and if you need the money, you often aren't), your plan may not even get glanced at, even if your business has merit.

If you decide to forgo taking on an equity investor, you may decide to go the loan-taking route. This isn't easy either. It may be hard to find an attractive loan without connections. Furthermore, because your new business doesn't have major assets, most lenders will want you to guarantee the loan with your house or other major collateral, which adds to your personal financial risk. If you don't have appropriate collateral, you may find it nearly impossible to get a loan for the business. Basically, you have to be somewhat successful and have proven your financial abilities to save toward your business in order to get a loan to start a business.

Whatever route you choose, raising capital takes a lot longer than you expect. Take whatever time frame you think it will happen in and multiply that by one-and-a-half to two times as much. If you have budgeted six months, it will probably take nine to twelve months—and if you are thinking one month, wake up, because you are dreaming. This is especially the case when raising money from individual investors. Even when people commit verbally to an investment, it is really hard to get them to write the check. Getting people to part with their money is challenging; people will wait as long as possible to part with their money (just ask the government what percentage of tax returns get sent in at the last possible moment and how many taxpayers file for an extension).

The worst part of raising capital is that it is rarely a one-time occurrence. If you ever want to grow your business (which you should, since the point of having a business is creating equity value and growing your business is a necessary part of that), you need to constantly be raising capital. There are a lot of businesses that start raising a new round of capital just months after they close on a round of financing, given the amount of time and effort that it takes to complete. If you want to open new locations, add employees, add new equipment or machinery, or make an acquisition, these are all going to require capital. Make sure to stock up on lots of Tylenol, because you are bound to endure the capital-raising headache for the long haul.

Financial Statements Aren't a One-Time Event

Once you have capital in the business, you need to continually evaluate your financial statements. These tell a story about your business and the more astute you are at evaluating what these statements are telling you about your business, the better business decisions you will make going forward. You won't be like my former clients (whom you will read about in chapter 24) who didn't understand that they were losing money on a certain product line and shouldn't have expanded their overhead (or even have been in that business).

And you won't be like the managers (whom you will read about in chapter 28) who didn't realize their company was not selling its products for enough money because its financial statements were both incorrect and skewed from of all of the gift certificates it was selling.

You will need to evaluate the potential return on your investment for any new business line you seek to launch or major business purchase you are contemplating. Sometimes, it seems like you need a super-secret decoder ring to really understand everything, but it is critical that you are able to understand the financial story of your business for it to be a successful venture in the long run.

Managing your business from a financial perspective is both an art and a science, not to mention intimidating and ever-present. The financial story of your business is the one part you will want to skip up front, but it is the most important and creates just another job and hat for you to wear when you venture out on your own. If this is not a hat you ever want to wear, then do not think about leaving your day job.

EXERCISE 12

TARGET FOCUS—OPPORTUNITY:

Understanding the Numbers So You Can Evaluate Risk and Reward for You and Your Venture

Write down the answers to all of the following questions:

1. What assumptions are you making that will drive your financial model? Some examples of the many assumptions you may make include:
   - How many customers will you be selling to?
   - How long will it take you to make sales?
   - How many repeat purchases will you have in what time period?
   - What are the costs of the goods or services you will be selling?
   - What kind of administrative expenses will you have to start and continue on an ongoing basis?

You may want to consult with someone experienced in accounting and financial models to make sure you have thought through all of the assumptions.

2. Are your assumptions realistic? To evaluate this, review each assumption in context. For example, if your potential market has one million people and you have to reach 990,000 of them to start turning a profit, then your model probably isn't realistic.

For these two items, your answers will help you evaluate the viability of your business model as it stands now and also assess later on whether the upside potential is worth the risks you will be taking. If you find the business model isn't viable or doesn't create enough rewards for the risk you bear, you can either try to revise the business model so that it becomes viable and creates the right risk/reward balance, or discard the business model altogether. When you have a business model you feel is worthy of evaluation, you will later put the potential financial and qualitative rewards of the opportunity on the "rewards" side of your Entrepreneur Equation.

3. How much money do you need to start and run your business for two years?

4. Do you have the amount of money required by item 3? If so, are you comfortable with risking all of it?

5. If you answered no to either item in number 4:
   - How much money do you need to raise?
   - Who are you going to raise the capital from, and how much "skin" will you have in the game?
   - Are you going to seek equity (giving up a portion of the ownership of your business), debt (creating an obligation for you to repay and perhaps having to guarantee the debt with a major asset that you own), or both?
   - What are the pros and cons for your accepting money from each potential source of capital?
   - How does raising money affect the risks and rewards of starting the business?

6. Will you have enough money to live on while you start and run this business (for at least a year-and-a-half to two years)?

7. If you answered no to item six, or if something unexpected happens, if you have to choose between paying your personal bills and your business bills, what will you choose?

8. How much do you need to save to have enough money to live on and fund the business?

Use the answers to items 3 through 8 to assess whether you would be better served by waiting until you had more money yourself to invest in the business. Undercapitalizing a business will set you up for failure. If you are raising capital, evaluate what impact (both financially and qualitatively) accepting that capital has on your risks, issues, and potential rewards to assess the risk and reward balance for you. Later, you will put any risks, financial or otherwise, on the "risks" side of your Entrepreneur Equation later.

ENDNOTES:

1. Norm Brodsky and Bo Burlingame, *The Knack* (New York: Portfolio Hardcover, 2008), 75.

21

The Most Competitive Time *Ever*

THERE HAS NEVER BEEN a worse time to try to start a business. Why, you ask? Because there has never been a time in history where there has been more business competition. *Ever.* We have come off one of the most innovative centuries in all of time. Virtually everything imaginable, useful or not, has been thought of, as well as at least a dozen derivative products or services for each innovation. Pop on over to the U.S. Patent and Trademark Office website at www.uspto.gov and take a look through the registrations for patents, trademarks, and service-marks for new product innovations, brand marks for goods, and brand marks for services, respectively. Think of anything you can imagine and then look at how many patents and trademarks have been filed related to that topic. It is a staggering amount that will make your head spin.

We have more choices for every product and service you can think of than we will ever need. From hamburger joints to toothpaste to child care options, we have myriad choices for everything we want, everything we need and even for things we don't give a crap about. Plus, because historically there has been no screening process for entrepreneurship, all kinds of people jump into business. While it is very difficult to make a business succeed, it is really easy to try and start one.

For anyone legitimately trying to start a business, the competition faced by entrepreneurs today creates all sorts of issues. For one, novelty isn't going to carry your business the way it did fifty years ago. With the perceived ease of trying to start a business, even if you come up with a somewhat novel idea, the chances are that there are dozens of people working on the same thing or something that is similar. If not, the moment you launch your business, there will be dozens of imitators—and, if there is any hint of success, hundreds more.

Your business competes for customers' time, attention, and money against indirect competition as well. If you come up with a new food product, you are still competing against the tens of thousands of existing food products out there. Even if your food product is slightly different, it is still food and has to compete with all of the other food choices, because there are only so many occasions each day that people eat and only so much money they will allocate to food.

If the companies you are competing against are good competitors, this is bad for you. They will be slugging it out with you for market share on a daily basis. You will have to innovate at lightning speed in every aspect of your business because there will always be at least one business right there (and likely multiple businesses) trying to steal your customers and your market share. This may include larger businesses that have more capital, more resources, and a better brand name than you.

You may think that a large company wouldn't bother competing with a small player; however, this happens all of the time and is happening more frequently as competition has increased. Instead of just competing with their larger competitors, big companies will sometimes go "down market" and compete against small competitors.

This happens in every industry and across industry segments. When my husband and I started Intercap Merchant Partners' investment banking practice, we started an investment bank to fill a void in the market. At the time, most large investment banks wouldn't take on mergers and acquisition transactions under $75 million in value, because smaller transactions didn't generate the minimum fees required by the larger investment banks to take care of their staff and overhead. Most large investment banks had a fee minimum of at least $1 million per transaction and wouldn't even consider something below $500,000. Therefore, smaller and middle market clients whose deal sizes didn't reach that range had to find other merger and acquisition advisors, many of which didn't have the same expertise as the large investment banks. Having been trained by and using the same standards as large investment banks, Intercap Merchant Partners set out to service those lower middle market businesses. We could offer bulge-bracket investment banking capabilities for those smaller businesses whose deals were in the $20–50 million value range that netted fees of $250,000 to $500,000 per transaction.

This was a great differentiator for a small period of time. However, once the large investment banking niche got ultra-competitive, the large investment banks started coming after our niche. Where before they wouldn't touch deals that had a potential fee under $500,000, now they were vigorously pursuing those exact transactions. So, instead of competing against Joe Schmo advisory firm, Intercap Merchant Partners was now competing against Banc of America Securities (the very firm we had left years earlier and which previously would have never thought of doing the size deals we were doing). That is how quickly the marketplace moves, and if there is money to be made, lots of competitors, including some formidable ones, will be flocking there.

This example with Banc of America Securities is not an isolated incident. When a big company's growth opportunities start to slow in its traditional marketplaces, it will go after the smaller niches. There are many instances of this, such as mega-retailer PetSmart going after the traditionally mom-and-pop pet-lodging and pet-watching niches with its PetSmart PetsHotel and Doggie Day Camp services. We all have seen Hershey's go from a mass-market chocolate manufacturer to the ultra-premium artisan chocolate niche with its acquisitions of upscale chocolatiers Scharffen Berger and Joseph Schmidt. If there is a growth opportunity, even a small one, all potential competitors will be aware of it and most likely, some will come after it.

Bad Competitors Are Bad for You, Too

You will face a lot of strife from good competition. However, bad competitors can be even worse. Bad competitors can screw up a market opportunity for you as much as, if not more than, good competitors. Bad competitors can give consumers such a bad experience that they never want to try a similar good or service again. Customers will trade to an indirect competitor's product or service simply because you are guilty by association of serving the same niche as your bad competitor. For example, if you make a natural cola and a potential customer tried one of your competitor's products first, which happened to taste like dirt combined with vomit, the customer may get a bad association with natural cola in general and never try your superior product. If a potential customer was scammed by a company that supposedly provided debt consolidation services, even if your debt consolidation company is legitimate and effective, you may be lumped in with the scammer in the customer's mind. Bad competitors poison the well, which can spell real trouble for you. With the ease of starting businesses, this is a growing concern for aspiring entrepreneurs.

Wade Beavers and Joe Sriver of DoApp couldn't believe how fast a market can move and change. Their team began to create concepts for iPhone applications ("apps") prior to the launch of Apple's App Store. By the launch date, they had conceptualized four hundred and fifty different apps. Wade estimates that somewhere between eight to twelve weeks after Apple's launch of the App Store, 90 percent of those apps had already been created by competitors. He says, "You may think your idea is brilliant, but the chances are that someone has already thought of it. Take for example our 'Whoopee Cushion' app, which was initially banned. By the time it was approved, there were already fifty other flatulence apps available!"

While the market may move quickly in the technology industry, every industry is exposed to the same issues, at varying degrees of speed. Business is a daily war, and you have to defend your turf against the competition. There is no room for complacency or taking a break. Just as you celebrate a victory, you have to get back in the trenches, as there is always someone trying to one-up you.

Hey Mr. Customer, I'm Over Here...

But to celebrate a victory, you have to reach your customers. Competition is so fierce that it has become very difficult to reach your target customers in the first place. The amount of business products in any given market is staggering. Whether you are targeting end-consumers or businesses, mass market or a niche, people are hard to find, and it is even harder to get their attention once you do find them. There is so much noise in the marketplace that every business competing for your customers' attention makes it that much harder for you to get your message across.

THE AMOUNT OF BUSINESS PRODUCTS IN ANY GIVEN MARKET IS STAGGERING. WHETHER YOU ARE TARGETING END-CONSUMERS OR BUSINESSES, MASS MARKET OR A NICHE, PEOPLE ARE HARD TO FIND AND IT IS EVEN HARDER TO GET THEIR ATTENTION ONCE YOU DO FIND THEM.

Think about your daily life and how many marketing messages you see every day. You get flyers in the mail. You see billboards on the sides of roads, on buses, and at train stations. There are commercials on the radio and television, and in magazines and periodicals. If you have an email account, no doubt you have received email from companies you have done business with, as well as those who are spamming you, peddling everything from advanced degrees to penis enlargements. Online, banner ads, pop-up ads, and advertorials litter the web. Now, for all of those advertisements and marketing pieces you have seen, how many do you remember, and how many have encouraged you to try a product or service? The answer is probably a tiny fraction of what you have been exposed to. In fact, you and I see so many marketing pieces each day that we are starting to become desensitized to marketing in general.

I know our company receives all sorts of mail solicitations, many of which have no relation to our businesses whatsoever. We get glossy brochures on everything from recycling programs and corporate gifting to janitorial services and venues to host client events. We get letters, phone calls, and emails, as well as advertisements disguised as flyers, keychains, mousepads, magazines, coupons, gift certificates, and more. I am sure that there are probably some gems hidden amongst all of the rocks—that is, services and goods that we actually want or need—but most of the solicitations get put into the circular file (a.k.a. the trash can) because we simply don't have the time to go through the sheer volume of solicitations. These advertisements have become so omnipresent and intrusive that everyone is predisposed to either say no, or totally ignore your message in the first place, even if you have a good or service with merit.

And on top of the noise in the market, your potential customers are more fragmented than ever, so it is hard to target them in the first place. It may have been obvious twenty years ago to target a certain business group through an industry conference. Now there are dozens of smaller conferences servicing the same industry. Instead of going to one big event, there is an event in every major city twice a year. Consumer products companies used the television for advertising when there were only a few channels and few distractions. Now people are spending less time watching television, and their viewership is split among hundreds of channels. Finding the customers is a challenge, and then, if you do find them, you may not be able to get their attention. Not exactly what you would call "fun," right?

A World Wide Web of Choices

Many aspiring entrepreneurs don't think through the issues regarding competition and reaching customers before starting a business. For example, one entrepreneur (I will call her Katy) who was referred to me made custom purses. I asked her how she was planning to sell them. Katy told me she'd do it through websites like eBay and on "the internet." I then asked her how the customer was going to find the purses on eBay and the internet.

To make my point, I went straight to eBay. When I typed "purse" into eBay's search box, there were 229,888 listings that included the word "purse." I am sure it varies a bit depending on when you check the site, but there are still hundreds of thousands of purses on eBay every day. I then narrowed the eBay search by putting the more descriptive "black purse" into the search box and that narrowed it to a mere 34,067 black purses available on eBay. Switching from using the search function to the category function, there were 195,978 listings in eBay's purse-equivalent category called "handbags and bags."

Going to Google was even worse. The word "purse" returned 32.7 million results and "black purse" returned 1.13 million results. Katy could put the purses on eBay or on her website all day long, but how the heck was anyone going to find them?

Clearly what Katy didn't realize is that on eBay or anywhere else online, if a business wants a customer to be able to find its products, it needs to be very specific. Most of the time, the search for a black purse is done with a specific brand name attached, such as "Louis Vuitton black purse" or "Gucci black purse," or even more specific with a style attached like "Coach black soho ski hobo purse." This is to hone the search results to a more reasonable number of options.

Unfortunately, nobody has heard of Katy's new business, so nobody will be typing "Katy's black purse" into any search engine, and certainly nobody is going to take the time to browse through thousands of results and just magically discover Katy's purses. She has to build her brand first and that, given all of the competition and noise we have been talking about, is neither easy nor inexpensive to do.

So, if you like the idea of never-ending competition with major competitors with tons of resources and bad competitors who could damage your reputation, all to gain the attention of customers who are hard to find and even when you do find them they are so overloaded with information that they ignore you anyways, you are going to love being in business. If that doesn't sound fun, start heading in another direction.

EXERCISE 13

TARGET FOCUS—OPPORTUNITY:
Do You Have a Competitive Advantage?

Write down the answers to the following:

1. What other businesses are you or will you be competing with either directly (i.e., providing the same types of goods and services) or indirectly (i.e., providing a different type of goods or services to the same target customers, like movies and video games both competing for customers' entertainment spending)?
   - If you are having trouble identifying competitors, you can ask friends, visit stores where similar products would be sold, and search for key words related to your business in Google, among other research options.

2. Write down next to each competitor how your business will compete with those businesses. You should include what you will bring to the table that is innovative and difficult to replicate in terms of:
   - Value
   - Customer service
   - Relationships
   - Functionality
   - Marketing
   - Intellectual property
   - Technology
   - Or any other competitive advantages that would be hard for another competitor to reproduce

3. How easy is it for another company to enter your business segment and compete with you?

A large number of competitors, ease of entry into your industry segment, and fewer competitive barriers for your opportunity will make it more difficult to succeed and decrease the upside potential of the opportunity. Use your evaluation of the competitive landscape for your business model to assess whether your assumptions about your business are realistic. You may need to adjust the business model to make it more viable and attractive before you get to your risk and reward evaluation.

RECOMMENDATION

If you do decide to move forward and want to learn about the slow but effective process of building relationships with your customers, I recommend *The Contrarian Effect* by Michael Port and Elizabeth Marshall.

22

Too Smart for Your Own Good

THE WEIRD THING is that sometimes, the more successful you are and the more talents you have, the harder it is to run a business. This may seem counterintuitive. If you are super smart, motivated, and talented, then you would logically be the best possible candidate for entrepreneurship, right? Unfortunately, this is often not the case because you are always going to be better at doing every job than your employees.

The "smart people" problem starts back in school—definitely in college, sometimes in high school and depending on your school system, even as far back as junior high, when teachers first assign the dreaded "group projects." Knowing the 80/20 rule (80 percent of all work is done by 20 percent of the people), what do you think happens in every group project? The smartest and most talented people in each group do the lion's share of the work. They don't want to risk their grade in the class by dividing the work equally, and just hoping that Timmy (the guy who is absent from class two days a week on average and sleeps through class on the other three days) does his part well, if he remembers to do it at all. In school, there isn't any benefit in trying to get Timmy up to speed quickly. Forget that. No, the smart people just take over and do the whole project themselves.

And thus begins the smart people work cycle. The smartest people do just about everything better than most everyone else. They write better, plan better, reason better, and sometimes, even look better. They are better, until it comes to running a business. Then they are not better—they are screwed. There are only twenty-four hours in each day, and a person does need to sleep, eat, shower, and do certain other things. So, each day this smart person tries to do everything himself, because he can't stand someone else doing a job badly. Then, he is stuck with the one-man-band "job-business" with no way to grow.

SOME OF THE SLACKERS—SOME OF THE PEOPLE WHO KNEW BEST TO SURROUND THEMSELVES WITH SMART PEOPLE WHO WOULD DO THE WORK—ARE BETTER-SUITED FOR ENTREPRENEURSHIP THAN THE SMART PEOPLE THEMSELVES.

It is interesting to note that some of the slackers—some of the people who knew best to surround themselves with smart people who would do the work—are better-suited for entrepreneurship than the smart people themselves. They know how to delegate and sometimes, how to manipulate other people into doing things that they don't want to do.

Ideally, the smart people would just be able to convey their talents. But since the smart people are so used to doing everything themselves, they don't learn the key skills to make their businesses successful, including automating and delegating as many tasks as possible. As a smart person, you need to use your smarts and talents to boil down their essence in an easy-to-follow format that even a monkey can replicate. (See "Recommendation" at the end of the chapter for a book on this.)

Also, smart and talented people often have a flair for the unusual, complicated, or different. They don't like to follow the KISS principle (Keep It Simple, Stupid), which is required to make a business succeed. If you think of the assembly line in a fantastic manufacturing plant, or the global presence of McDonald's, they both seem complex, but in reality, they are a series of incredibly simple functions. Every single task is broken down into easy-to-follow steps. The assembly line worker repeatedly performs a few tasks that are specifically defined. So does the McDonald's cook, cashier, and drive-through order taker. There is little input from these individuals, as everything has been standardized for them.

In fact, some of the largest, most successful businesses in the world are staffed not by the smart people but, in large part, by regular, average, and sometimes, stupid people. These successful entities have just a few people who are smart enough to standardize, automate, and delegate the majority of the tasks in a way that can't be screwed up by their average employees.

So, being smart or talented isn't going to help you unless you can use those smarts to figure out a way to simplify those tasks that will make a business successful. This isn't easy, because it goes against everything you have ever done and is counter to how you were taught to think. However, it is necessary for a business to succeed, and it is why smarts and talent alone don't predict entrepreneurial success.

The Smarter You Are, the Bigger the Opportunity Cost

The other issue with the smart people starting businesses is that smart people have the most to lose. The smarter you are, unless you have the social graces of a wild ape, the more options you have available to you. You have the ability to make a lot of money in a variety of fields and have room in your career for promotions and raises. This means that when you start a business, you have a lot more to risk than someone who makes less money and has fewer career options. This is often referred to as the "golden handcuffs" dilemma. Because you have more to risk, this means that you need to have a business opportunity that is going to provide an even bigger reward for it to be worth it to you.

If you currently make $250,000 a year (or have an opportunity to do so), your business is going to have to be five times more successful than the business of someone making $50,000 a year to get the same return. Additionally, it is a lot harder to establish a business that will double your yearly profit when you make $250,000 a year than if you make $50,000 a year.

So, with the most to lose, a wide range of other options available, and the penchant for more intricate, complex endeavors, don't be surprised when the valedictorian of your high school keeps his day job and it is one of the more average students that finds success (or at least tries to find success) in his own business.

EXERCISE 14

TARGET FOCUS—OPPORTUNITY:
Is Your Business Scalable?

Write down your answers to the following questions:

1. Does your business model require you to be doing the bulk of the work because of your "own special flair"?

2. Can you simplify the business to teach others to do what you do and still provide outstanding value to your customers?

3. Can you automate your business process?

4. If you delegate work, can you still manage and stay aware of what others are doing (i.e., not abdicate when you delegate, not out-of-sight, out-of-mind)?

If you answered yes to question one and no to any of the other questions, your business is not scalable and will fall into a jobbie or job-business category (as discussed in section 2A). At this point, you may want to retool your current business model. If you are set on evaluating this particular business model as it stands, use your awareness of the additional risks associated with jobbies and job-businesses as part of your evaluation of the overall risks and rewards of the business.

RECOMMENDATION

To gain some different perspectives on and insights into automating and delegating in your business, you may want to reference Tim Ferriss's *The 4-Hour Workweek* and again, Michael E. Gerber's *The E-Myth Revisited.*

23

Buying a Business Is Acquiring Someone Else's Problems

I hope that you now have a better picture of the unique risks and issues associated with starting or franchising a business. Getting a business going is the most difficult part of a business's lifecycle, one that most new businesses do not survive. So, logic may tell you that the path to minimize that risk is by circumventing the start-up issues through buying an established business. Sure, it costs more money up front, but an established business has a track record, vendor relationships, and a customer base. It has employees that already know what they are doing. Plus, you can get out of doing a lot of those annoying start-up tasks. So, I know what you're now thinking: perhaps buying a business is the easy path to entrepreneurship. Right? Wrong.

Buying a business can equal buying someone else's problems. Here's the thing about people, business owners included: they are greedy. If a business is doing well and expected to continue to do well, most entrepreneurs won't want to part with it. I have advised dozens of businesses to sell when they are nearing the peak of their growth rate, knowing they will get a premium price for selling their business at that time. Almost every time (I would say at least 90 percent of the time), the business owners don't sell when things are going well and they have visibility on future growth, because they think they will be missing out on more value (this is often referred to as "leaving money on the table"). The greedy entrepreneurs want to wring every last dime out of the business, so they convince themselves if they can wait just another year, their business will be worth more, and then they will sell it. Then, the next year comes, and they go through the same rationalization. They risk their their business encountering a blip just to get a few more dollars in value each successive year.

Ultimately, they see this business blip (or perhaps more than a blip, such as a total catastrophe) coming and *then* decide to sell (which, of course, always means that they end up getting a lower value for the business than they would have received if they had sold it years earlier, but that is a subject for a different discussion). What this means is that when a business is up for sale, most of the time it is because things are going south or the writing is on the wall that something negative is on the horizon that allows for the entrepreneur to decide it is an appropriate time for him to cut bait. So, if you're considering buying a business, you should just assume going into your evaluation process (which is called the "due diligence" process) that you are going to be inheriting someone else's issues, whether they be minor, medium, or major.

When an entrepreneur puts his business up for sale, his job is to sell it. He puts on his salesman hat, as it behooves him to portray the business in the most positive light possible. He (and potentially his advisors) will tell you that the business is only for sale because of some very believable reason; it could be that he is retiring, moving, taking care of a family member, or some other story that may be plausible or even part true, but is also part of the marketing spin of the selling process. However, if the entrepreneur really loved the business and thought it was going to continue to grow and increase value, would he be walking away entirely or finding some way to keep his hand in the cookie jar?

When you meet the owner, you may be shocked that the business could be successful at all under his management. Your ego may tell you that the current owner is a blowhard, nincompoop, or complete airhead and that you would be able to run the business much better than he did. If someone like him could achieve the current level of sales, think of all of the things you could do to make it grow even more!

However, despite the fact that he may not be the brightest bulb in the shed, there is one very important thing he has that you will never have before purchasing the business: *full information*. As I have said, information is power, and in relation to this new business, you are at a significant disadvantage in the area of information.

The current owner knows a heck of a lot about the business. He knows where the skeletons are buried. He knows the status of the relationships with the vendors. He knows how much of the business is reliant upon him and his connections (and how hard it may be for you to take those over once he leaves). He knows which employees do good work and which do not, as well as how much productivity comes from the work he does versus that of

> INFORMATION IS POWER, AND IN RELATION TO THIS NEW BUSINESS, YOU ARE AT A SIGNIFICANT DISADVANTAGE IN THE AREA OF INFORMATION.

his employees. He knows which employees will hate the fact that there is a new owner and will probably quit after the business is sold. He knows which systems are out of date, which equipment is on its last legs, and what his competitors are up to that jeopardizes the company's very existence.

There are also things he probably doesn't even realize about his own business that he couldn't convey to you even if he wanted to. Whatever the case, these are things that you will not know and are hard to evaluate through due diligence and the inspection process.

The owner is then going to put a marketing spin on whatever questions you do ask. He may not out-and-out lie, but his objective is to sell the business, so he will find creative ways to answer the tough questions. If you don't ask certain questions, he won't feel compelled to remind you that you may want to ask about why payment terms with their largest vendor have changed three times this year or how risky it is that 70 percent of the company's business comes from one customer (which happens to be the business owner's brother-in-law).

Also understand that you are never going to be able to get answers to all of the questions you have, nor get access to every piece of information necessary, as the sale process is usually confidential—meaning, the top vendors, customers, and employees that you would love to interview you can't (or at least not fully) because conversations with them could put these relationships with the company in jeopardy if these important entities believe that there is a sale process going on. So, you will always be at an information handicap when evaluating the business.

Even if you had all of your questions answered to your satisfaction—and you asked the right questions—you still will not know all of the pitfalls and issues. Maybe the employees won't like you or won't feel like they need to work as hard for you, whom they don't know, versus the man they have been loyal to for the last decade. Maybe the existing systems aren't something with which you are comfortable. The vendors, customers, or even the landlord (all whose approval may be required to transfer existing contracts like vendor contracts, leases, and more) may decide that it is a good opportunity for them to try to renegotiate terms or try to hold the business "hostage" in other ways (this happens all of the time during business sale processes). And just maybe the business has been successful only because the owner got lucky and that luck is about to run out.

Buying a Business Is Not a Shortcut to Entrepreneurship

You need not look any further than your local newspaper (okay, maybe a little further, since a lot of those are going out of business too; so let's say any news outlet of your choice) to find stories about businesses that have been damaged by making bad acquisitions. The biggest, best run, and most well-funded companies in the world have stumbled over and over again from buying competitors, so to think that you can just buy a business and it will be a cakewalk is simply naïve.

Additionally, just because you are buying a business rather than starting one from scratch doesn't mean that the other business operational issues that we have discussed don't apply. You still have the same business problems. You still have to answer to your customers; in this case you must hope that the customers you "paid for" when buying the business don't use the sale of the business as an opportunity to leave or renegotiate terms that put the business in a bad position. Likewise, as the new owner, you have to hope that the employees you "paid for" when buying the business don't use the sale process as an opportunity to quit, demand a raise, or slack off. You still need to be able to multitask and wear different hats. You still need to know everything that is going on because it is still your money and time on the line.

> WHEN YOU BUY A BUSINESS, IT IS NOT A SHORTCUT TO ENTREPRENEURSHIP. YOU STILL HAVE COSTS AND EXPENSES. YOU STILL HAVE TO MANAGE CASH FLOW. YOU STILL HAVE TO WORK BECAUSE BUSINESSES DON'T RUN THEMSELVES.

When you buy a business, it is not a shortcut to entrepreneurship. You still have costs and expenses. You still have to manage cash flow. You still have to work because businesses don't run themselves. Once the previous owner leaves, he doesn't really owe you anything. You then have the delightful task of wearing someone else's shoes and not only trying to fill them but trying to run in them as well. You still need to be able to do all of the things a business owner does, but now you may be even more financially invested in the business since you had to pay for what you believed is the "going concern" value of the business plus additional "goodwill," which may be many more times than what it would cost to start a similar business.

Your day job is looking better and better, huh?

EXERCISE 15

TARGET FOCUS—OPPORTUNITY:
Assessing an Acquisition

If you are seriously considering purchasing a business, make sure that you can answer the following questions. You will probably want to engage one or more experienced service providers with substantial knowledge of the acquisition process to help with due diligence (such as an investment banker, lawyer, and/or accountant; the first two can also help with the process and negotiations). The key points are *experience* and *knowledge*: you don't want your Uncle Ira, who happens to be a divorce lawyer, to advise you regarding an acquisition.

Ask yourself the following questions:

1. Which intangibles are you paying extra money for? How are you valuing them?
2. What assumptions are you making about the business?
3. How will changes in the assumptions affect the value of the business and, ultimately, the value you are paying?
4. Can you put a mechanism in place (such as an earn-out provision, where the purchase price is tied to the business reaching future milestones) to help mitigate some of the downside risk?
5. Do you need to buy this business? What are the competitive benefits of the business that would be more costly and difficult to replicate with a new business?

Your answers (and advisors) will help you to define the risks and opportunities associated with buying the business, which you can use to create your Entrepreneur Equation.

24

Just Because You Won the Genetic Lottery Does Not Mean You Were Born with an Entrepreneurship Gene

H ALF A CENTURY AGO, a family business guaranteed to the children growing up in such a fortunate family a specific life path and a somewhat certain future. Businesses started by entrepreneurial family members were often a logical place for the whole family (or at least a good part of it) to work and learn. Many offspring worked in the business in some capacity as they grew up. Many kids even passed on pursuing higher education and went right into the family business. These kids started low on the totem pole, learned the ins-and-outs of the business as if it was their schooling, and, eventually, climbed up the family-owned corporate ladder. As the older family members were preparing to retire, the younger generations were the obvious successors to the business. Family businesses typically stayed in the family and were passed down from generation to generation.

A whole lot has changed in our country's recent history. This has changed the business and competitive landscape, as well as the mindset of the privileged and the opportunities for entrepreneurs.

Growth and Opportunities

Back in the day, entrepreneurship had a different flavor than it does today. There were far fewer business entities. There were new ideas to be implemented around every corner and there was a lot of running room, making the creation and growth of a business totally different from what it is today.

Think of what we have access to today. If you want a cola, under the Coke brand alone you can have Coca-Cola, Coca-Cola with Lime, Diet Coke, Diet Coke Plus, Diet Coke Black Cherry Vanilla, Diet Coke with Lemon, Diet Coke with Lime, caffeine-free Coca-Cola, caffeine-free Diet Coke, Coca-Cola Zero, cherry Coke, cherry Coke zero or Diet cherry Coke. If you don't like Coke, you could have a Pepsi…or Diet Pepsi, Pepsi Wild Cherry, Pepsi Natural, Pepsi Max, Pepsi One, Diet Pepsi Wild Cherry, Caffeine Free Pepsi or Caffeine Free Diet Pepsi. If you don't like either of those brands, you can choose to have an RC Cola or store-brand cola—or even an organic cola. That doesn't even include other carbonated beverages from root beer to cream soda to lemon-lime, if you perhaps want a soda (or *pop* as us Midwestern folks like to call it) but not a cola. If you expanded to beverages such as flavored waters, juices, smoothies, and more, it would take me at least five pages to list out all of the options to quench your thirst!

We have too many options now, which means that the business environment has changed from innovating products and services to innovating cost reductions, marketing, customer relations, and distribution strategies. These tasks are not typically viewed as creative or fun the way idea and product innovations are; they are more of the "blocking and tackling" aspects of business. This may be less appealing for many potential entrepreneurs and certainly requires a different set of competencies for the business.

A key reason that many kids historically went into the family business is that there were not a lot of other well-paying options. Higher education, especially at prestigious universities, was available only to the toniest of families. So the family business became the default option for many kids. Now there are myriad options available to children for their futures. Education is widely available and strongly encouraged. Services firms have exploded, creating high-paying, challenging career paths. The world is a young person's oyster in terms of possibilities, so the family business is sometimes not that interesting.

If the young person is not interested in the family business, she is not going to be passionate about it. And having a dispassionate entrepreneur is a clear starting point for failure.

> PARENTS HAVE ENGAGED IN LOTS OF TOUCHY-FEELY B.S. THAT ELIMINATES MOST COMPETITION AND CREATES A SO-CALLED FEEL GOOD ENVIRONMENT.... WHEN CHILDREN DON'T LEARN TO COMPETE, STRIVE TO IMPROVE, OR DO MORE WORK AND PREPARATION FOR THE NEXT TIME, THEY DON'T DEVELOP THE CRITICAL SKILLS THAT ARE NEEDED IN THE REAL WORLD.

The Trophy Generation

Another thing that has changed, and continues to get worse, is the way that a lot of kids are raised. Parents have engaged in lots of touchy-feely B.S. that eliminates most competition and creates a so-called feel good environment. If you go to a swim meet, the winner isn't the only one to get a trophy. No, not even just the first, second, and third place finishers get a trophy. Some genius decided that *everyone* in the swim meet should get a freaking trophy for participation. Supposedly, this way nobody feels like a "loser."

This all sounds great in a sunshine-and-sprinkles environment, but I live in reality. So does business. When children don't learn to compete, strive to improve, or do more work and preparation for the next time (because, hey, why should they if they are going get a trophy anyway?), they don't develop the critical skills that are needed in the real world and certainly in the business world.

Trophy kids do not make good entrepreneurs and business managers. There are no trophies for everyone in business. There are no bonus points for participation if you don't "win" against your competition. The special prize for that is called *bankruptcy*.

You don't want someone with the "Hey, I gave it a good-old college try" attitude running your business. You want someone scrappy who is going to find a way to make it work, even in the face of adversity. Therefore, non-competitive, touchy-feely people shouldn't be running businesses, even if their parents want to hand it over to them.

Mergers and the Capital Markets

One reason that businesses were historically passed down from generation to generation is that there weren't enough ways for the family members to get the value back out of the business that they had spent years to create. Creating significant equity value, they logically wanted to be able to have their families benefit from that value. The easiest way was to have the business continue in their family to their benefit. Selling for a premium price wasn't really an option. There were no private equity firms, there were few competitors with the resources to pay a premium price for the business, and other suitors may have not had access to capital to purchase a business for a desirable (to the company) valuation.

The capital markets and access to financing have significantly changed the game for family businesses. With the explosion of capital availability, there are now other viable options that, frankly, hedge families' risks much better than a succession. These range from more aggressive lending for potential buyers (strategic or otherwise) to private equity firms doing sales in stages (such as recapitalizations) or bringing in their own management teams. Depending on the size, financial position, and growth history of the company, among other factors, a company can garner a price of many multiples of its profit during a sale or merger.

By selling the business, older generations can put a much stronger guarantee on future generations' success because they have locked in a price and secured cash for their heirs, which can then be invested through diversification (in simple terms, not putting all of their eggs in one basket). If you hand over the company and it goes south, then the heirs have nothing. If you hand over the cash, they can invest it in a variety of investments ranging in risk to preserve capital or to pursue opportunities for growth.

If you don't believe that the risk is that high in passing down a family business, keep reading.

Just because you won the genetic lottery doesn't mean that you got an entrepreneurship gene passed down to you. In fact, if you have a fairly well-off family, you may be more averse to risk, as you have more on the line.

Another issue is that parents like to throw their hopes and dreams upon their children. Some want their kids to follow exactly in their footsteps; others want their kids to have everything they wanted but weren't able to achieve for various reasons. This may create pressure on you from your family to take over the business. But if you truly don't want to—if you are not interested in the industry, the business, or being an entrepreneur or business owner (or at least of that particular business)—don't let your parents or other family members push you into it. They had their opportunity to live their lives; you need to do what you want and are meant to do, or you will perform that job at a level somewhere less than 100 percent. Businesses need 100 percent effort. Have that uncomfortable conversation up front. As awkward as it may be, it will be a lot less awkward than having a conversation down the line after you have squandered a good portion of the value that your family has worked decades to create.

Widgets Are Different From Kidgets

Let me provide you with a solid example of why you shouldn't go into business just because it was in the family. Twenty-five years ago, a very smart and determined gentleman (I will call him Mr. X) had a passion for producing a product (to further protect his identity, I will call the product a widget). He was really interested in the widgets and spent time carefully crafting his first ones. These particular widgets were sold to specialty retail stores and marketed to adults (no, they weren't "adult products").

Mr. X was a thoughtful, methodical, and conservative man. He continued to build more widgets. He continued to sell to stores that allowed him a high margin for the product. He was able to modify some of the widgets slightly, repackage them, and create new products that appealed to new customers. It was a fantastic business that kept growing.

A few years in, it was clear that the widget business was a good one. It has some fantastic attributes, carefully cultivated by Mr. X, including:

- *Very high margins.* For each product sold, the company had a gross margin (wholesale price less the direct cost of goods sold) of more than 50 percent. This is a fantastic margin in any industry, and it made Mr. X's widget enterprise quite profitable.
- *Ideal retail relationships.* The channels in which the widgets were sold had very attractive qualities. In addition to the margins on the products, the products were sold firm; that meant that they were non-returnable by the retailers, taking away the prospects of major inventory risk from the company. Also, the retailers had set ordering cycles, which, in conjunction with the products being fairly easy to assemble, meant the company wasn't required to carry a lot of inventory.
- *Evergreen product lines.* The type of widgets that the company created were not fads or trendy products; they were tried and true and could generate sales year in and year out.
- *Small staff and overhead.* The company's products were relatively easy to produce, not requiring a lot of production support. The retail relationships were manageable by a tight staff. The small inventory allowed the company to exist without needing extensive warehousing operations.

The widget business was a nice, profitable business. It grew into the high-seven figures in revenue and also generated a seven-figure profit each year.

As time went on, Mr. X knew he eventually wanted to retire. He had two adult children, a daughter who was a stay-at-home mom and a son who was an advertising executive. He decided he would pass on a portion of the stock in the business to both of his children and tap them to come on board.

The daughter didn't want to join the workforce, so she offered up her husband, whose professional experience was in a different industry, to join the company's board of directors since, as a family unit, they were now substantial stockholders.

The son, X Jr., was tapped by his father to become CEO. X Jr. wasn't really interested. He was extremely creative and loved advertising. He particularly enjoyed advertising in the kids' products arena. His father's company made widgets marketed to adults, so it really wasn't a great fit for him.

After many months of conversation, a little something called guilt won out. Mr. X didn't want his legacy to die, and so he convinced X Jr. he could take this profitable company to the next level. X Jr. came on board, about twenty years after the company's founding, as its CEO.

So, what happened? Here is the summary version. X Jr. couldn't shake his enthusiasm for the kids market. He figured that maybe there was a way to make widgets directed at kids. He decided to develop a kid-oriented widget (I will call this the kidget) as the company was already great at widgets and he wanted to be involved with kids.

However, X Jr. was not particularly strategic, and while widgets and kidgets seemed similar on the surface, he didn't appreciate that the businesses were entirely different. Sales of kidgets took off, but X Jr. didn't fully understand that:

1. Kidgets needed to be sold to a different channel, which meant a difference in the business model. Instead of selling them to the specialty retail channel (who weren't particularly interested in kidgets), kidgets were sold to mass retailers like Walmart and Target. Because a large percentage of the kidget business was sold through these mass retailers, the business was taking on increased risk in terms of carrying more inventory and having goods that these mass retailers demanded could be returned at their sole discretion.

2. Kidgets, because they were directed at kids, needed to have more bells and whistles to make them attractive and interesting. It cost more to build a kidget than a widget, plus, mass retailers required lower price points. Therefore, the kidget was a substantially lower-margin product line for the company.

3. Because of the more complex kidget product, and the fact that mass retailers had different ordering cycles from specialty retail stores, more staff and overhead were required to make, sell, and warehouse the kidgets.

4. Kidgets, because they were directed at kids, were more of a fad product. Kidget product lifecycles were much shorter than the evergreen widget products the company was used to dealing with.

To X Jr., kidgets were taking off, which was a good thing. Sales grew rapidly, so the company neglected developing more widgets and instead put more resources into kidgets. Over the next several years, overall sales more than doubled, mostly due to the growth in the kidget business. However, these sales came at a lower profit margin; so while the company was profitable, it was so on a paper-thin, net-margin basis. It was earning nearly the same amount of profits in dollars it did when it was less than half its size and only focused on widgets. That meant that even though the sales were twice as large, the dollar profits were the same, reflecting lower profits on a percentage basis for the company.

Now, it never occurred to X Jr., his board of directors, or other key management that this newer kidget business was creating risks and lower margins. A large percentage (around 25 percent) of the growth was based on the sales of one single type of kidget, a fad that would prove to burn out after a few years. After the banner year of sales, X Jr., oblivious to the risks, recommended that the company move its headquarters to a larger facility to accommodate the huge growth and inventory requirements of the kidget business.

Maybe you can guess what happened next. If you haven't "seen this movie before," two months after the move was complete, the mass retailers decided to restructure their businesses and returned millions of dollars worth of merchandise. The once super-high-growth kidget turned out to be an extraordinary circumstance, and after the fad wore down, it contributed little in sales. And because of its earlier decisions, the company was supporting a huge staff and rent for the new, larger facility—but its sales had declined nearly 30 percent. So the company started to lose millions of dollars. Yes, *millions.*

I had the wonderful "luck" of becoming involved with this particular company right at the beginning of the meltdown. We performed rigorous analysis for the company (the kind of analyses that should have been performed by X Jr. and his team before increasing the rent expense by 300 percent) and found that without the support of the fad kidget, the overall kidget business, although producing more than double the revenue of the widget business, was actually losing money for the company. For every dollar of sales produced by the kidget business, it cost the company more than a dollar to create and market that corresponding item.

Now, this story continues on about how to turn around the business, but that is not the point today. The moral of this story is that the creative, advertising-oriented X Jr. was not cut out to run a business and be an entrepreneur, particularly at that point in time for a business that sold widgets. He didn't have the right skill set, and he didn't have a passion for the company's core product. By trying to relate the business to his own passions and interests, they ended up with kidgets, which created a lot of sales but no profits and in fact eventually ate up the profits of the neglected widgets.

I also can tell you that this is not a unique story. This is not the first time this has happened, and it's not the last time it will, either. The worst part is that Mr. X thought he was helping to secure his kids' futures by handing over the business to one (and allowing the spouse of the other on the board). He and they would have been much better off selling the business, with the proceeds going to the children so they could invest those dollars and pursue their own dreams, not try to continue to pursue their father's dream.

So, what's the takeaway here? There are other ways for kids of family business owners to have a secure future. Going into the family business may not be one of them. If you are not meant to be an entrepreneur and you don't have the passion, skills, experience, or desire for your family's business, don't let the family pressure you, and don't take it over because you think it is an easy out to slide into an established business. No matter how you slice it, work will be involved, and you won't be able to keep riding on someone else's coattails, even when you are related to those coattails.

EXERCISE 16

TARGET FOCUS—OPPORTUNITY:
Is the Family Business the Right Opportunity for You?

If you are asked to take over the family business, ask yourself the following questions:

1. If the business was owned by someone other than your family, would you apply for the CEO position? Why or why not?

2. What aspects of the business are you passionate about?

3. Do you understand the business?

Your answers should give you some clarity on whether or not you are best served by taking on this business opportunity.

As a secondary exercise:

1. Write down your strengths, skills, and experience.

2. Ask your family members to make a list of skills, strengths, and experience required by the job.

Compare where these two lists match up and where the discernable holes are to help you decide if you are the best person to take over the business and if this is the right opportunity for you.

3 B

Assessing the Risks, Issues, and Rewards of Entrepreneurship

Assessing the trade-off between the risks and issues of starting a particular business, and the potential rewards, is arguably the most critical part of the Entrepreneur Equation. Entrepreneurship's risks and rewards can be both quantitative (savings account stuff) and qualitative (quality-of-life stuff).

Quantitative risks and rewards are financial or numbers-oriented, including risks, such as how much money you are putting into the business, and rewards, such as how much money you can make from the business.

Qualtitative risks and rewards, on the other hand, involve intangible issues and risks as well as rewards or benefits. Qualitative risks would include having less time to spend with your family; issues here might be having to spend time doing work you don't like; and rewards could include a shorter daily commute. The qualitative risks, issues, and benefits are obviously more difficult to evaluate as there isn't always an apples to apples comparison.

The most important thing is to find the right balance of risks plus issues versus potential rewards. It is your job to take all of the risks and issues inherent in business ownership and in a particular opportunity, along with your current circumstances, and evaluate if there is enough of a reward. This assessment will help you decide if a given opportunity (or business ownership in general) is worth pursuing.

The key thing to remember is that while the risks and issues are typically required by the business, the rewards are just a possibility, so that possibility has to be big enough and important enough to you to make sense for you to take on all of the risks and endure all of the issues. This is an assessment that most entrepreneurs historically have not performed up front (particularly since many of them didn't have the tools to identify all of the risks and rewards) and is the most important step you can take in your overall evaluation of entrepreneurship.

25

The Business Version of
Let's Make a Deal: Is There Enough
Upside to Justify All of the Risks?

REMEMBER HOW I SAID that just because you can do something,
doesn't mean that you should? Well you figure out the "should"
part by evaluating both the risks and rewards of entrepreneurship. You
need to look at the entire picture of how much you can make financially,
and what else you are giving up, and decide if there is enough of a trade-
off in terms of a big potential payday to justify all of the risks involved
in trying to attain it.

Evaluating risks and rewards requires you to do a few things:

- Evaluate how much you are putting on the line in terms of your
  money, time, effort, and emotions. This means that in terms of
  money, you need to look at how much of your savings and personal wealth you are investing in your new business (or guaranteeing
  by using a major asset like a home to guarantee a loan).
- Assess how much you make—or could make—in a job working
  for someone else, including any benefits.

- Evaluate the opportunity costs of your investment. This means considering what else you could be doing with that money that is now tied up as an investment in your business. This opportunity cost could be a lost investment opportunity (such as putting that money into savings and earning interest on it) or a lost spending opportunity (forgoing a family vacation, new car, or other purchase), or even a lost opportunity to donate to your favorite charitable organization.

These monetary considerations, plus all of the hours you will be working and the stress you will endure, are your risks and issues. These risks and issues need to be evaluated versus the second part of the equation, which is evaluating how much upside potential you realistically could achieve from the business (the reward), based on your thoughtful financial model, assumptions, and level of investment.

The potential rewards of a business opportunity have to significantly outweigh the upfront and ongoing risks you are going to take and the issues you will have to endure for you to be willing to try to reap those rewards. There is no one right answer for everyone to say by how much those possible rewards needs to outweigh the risks and issues, but it needs to be substantial, and it needs to make sense for you. Graphically, you can think of an acceptable risk/reward balance, applied against your personal circumstances as:

POTENTIAL REWARDS   >   RISKS & ISSUES

Risks and Rewards the Game Show Way

Most investors look at this type of equation for every investment they make using financial benchmarks. For those of you not well-versed in financial terms, such as looking at return on invested capital or cash-on-cash returns, you may find this difficult to do. Therefore, I will turn to an easy proxy for explaining this financial risk and reward evaluation: game shows.

Now, I don't know why, but I *love* game shows; I always have. I think I even want to be a game show host in my next life (think Bob Barker, not Vanna White). Game shows are great for demonstrating evaluation and trade-offs. Even though game show contestants don't have to put up their own money to go on the game show, their evaluation skills are always tested, and there is always something, sometimes something substantial, on the line. No matter what is on the line, even if it is beaucoup bucks, a lot of contestants have an all-or-nothing, borderline gambling mentality. Take, for instance, the hit primetime game show *Deal or No Deal*.

If you are one of the five people in America who isn't familiar with *Deal or No Deal*, it is basically a game of statistics and chance. The way it works is that there are twenty-six suitcases that contain prizes ranging from one measly cent up to one million dollars. There are considerably more "small" prize amounts and just a few "large" prize amounts, all of which are known to the contestants in advance. What the contestants don't know is which suitcase holds which amount. That is the game. The contestant picks a suitcase to start that contains the prize he will retain if he keeps playing. This suitcase remains closed. Then, the contestant is required to pick other suitcases to be removed from play. As each suitcase is opened, the amount inside is revealed, letting everyone know what prize amounts remain in play (including in the contestant's chosen suitcase). The hope is that the removed suitcases will contain low prizes, making the chance of getting a high prize much greater.

After every few eliminated amounts are revealed, the show offers the contestant an amount of money to quit the game. The amount is somewhere between the lowest prize remaining and the highest prize remaining, depending on the amounts of low and high prizes left in play. The more high amounts available, the higher the prize offered to the contestant to quit. If the contestant wants to take the offer, he says, "Deal;" if not, meaning he wants to keep playing (thinking he has a bigger amount in his chosen suitcase), then he says, "No deal." What amazes me (and apparently the people working for the show as well, as I have heard from one of the producer's brothers) is how many people make poor evaluation decisions. A contestant may be down to seven suitcases, six of which are all worth under $10,000 and one worth $250,000. They are offered $50,000 to quit and they keep going—*no deal*. They convince themselves that they aren't risking anything since they came in with nothing. They would rather leave with five dollars and gamble for the $250,000, even though they are in fact risking $50,000 real dollars that would go home with them if they simply said, "*Deal.*"

If these people were playing *Deal or No Deal* with their own money at stake somehow, you would hope that they would take the *deal* more often. However, entrepreneurs often do just that; they say *no deal* and risk their own money on a business gamble. Whether it is due to poor evaluation skills, a gambling mentality, or something else, potential entrepreneurs poorly evaluate the risk and reward balance of a new business—if they do it at all.

As I said, you may not understand return on investment calculations, but everyone understands *Let's Make a Deal* (which, by the way, is one of my all-time favorite game shows). *Let's Make a Deal* gives you something, and then you decide whether it is good enough for you or if you want to trade it for something else. That something else could be better or worse than what you already have, so you have to decide if you want to make the trade.

Now, if you were given one dollar to trade for what's behind one of two curtains and were told that one curtain was worth nothing and one was worth $1,000, would you make the trade? Most of us would. One dollar isn't a lot to risk for the chance at $1,000, even if the downside is zero. Now, what if you were given $990 and asked to make the same trade—one curtain is zero, the other is $1,000? I hope that none of you would make that trade. You would be risking $990 for a chance to improve your situation by a mere ten dollars, a 1 percent increase. For each one of us, there is a different combination of amounts at risk and potential upside we would be willing to take the risk for, but for everyone, the risk needs to make sense. Certainly, in this case, a 1 percent upside doesn't make sense when the alternative is losing everything.

Imagine that in the previous examples, the amount you are trading stands for the amount you are investing of your own money in a new business. The two curtains represent the extreme possibilities for your business. You could fail, and it could be worth zero, or you could get the curtain with the big prize. Does the trade make sense? Before you answer that, you have to also factor in your current salary, your time, your opportunity costs, and all of the qualitative risks and rewards, among other things.

Let's play the game with more concrete numbers. Let's say that you are making $50,000 a year (plus benefits) at your current job and you have a gadget company that you can start with $60,000 of your own money. You need to evaluate whether you should make a deal. Should you trade your job and the investment for what is behind curtain number two—starting your own business? You don't always get full information on *Let's Make a Deal*, but let's throw in some additional details. Let's say curtain number two is a gadget business that sells $300,000 worth of gadgets from each year. Do you trade?

Well I hope you ask Monty Hall for additional information here. Let's further evaluate the choices. If you are employed, you make $50,000, and you get some benefits on top of that. Now, the $300,000-a-year gadget company may sound exciting because there is that big number there. But remember, that is sales, not profits, meaning that is not what you take home at the end of the day.

To find out what is leftover for you to put in your pocket, you have to take away from sales the cost of making the goods. Then, you have to take away the expenses of sales, marketing and administration, rent, employee salaries, advertising, professional fees, insurance, office supplies, shipping, postage, telephone and fax expenses, website expenses, and interest on any debt the business has incurred, as well as all other expenses, before you know what you are going to make.

The profit a business makes varies by how successful the business is, as well as the industry (e.g., commodity businesses have lower margins—the gross profit for each item after subtracting the direct cost of the product from the sales price of the product, expressed as a percent of the sales price—on average than a similarly branded business and service businesses sometimes have higher margins than product-oriented businesses). However, if you are doing well in this particular business based on the profits of competitors, you would be happy to have a business that has pre-tax profits in the range of 10 percent of sales (we look at pre-tax profits so that you can do an apples-to-apples comparison to your pre-tax salary of $50,000). Ten percent, by the way, is the level of profits that many professional private equity investors consider as a minimum gauge of a healthy mature products business. So, using the 10 percent proxy, that would mean that for a $300,000-in-sales gadget business, the amount available for you to take home is $30,000 (please note that these numbers are just for illustration; many businesses won't get to $300,000 in sales the first year—if ever—and many businesses aren't even profitable the first year). This profit ignores (only for this example, do not ignore this in reality!) that you may need to reinvest some of that money to make the business grow next year and the timing of cash flow. It also ignores (again, just for this example) that your perks and benefits from your old job, as with most "benefits" when owning your own business, now come directly out of your pocket.

The 10 percent is a proxy, a litmus test, or "sanity check" if you will, but it provides a good guideline for starting your evaluation. You won't have perfect information when you start a business, but you still need to sanity check your assumptions to see if they are in the realm of reality.

So, before even considering how the other, non-financial parts of the evaluation (such as the headaches and extra hours) come into play, you are taking a 40 percent (plus benefits) decrease in salary. And this is when you are selling $300,000 worth of gadgets, which is not a number to sneeze at and may not happen the first year. Sure, you say that the business may grow well past that over time and that you may also build equity in the business that you can one day sell at a multiple of several times pre-tax profits. That may be true, so you should evaluate your future business projections versus your current salary, plus any raises you would likely get over the same period of time you project that you will own the business. Even better, look at it over one-, five-, ten- and twenty-year time periods. Don't forget to take into account the initial $60,000 it cost you to start the business and the loss of using that money for other investments (or for other purposes). You should add in the value of the missed benefits, plus deduct any money that you need to put back into the business (from your pocket) to evaluate the financial trade-off.

If we look at the chart below and assume that with a starting salary of $50,000 and a 5 percent raise every year, after ten years, you would have earned (pre-tax) almost $629,000. Would you trade that for the chance that the gadget business, which after growing a generous 18 percent per year, *might* earn you almost $706,000, knowing that the other curtain could contain less than that, even zero? What if you took into account the extra $60,000 in start-up costs that it takes to make that trade? Now, what if you take into account that instead of putting that $60,000 into your business, you could put it into another investment that earns a conservative 5 percent a year on average? After ten years, that interests compounds to earn you another $38,000! If you take that into account, the no-risk scenario earns you both your pay and the interest on your savings, which together is almost $667,000.

If you include your initial $60,000 investment, that brings you to having more than $726,000 at stake, which means that you are risking more than your projected upside from investing in the business.

JOB No Investment at Risk			BUSINESS $60,000 Investment at Risk	
Year	Salary 5% Growth	Compound Interest on Investment of $60,000 (5% Interest)	Year	Take Home Profits (18% Growth)
1	$ 50,000	$ 3,000	1	$ 30,000
2	$ 52,500	$ 3,150	2	$ 35,400
3	$ 55,125	$ 3,308	3	$ 41,772
4	$ 57,881	$ 3,473	4	$ 49,291
5	$ 60,775	$ 3,647	5	$ 58,163
6	$ 63,814	$ 3,829	6	$ 68,633
7	$ 67,005	$ 4,020	7	$ 80,987
8	$ 70,355	$ 4,221	8	$ 95,564
9	$ 73,873	$ 4,432	9	$112,766
10	$ 77,566	$ 4,654	10	$133,064
	$628,895	**$37,734**		**$705,639**

Salary (with raises) of $628,895 + investment of $60,000 + interest of $37,734 = $726,629
Business after ten years with 18 percent annual profit increase = $705,639

You wouldn't make that trade based solely on the financial risks and rewards. But a lot of people do, because they never go through this math exercise at the onset.

You can see that this evaluation is particular to your circumstances and the opportunity. If you had less salary at risk, a lower investment to make, and a bigger potential opportunity, it may be a better trade for you. Plus, if you can sell the business at the end of the day, that creates additional upside for the rewards side of your equation.

While your projections show a snapshot of the business and can never account for every factor or scenario, they are a good starting point for evaluating if your risk and reward trade-off makes sense. If the numbers don't work, then you shouldn't make the trade. No supposed freedom of ownership is worth it if you aren't making profits.

Given the risks of starting a business and all of the ancillary headaches associated with it, the potential amount you can make from owning your own business should greatly outweigh the amount you can earn from your current job or a similar one. I can't tell you exactly how much it should outweigh it—that is up to you, but make sure you are comfortable with the reward benefits that you are taking the risk for.

Another way to sanity check yourself is to understand how much you are making per hour. Let's go back to the $300,000-in-sales gadget company that gives a pre-tax profit of $30,000. That business is going to require a lot of time and effort to get off the ground. There are fifty-two weeks in a year, and let's outrageously assume that you can actually take two weeks off for vacation (pipe dream!), so you have fifty work weeks a year. While it isn't uncommon for entrepreneurs to work seven days a week, let's say you decide to put in long hours during the week to have some free time on the weekends (yeah, right) and so you work five days a week instead. That is five days each week times fifty work weeks, or 250 work days per year.

To be able to take off the weekends, run the business, do the extra paperwork, etc., you are putting in twelve hours a day at work—7 A.M. to 7 P.M. This is probably conservative (fourteen-hour days are more likely), but just for illustrative purposes let's assume that it is accurate. Twelve hours each day times 250 work days is 3,000 work hours per year.

That year, you take 3,000 work hours to make $30,000 profit (less any money you may need to reinvest in growing the business) from your business with $300,000 in sales. That means, for all of your risk, headaches, and hard work, plus the $60,000 that you have invested of your own money, you are getting paid *ten bucks per hour*.

And that doesn't even begin to take into account the opportunity costs of the business. The money you invest in the business can't earn interest. The time you spend working on the business isn't spent doing fun things; you may have to forgo vacations, your kids' baseball games, family events, favorite television programs, or a hobby to be able to earn ten bucks an hour. Does that seem worth it to you? Does risking $60,000 of your hard-earned money that you invested to get the business going, the sleepless nights, the paperwork, managing employees, and working twelve-hour days seem worth the *opportunity* (because it is not a given that you will achieve your projections) to earn ten dollars per hour? Again, I can't answer that for you, but likely, you never thought of it that way.

The point is that you need to evaluate what success is and what it requires. You need to understand what you are trading and if it is a fair trade-off. You need to use the hard numbers as a benchmark and then factor in all of the other intangibles before you decide *deal* or *no deal*.

Your Business as a Portfolio Investment

One other part of evaluating the risk and reward balance is taking into account diversification. We have all been told that it is important to diversify your investments. You don't want to have all of your eggs in one basket (sorry for the overused phrase again, but it is really the best one). This is why many stock market investors choose to invest in mutual funds versus picking individual stocks. If you have diversity, one bad investment isn't going to ruin you financially. It will hopefully be balanced out across your entire fund or portfolio; the really bad will be averaged with the really good and the mediocre, to give you a fair, combined investment return.

When you are starting your business, you are also investing in it. If all of your money is in your business, you will not have the opportunity to

WHEN YOU ARE STARTING YOUR BUSINESS, YOU ARE ALSO INVESTING IN IT. IF ALL OF YOUR MONEY IS IN YOUR BUSINESS, YOU WILL NOT HAVE THE OPPORTUNITY TO DIVERSIFY WITH OTHER INVESTMENTS. SO, IF YOUR BUSINESS DOESN'T DO WELL, ALL OF YOUR EGGS WILL BE IN A BASKET THAT IS BROKEN.

diversify with other investments. So, if your business doesn't do well, all of your eggs will be in a basket that is broken.

It is important for an entrepreneur to show his commitment and have a significant stake in his business. This is a safeguard to ensure that the entrepreneur does everything he can to make the business successful. However, if you are putting every last dime into the business, your eggs will be all in that basket. If I were in that situation, I would want that basket to be bulletproof with fifteen inches of premium padding and a bodyguard to make sure that something didn't happen to every single one of my eggs.

Evaluating your risks and rewards by doing the entrepreneurial math is one of the most important things you must do before you commit to the entrepreneurial path. This involves looking at the hard numbers and evaluating both quantitatively, as well as qualitatively, what you would give up versus what you may gain. Then, imagine yourself standing in front of two curtains representing the upside and downside possibilities of your new business (to make it more interesting, imagine Monty Hall there with you wearing a plaid jacket from 1962). You are holding the amount of money you will be risking to start the business, including your start-up costs and existing salary. Then, think about the other trade-offs you will have to make. Look at the two curtains before you again. Will you make that deal? Only do it if it is really worth it.

EXERCISE 17

TARGET FOCUS—RISK/REWARD:
Assessing Risk and Rewards from the Numbers

This exercise is comprised of three different evaluations.

A. The financial "deal" evaluation:

1. Write down the value of the salary and benefits you would be giving up to start your business. Be sure to include raises and bonuses for each year over the next ten years. If you are unemployed, make an assumption on your next job using reasonable expectations for when you might get the job and the potential salary.

2. Next, write down how much money you will personally invest to start and run your new business.

3. For any money you plan to invest, write down what other investments you could alternatively invest that money into. What is a reasonable rate of return you can expect to make on that money? If you don't have a good benchmark, you can look at a range of scenarios (from losing 10 percent to making nothing to gaining 10 percent).

4. For any money you plan to invest, write down what will happen if you lose part or all of that investment.

5. If you need to take out a loan, write down how much the loan is for and the amount of interest you will be required to pay on that loan.

6. Write down what you need to put up in collateral for that investment.

7. For any collateral you will need, write down what would happen if you lose that collateral.

8. Write down how much you reasonably believe your business will make over the next ten years. Like in number three, look at normal, bad, and good scenarios based on varying the assumptions behind your business.

Now, evaluate if you should you "make the deal" based on the financial merits of the risk and reward trade-off. Do you trade your salary, benefits, investment, and/or collateral for the possibility of making what you may be able to make, purely based on the financial return?

You can first look at the value of item one plus item three above over that ten-year period and compare it to item number eight, taking into account any interest you will have to pay in item five. Is the return big enough to justify the risk? What if you take into account the collateral you have to put up (items six and seven)? Is there a financial merit to the trade-off? If so, how substantial is it? Remember, you probably won't want to trade $49,000 a year for *the chance* to make $50,000 a year. If you aren't 100 percent comfortable with numbers, enlist someone to help you with your evaluation—it is that important!

B. The hourly evaluation:

1. Write down how many days a week and hours per day that you think is realistic to achieve your financial model. Find out how many hours per year you will be working. *Note: you should interview other entrepreneurs in similar situations for some honest feedback, and take into account all aspects of the business, from marketing to paperwork to customer support to operations (performing the service you provide or making the goods you sell).*

2. Take the amounts you expect your business to make each year in good, bad, and normal scenarios (from step A8 of this exercise above) and divide each one by the number of hours you will work

that year from B1 above. This is your per-hour wage under the different scenarios.

Assess the per-hour wage. Is this a wage that you feel good about and you feel is a good reflection of the value of your time? If not, the reward of your business may not be substantial enough to justify the risk.

C. The prudent investor evaluation:

1. Ask yourself if you are "betting the farm" on your business.

2. Is the level of investment that you will be making wise, given your financial situation?

3. Would you consider making a similar financial investment in any other potential investment?

4. Do you have other investments?

5. Will you remain diversified from an investment standpoint, or will all of your money be tied up in the business?

6. Would you advise a friend or family member (that you like) to take on the same level of financial risk that you will be taking on by starting a business if the roles were reversed?

If you answered yes to items C1 or the second part of C5, or no to the other items, you are not making a prudent financial decision and should reconsider starting a business at a time when your circumstances have changed, so that your Entrepreneur Equation is not out of whack.

26

People, Spaces, and Things... What You Give Up When You Leave Your Job

THE WHOLE JOB THING gets a bad rap. First, you wake up in the morning and to perform your job, you have to go off to a place called "work." Work, by definition, is somewhat unpleasant—it's not called fun, party time, or relaxation for a reason. If you were perhaps instead to go to "fun" every day instead of work, you may begin the day in a better mood. So, work and the job associated with it start out with a strike against it.

Then, you have to go to the place where you do "work"—a business or company. The company, therefore, is guilty by association. And your job working at a company starts sounding really awful once you factor in that you may be smarter than your boss, that your co-workers smell like bologna sandwiches, and that your office hasn't been painted in the last decade.

You do your job for a while without issue but eventually, it starts to grate on your last nerve. You then start to fantasize. Maybe you fantasize about retiring to your own tropical island, but you don't have enough money, so you don't do that. Then you think maybe you should find another job, but you worry that it would be just as bad. Finally, you start thinking about how life would be better if you were out on your own. You could start your own business and escape your idiot boss, make sure to never hire anyone who smelled like lunch meat, and even pick the sleekest office decor in the world!

Maybe you have a brilliant business idea, or maybe you don't, but you start obsessing that having a desk without wads of chewed-up gum stuck underneath it and bathrooms that don't look like they belong in a third-world country would improve your quality of life exponentially.

Starting your own business sounds like heaven. Unfortunately, nobody has yet been able to prove the existence of heaven on earth.

With all of the fantasizing about how great it will be to set out on their own, what many future entrepreneurs forget to factor into the equation are all of the benefits they get from being a part of a company. Some may seem trivial, some may seem outlandish, but when they are your responsibility and on your dime, you see them in a whole different light.

Obviously, what you have access to will vary by the type of industry and company you are currently working for and the type of business you are thinking of starting. Regardless, whatever you had access to before as a company employee is now, as an entrepreneur, coming straight out of your pocket. These items are part of the qualitative risks and issues you face when you start a new job.

The Little Things, Like Paper Clips and Coffee

When I worked at Montgomery Securities (an investment bank headquartered in San Francisco) in the mid-1990s, we had almost a thousand people on staff and therefore, a lot of perks. Some of these perks were appreciated, and some were, frankly, taken for granted.

By the late '90s, our firm was acquired twice within a period of one year: first by NationsBank and then through a second merger with Bank of America. This sent my colleagues in the corporate finance department into a tailspin and a number of my colleagues decided it was an ideal time to explore starting their own businesses.

One of my first colleagues that left to pursue his own venture was Shane (not his real name), a senior associate a few years out of business school. He had been working at the firm since receiving his MBA and upon the merger chaos ensuing, decided to jump on the internet business bandwagon that was everywhere in Northern California at the time.

I went to visit Shane in his new offices a few months after his departure and asked him about his experience. He told me that he had been completely oblivious to the resources that he previously had access to while working at a larger company. At Montgomery he had a secretary, whom, at the time, he assumed didn't really do much for him. But now he confessed that he was spending too much time fielding phone calls, which was taking him away from working on other aspects of the business. He also had to book his own travel (on his own dime) and sit in the economy cabin instead of business class (not to mention that he chose to stay at the cheapest hotels possible rather than the luxury hotels our former employer sprung for).

His funniest complaint was that he missed the "awesome coffee." Montgomery had premium coffee always brewing in the kitchen on any floor that you visited. Now that the coffee cost was coming out of his pocket, he was using cheap, store-brand coffee rather than Starbucks Breakfast Blend. Even worse, he complained, was that he now had to make the coffee himself. It wasn't that it took much effort to make the coffee, but it was just one more thing he had to remember to do.

Who would have thought that it was for the tiny little perk of the access to good coffee that he didn't have to make for himself he was nostalgic? That little perk (and I am sure many other issues) had quite an impact, because he was back working for a major investment banking firm within eighteen months.

Two more colleagues, Kim and Johanna (again, not their real names), also decided to branch out and start their own company. A few months into the start-up process, Kim and Johanna were shocked at the cost of stocking their office. In addition to now having to pay rent for a dinky space, they needed to get office furniture and equipment—everything from desks to phones to high-end printers, all of which they previously had access to. Their big revelation: the ongoing costs of the office supplies. Kim said that she missed the supplies program at Montgomery where you could order anything you wanted, from highlighters to staples, out of a six-hundred-plus-page catalogue and it showed up on your desk the next day.

Now that every supply was an expense directly coming out of their pockets, Kim and Johanna became very conscious of every piece of paper they printed on, paper clip they used to secure a note, and stamped envelope they sent out. The little items added up and never went away once the supplies department became their responsibility. While I am sure it had more to do with the difficulty of securing clients than the cost of the paper clips, Kim and Johanna closed up shop in less than a year.

Office Space

And then there is me (oh, I am not immune from having overlooked a few key details either). Even though I had been educated at Wharton and advised some of the fastest-growing businesses in the world, I really did not understand all of the issues around entrepreneurship until I encountered them first-hand. Within a few months after all of the others had bailed from our previous employer, I followed suit and started my own advisory firm.

Among my biggest issues was space. Our first office didn't have much room because, hey, office space is expensive as it is. There was only enough room for me, my husband (who was my partner at the time and the company's co-founder), and one additional employee. We didn't have a conference room, so we had to meet with clients at their respective offices. We couldn't hire additional staff or even take advantage of college interns because we had no place to put them and with trying to pay ourselves, our single employee, and the business's operating expenses, we were tapped out as it was. This was a classic type of issue that wasn't given enough thought beforehand. Who would have thought that I couldn't take advantage of an intern (an employee who would actually work for *free*) because I didn't have a place to put him in the office, let alone want to spend the money on a computer for him to work on or a desk and chair for him to sit in (not to mention finding the time to train him)?

So, if you work in an office, you may take for granted that you have unlimited access to things like Post-it Notes, highlighters, printer ink and paper, a good working copy machine, a secretary, warm coffee, paper clips, a nice bathroom, a travel agent, envelopes that you don't have to lick, your favorite kind of pens, filing cabinets, notepads, and filtered drinking water. But don't be blasé; these are not trivial items when you have to provide and pay for them.

If you work in a non-office environment, the perks may not be the same in type, but they are just as important. If you work as an auto mechanic, hairdresser, or a massage therapist, having someone help schedule appointments means that there is more time for you to make money performing your craft. The expense of purchasing oil (whether for automotive, deep conditioning, or massage purposes, respectively) is now coming out of your pocket. You have to supply your own invoices or hair dye or clean sheets. Whatever company you work for now is providing equipment and other resources to you, and it is up to you to recognize their value.

Big Things—The Three Cs: Credibility, Clout, and Contacts

Exponentially more important than providing paper clips and coffee is the extra Cs that working for an established company gives you. These three Cs are credibility, clout, and contacts.

It makes no difference if you provide better service and preferential pricing, or even have the same person doing the same work—your new business card is worth a fraction of the business card that has an established company's name on it. There are many reasons for this, but most companies like to hire established firms, even if you had previously been their account representative. It may be that customers really believe that at a big company, "the whole organization is behind you," even if you were the one and only person doing the work when you worked for Established Company, Inc. Maybe they like the cachet of having a big-name service provider or business partner. Perhaps they enjoy some other corporate perks (like being taken to the stadium box for an NBA game, to a golf tournament, or even receiving a giant fruit basket during the holidays). Or just maybe, they understand all too well how many new and small businesses fail each year and don't want to risk being supplied or served by a "newbie."

My husband was amazed by the power of a name change when he left our advisory company and went back to work for a major investment banking firm. The same prospects that we had called on under our smaller banner were now calling him back more quickly. They were taking more meetings, and he was signing up engagements more rapidly. Why? His skills hadn't changed. Frankly, the person doing the work hadn't changed either. However, the perception of his resources from the customers' perspective had changed, and that made a huge, discernable difference.

For whatever the reason, even your best existing customers and clients may not follow you to your new firm. And while you may provide needed goods or services at an outstanding value, given the competitive marketplace businesses face today, it is very difficult to find new clients and customers, especially ones that pay (and pay regularly and on time). Many of the potential customers and clients willing to take a chance on a newer and smaller business are willing to do so because they are desperate. One business owner characterized that phenomenon to me as "[new businesses] are the best friends of desperate men." Unfortunately, these are probably the customers you don't want. If these customers don't pay, or delay paying, remember who it is that has to track them down (hint: it's you). And if you don't have customers or clients that pay you, you don't have a business.

A plan of having customers or clients follow you to your new business may be one of your biggest challenges. Actually, it may also be against your employment contract, too. Remember that paperwork you signed on the first day of work? You probably never even read half of it or even kept a copy for your files. But you need to get your hands on that paperwork because there may be a non-solicitation or non-compete provision, which states that for some period of time (six months, two years, five years, etc.) that you cannot call on or try to service any existing client of the company. Some take it as far as to say that you can't call on any prospective client of the company, really limiting your ability to take off and open a competitive business or use any contacts that you have. So legally, you may not be able to open a competitive business, or if you do, your top prospects may be completely off-limits.

Customers are not the only ones with whom you lose credibility, clout, and contacts. Vendors and suppliers are much the same. You may have even been the point person for a given vendor at your previous company, but then you were acting as a representative of Established Company, Inc. and the vendor had a relationship with the company as much as with you. They know that Established Company Inc. can pay its bills on time (they have been doing so for years), so they are happy to extend Established Company great credit terms. They may know you personally, but your New Business Inc. is an unknown quantity. This means you don't get the great credit terms, so you have to pay for your goods and supplies sooner or even up front, putting a crunch on your cash flow.

> LEGALLY, YOU MAY NOT BE ABLE TO OPEN A COMPETITIVE BUSINESS, OR IF YOU DO, YOUR TOP PROSPECTS MAY BE COMPLETELY OFF-LIMITS.

Established Company Inc. is also larger, so it probably orders more items from each vendor and is able to take advantage of that purchasing power in terms of discounts. New Business, Inc. has no purchasing power, therefore you have to pay full price. Not to mention that being a smaller company, you and New Business Inc. are no longer at the front of the line. Your sales representative may not rush to take your calls, help you out in a pinch, or show you any love whatsoever for quite some time. Let's face it, the more important you are as a customer, the more fawning and ass-kissing you will receive from vendors and suppliers. When you are a small guy, they may feel as if they are doing you a favor, which is not a favorable (again, lame pun intended) position for you to be in with your suppliers and vendors.

Calling in the Technical Support Team— Oh Wait, You Don't Have One

When you work for a company, usually there are people on staff (or for smaller companies, outsourced) that help take care of problems. If your computers are acting up, you call technical support. If the copy machine breaks, you call the copier service staff. If someone strange is trying to get into the back offices, you call security.

Let's play a guessing game. When you start your own business, guess who is in charge when things go wrong? Survey says...you! If your computers are acting up, you need to deal with it. If you are an IT professional, this may not be the end of the world, but if not, then it is a headache, one that takes away time from doing other things. You probably don't have a technical support group on staff. You may not even know who to call. You may have to get into your car, go to the nearest Best Buy store, hand your computer to the Geek Squad, and hope that it doesn't take too long to fix it. If your computer does need to be fixed, you may not have another one sitting around the office to use while you are waiting, or if you do, it may not have the information you need to effectively do your work. Then, you have to figure out a work plan in the meantime while you wait to go back to the store to retrieve your computer, which may not be for several days. This takes away valuable time that could be spent working on your business and puts extra hours and stress on you.

If you have a physical location for your business, such as an office space or retail storefront and you are lucky, your landlord may have a janitorial crew that cleans at night. Of course, if your landlord provides a janitorial crew, that means you are paying for it as part of your lease. If the landlord doesn't provide that service, or if they only clean the common areas, guess who is now in charge of janitorial services? Survey says...you (yet again)! You can either hire a service (which costs you money), or you or one of your employees can clean. If you are the only employee, your choice is either money out of your pocket or time out of your day with a vacuum and a feather duster. Not necessarily how you pictured the American Dream, eh?

When you are at an established company, there are resources to draw upon. When you own your own business, you lose that. It falls on you to figure out, manage, or fix whatever it is that has gone wrong.

Benefits: Is It Really a Benefit When It Comes out of Your Pocket?

In addition to salary and bonus potential, one of the important considerations job holders take into account are employee benefits. These benefits vary widely by company, industry, and position, but benefits are a key component of many jobs. When you apply for a new job, you evaluate the benefits as an extra factor on top of your cash pay to assess the overall value of a job offer.

When you own your own business, almost every so-called benefit comes directly out of your pocket. So, your benefits are not in addition to what you make, they are actually subtracted from what you earn when it is your own business.

Here are just some of the benefit differentials to take into account.

HEALTH INSURANCE

If you have ever tried obtaining health insurance as a self-employed person or small business owner, it absolutely sucks. It costs a small fortune, and it is a pain in the butt to apply for. I know there are a number of well-known folks who contend that this isn't as difficult as it sounds. I am guessing these people have a very clean health history, because it has been my personal experience (and that of many other small business owners that I know) that if you have a history of having a "health issue" as minor as say, hangnails, the insurance company is going to find a reason to charge you more or potentially deny you coverage, for your health care package.

Many established companies offer their workers health care benefits. In most cases, established companies have better health care policies available to their employees than you can get as a new business owner. The established companies have more workers that they are buying or negotiating policies on behalf of, which allows them to enjoy discounts (which are ultimately passed on to you as an employee). If you work for a company, health care will usually cost you less than it will on your own. In many cases, your employer may also pay for a portion of the health care cost as an additional perk. The plan may be open to your spouse and children. Your plan benefits in many cases will also be superior, again because of the negotiating power the larger company has. Best of all, the health history requirements when you are in a larger group are much less stringent (i.e., a history of hangnails does not disqualify you or jack up your coverage rates) than they are for you as a small business owner.

There is, more often than not, a significant tangible penalty that you will incur from health care costs when you start your own business. While the national healthcare bill (*a whopping 2,400 pages*) that was signed into law last year is intended to help reform the healthcare system, it will be implemented over eight years, and health care will likely remain a burden for small businesses for quite some time.

VACATION TIME

Paid vacation time is a great perk that many employers offer. It is good for the employer because it is a perk they can deliver that doesn't cost them extra cash. It is appreciated by most employees because they value having free time. It is a fantastic bargaining tool for both employers and employees. Even in companies that are not quick to provide cash raises, if you have been employed for a while, you can usually bargain for more vacation days.

When you have your own business, there is no such thing as paid vacation time. Especially early on, and for sure if you are a one-man band (i.e., the only employee), the thought of taking a vacation is somewhat ludicrous—you have too much to do to be able to go enjoy a week at the beach. If you do plan to take the time off, it is not paid—in fact it actually costs you because there will be nobody available to run the business. If the business is not open and running, then you are not making money, which takes dollars directly out of your pocket.

So, where vacation is a perk for an employee, it is a cost (and a pipedream!) for a new business owner.

SPECIAL PERKS:
FROM DAY CARE TO BIRTHDAY CAKES TO HOLIDAY PARTIES

Many employers offer a whole host of perks for employees, from the bold to the basic. Some companies pull out all of the stops to offer special incentives for employees, from on-site day care to shoe shining and laundry services. Other companies keep the perks more streamlined, such as having birthday cakes monthly for employees to having bagels every third Friday morning. Summer barbecues, winter holiday parties, and hosting on-site massages are other items that employers offer to keep employee morale high.

When you own your business, you either do without these perks or you pay for them. If you have employees, every perk you offer is no longer a perk for you, it is an expense (remember my former colleague with the store-brand coffee?). Perks you provide can also be a use of your time. If you have a holiday party, it not only costs you money, but you have to plan it, too. If you offer an on-site dry cleaning service pickup and they screw up, you have to figure out how to fix it. Make sure to calculate the value of even the most basic perks when you evaluate the risks and rewards of owning your own business.

The "Benefits" of Working with Other People

Most of us have had co-workers that we could "take or leave" (or maybe just leave). We have worked with people who were loud, nosy, and obnoxious types, or were saboteurs or incorrigible kiss-asses (and probably some people who were all of the above). All kidding aside, there are a lot of great benefits derived from working with others.

A man we'll call Matt was a consultant who worked for a major consulting firm. He got tired of the so-called corporate grind and decided to become a freelance consultant. Within two years, he was back working in the consulting industry for a different established consulting firm. There were many reasons why he went back, but this one struck me as particularly interesting. He said:

One of the biggest issues was the professional isolation. Even though I didn't always agree with my co-workers, and maybe thought that their suggestions were stupid at times, they actually provided a lot to me, which I completely took for granted. Working with others allowed me to grow both personally and professionally. They helped me solve problems and see different perspectives on projects.

They created new networking opportunities. I know a lot of people, but with my co-workers, we together know a *ton* of people. They provided professional contacts, resources, and opportunities that I didn't have access to when I worked by myself. Having other people on your team and in your division gives you both perspective on what to do and what not to do. I learned some of the most valuable lessons by watching colleagues interact with customers.

As Matt's story illustrates, working with other people gives you continuing education and helps you to grow professionally. Plus, interaction is healthy—it keeps your mind sharp and helps you avoid feeling isolated.

Everyone's Two Favorite Game Shows... "Pass the Buck" and "The Blame Game"

An intangible benefit for many workers is the safety net at work called *other people*. Above, we explored how having co-workers can help you grow. They can also help you in other ways. We live in a culture where people like to do the least amount possible and don't like to take responsibility for their actions. When you work in a company with other people, this is easy to do. When you own your own company, this is nearly impossible to do.

Let's take everyone's favorite "game show" that I like to call *Pass the Buck*. Pass the Buck is played as follows. You get a task or responsibility that you don't feel like doing or being responsible for. Then you pawn this task off on someone else. It could be a co-worker, an administrative assistant, or even a junior staff member; it doesn't matter, as long as the responsibility doesn't remain with you. Let's say you don't want to write the company's monthly newsletter. In Pass the Buck, you tell your boss that you are swamped on a project and volunteer your co-worker Jimmy to do it instead. Or if you don't feel like planning a company off-site event, you Pass the Buck right over to your secretary and have her do it for you. Perhaps an annoying client is coming into town and needs to be picked up from the airport. You don't want to do it, so you Pass the Buck by declaring that you have to pick up your dog at the veterinarian that day and suggest that your team member Susie do it since she isn't that busy.

Pass the Buck is a game loved and played by many. It works well for small tasks that pile up, and sometimes even for big tasks as well. The larger the organization, the more often people play Pass the Buck and the more times the buck gets passed! If you are really good at playing Pass the Buck, those in charge of your compensation won't really notice, and you won't be penalized for it

> WE LIVE IN A CULTURE WHERE PEOPLE LIKE TO DO THE LEAST AMOUNT POSSIBLE AND DON'T LIKE TO TAKE RESPONSIBILITY FOR THEIR ACTIONS. WHEN YOU WORK IN A COMPANY WITH OTHER PEOPLE, THIS IS EASY TO DO. WHEN YOU OWN YOUR OWN COMPANY, THIS IS NEARLY IMPOSSIBLE TO DO.

come review or bonus time. If you are bad at playing Pass the Buck, it may come back to haunt you a bit. If you really suck at Pass the Buck, you will end up getting the buck passed to you more often than you pass it on. But at least you do have the opportunity to pass it on to someone else again.

When you own your own business, you can't play Pass the Buck. You can try, but ultimately, the buck stops with you. If none of your employees want to take on a given task (and if it requires any work at all, they won't), or if you have no employees, there will be no buck passing. You get to do the dreaded task. If the task doesn't get done, then you can't even be a contestant on everyone's second-favorite "game show," *The Blame Game*.

The Blame Game, which is sometimes referred to by its slang name, "Throwing Someone under the Bus," is another game show people participate in quite frequently at work. It often comes on right after Pass the Buck.

When something doesn't get done, gets done poorly, or is otherwise a disaster and you don't want to get in trouble for it, you immediately relieve yourself of all responsibility by shifting that responsibility (deserved or not) to someone else entirely. You point the finger at that person and declare that it was "all their fault." That is how you play The Blame Game. The newsletter you didn't want to write was done seventeen days late with a hundred typographical errors, but you shift the blame to Jimmy; it was his project, you were busy doing other things. The company's off-site event was at a terrible location with no cell phone access, and the lunch that was served gave half of your co-workers food poisoning. No worries; you can throw your secretary under the bus on that one, as it was her fault since she did all of the planning. The annoying client was picked up two hours late from the airport and was so mad that he pulled his account from your firm. Well, that was not your fault either; Susie agreed to do it. And so The Blame Game goes.

Just like Pass the Buck, if you are good at The Blame Game, you can get away with a whole lot by blaming others. You rarely ever feel the whole burden of something gone wrong, as there are always other people to cushion the impact of the issue you can share the blame with.

When you own your own business, you can't play The Blame Game. Even if it is someone else's fault, if something doesn't get done, or is done poorly or incorrectly, it is your problem. You can blame your employees, but the full impact of the problem falls on you. It is your business, and you will bear the ultimate burden because it is your money and reputation on the line. If things go really badly, you will go home with a nasty parting gift called *going out of business*.

Now obviously, this section is a bit tongue in cheek, but there is reality behind the joking, as there always is. If you are the type of person to shirk responsibilities or shift blame frequently to others, or just like having the comfort of a group of people to share the burden with instead of being responsible for all of it yourself, then entrepreneurship is going to be a tough and unpleasant road for you. You need to have very broad shoulders to carry the weight of all of the responsibilities yourself when it is your own business. You have to be honest with yourself. If you aren't willing to stand by yourself in a big way and take accountability for all tasks (no matter how menial) and take all blame for things gone wrong, don't quit your day job.

The Pond's Maintenance Is on You

From suppliers to supplies, credibility to benefits, you are getting so many hidden tangible and intangible benefits from being associated with an established business. You may think that you are going from being a small fish in a big pond to a big fish in a small pond by leaving your job and starting your own business. The reality is that you are going from being a small fish in a big pond to a smaller fish in a bigger pond, with the extra responsibility of taking care of the pond's maintenance. Make sure to take the financial costs, emotional costs, and opportunity costs of what you lose when you walk away from your job into account when you evaluate that option.

EXERCISE 18

TARGET FOCUS—RISK/REWARD:

Identifying Qualitative Risks

1. Make a list of the following:
   - All of the benefits you receive from your job (or would receive in a job if you are not currently employed). Include every benefit you can think of, no matter how small or large.
   - All of the advantages to having co-workers.

2. Go back and circle any of the items that you will have to give up or modify significantly if you leave your job (or forgo a job) and choose to start a business.

The circled items represent some of the qualitative things you will risk when you start a business. The items on the list should be added to the risks and issues side of your Entrepreneur Equation as part of the overall risk and reward evaluation of your business opportunity.

27

Employees—Damned If You Do (or Don't) Hire Them

T HE EMPLOYEE CONUNDRUM is one of the biggest challenges that you face when considering entrepreneurship. As discussed previously, employees help determine where you are and where you want to go on the Job to Business Spectrum. If you don't hire employees and are a one-man band, you aren't really creating equity, you are creating a job (a.k.a. a job-business). And for all of the reasons in this book already, if what you have is a job, you may find that given a job's risks and rewards, you are better off working for someone else's company instead of working for yourself.

So, if you are thinking big—big enough to create some equity in an entity that itself has value—you are going to need some employees to get there. In fact, if you don't have anyone else working with you, you will probably eventually go insane. You are human, which means you will, at some point, get the flu, or you might want to take a vacation. But even if you work 24/7, you just can't possibly do everything yourself. Hiring employees is necessary, but a necessary evil in many ways.

Fun with Employees

When you add your first employee, everything changes. And I don't just mean that you can no longer leave the bathroom door open when you pee. The moment you decide to hire an employee, just one measly employee, your paperwork and legal headaches increase by a factor of several hundred. If you haven't been through this before, here's what you are in for (and if you have, just consider this a friendly reminder). First, you have to hire the employee. That requires you to spend money to take out ads or hire a staffing agency to find interested applicants. Then, you have to weed through the applicants to find the candidates you might potentially want to hire. Then, you have to conduct interviews. When you conduct an interview, there are certain guidelines of things you can't ask or say; if you do, you violate the law. If you think that blue-haired memaw is too old to do a good job at your skateboarding company, you better find another reason not to hire her because you can't discriminate during the hiring process. If you discriminate based on factors like age, race, or sex, you open yourself up to lawsuits. Now, if you worked for a large, established company, your human resources department would be up to speed on all of these rules and guidelines. But you are now flying solo, so it falls on you to figure out the rules and guidelines and follow them.

While you conduct interviews, you have the fun task of trying to find the best, most qualified person for the least amount of money. You also hope this will be someone with some experience that will take a salary close to what you have budgeted for the position. This is not an enviable task, as you typically get what you pay for. The people who will agree to a low salary may be unqualified, sketchy, or otherwise broken; those who are qualified will want you to pay them their worth, which is more money out of your pocket.

So, you have to prioritize. Which is more important, your budget and therefore your profits, or having a more qualified employee? If you do find a great person who doesn't know their own worth (or the median pay for that particular job), don't get too excited. The chances are that they will figure it out and eventually require more money to stay with your company.

If you don't know the applicants for your job positions, you are going to have to do some research on their backgrounds. You obviously wouldn't want sex offenders working with kids, embezzlers managing your cash register, or murderers working with your customers (no matter how frustrating your customers can sometimes be). Background checks are advisable (and, of course, cost money and take time). Many companies also like to do credit checks as well; there have been an increasing number of stories about people in financial straits doing lots of shady things at their jobs, such as stealing from their employers. It is good to find an employee who is hungry, but perhaps not starving.

Then, of course, you will want to check the applicant's professional and personal references. This takes more time, but you should always do your homework, especially when you will be entrusting these people with your livelihood and your personal investment. You also may want to test for drugs. This may be a one-time deal or an ongoing procedure, particularly if the job you are filling is something where employee drug use can cause someone else harm (like an employee driving a company delivery truck for which you are liable).

If you find yourself in the awkward position of having people you know (friends, acquaintances, and/or family members) interested in the jobs that you need to fill, then you have a whole other set of issues to think about. It is very difficult to work with people with whom you have an existing personal relationship. On one hand, you know these people and hopefully have some level of trust in them. On the other hand, there is already an established protocol between you and that person for communication and interaction, which will get turned on its head once a professional dynamic is put in place. The person may be accustomed to viewing you as a peer instead of an authority figure, which will make it difficult for him to take orders from you once you are his boss. This can also be exacerbated if he is used to being some sort of an authority figure to you personally, such as an older brother or personal mentor.

Other issues arise when your friends or family members are used to a playful personal interaction, such as joking around with you most of the time. However, your business is not a joke, especially when you have a lot of your own money on the line, as well as your time invested in it!

Good people don't always make good employees. I have heard hundreds of nightmare stories about people working with friends and acquaintances. Just because someone is nice, fun, or related to you doesn't mean that he is qualified for a particular job. I once hired a friend who I thought would be perfect to work in one of my companies. He wasn't; he was all over the place like a little kitten that needed to be constantly refocused. He wanted to chat about life, not about business. The business was my life, and eventually we mutually parted ways.

> GOOD PEOPLE DON'T ALWAYS MAKE GOOD EMPLOYEES. I HAVE HEARD HUNDREDS OF NIGHTMARE STORIES ABOUT PEOPLE WORKING WITH FRIENDS AND ACQUAINTANCES. JUST BECAUSE SOMEONE IS NICE, FUN, OR RELATED TO YOU DOESN'T MEAN THAT HE IS QUALIFIED FOR A PARTICULAR JOB.

It is difficult to maintain an important personal relationship and do business at the same time. That is perhaps where the phrase "business is business" comes from. Moreover, it makes for an awkward birthday party or family dinner after you have had to fire a friend, a cousin, a spouse, or a sibling, so think long and hard about it before you take the plunge. It may be easier to have the uncomfortable conversation up front (i.e., I don't want to ruin our friendship, relationship, sex life, etc.) rather than endure the issues if it doesn't work out.

Fun with Logistics, Paperwork, and Benefits

Okay, now back to employee logistics. While you are interviewing, you need to make room for the employee. In a retail store, this may be easier. In an office environment, this may be exponentially more difficult. Either way, once you make the space, you have to outfit the workspace with all of the tools needed for an employee to do his or her job, including a desk, garbage can, chair, computer, pencil holder, filing cabinets, uniform, cleaning supplies, delivery van, makeup brushes, or whatever other items are needed.

You have found an employee candidate that agrees to your salary package. Great! Then, they ask about benefits. ##!!*@—you forgot about benefits! Some businesses can get away without offering benefit packages, but to be competitive, many businesses have to offer benefits at least comparable to those offered by other companies where employee candidates might also consider applying. This means that you have to put together or expand your health care plan. You may have to institute or expand your 401(k) program. You may have to plan a holiday party. Whatever benefits you choose to offer, they constitute more time, more paperwork, and more money out of your pocket. In fact, taxes and benefits can be an additional 20–30 percent or more (depending on your state and your benefits package) above the cost of the employee's salary. So, if you thought you were paying someone $30,000 a year, you may find that you are really paying them $39,000 a year after benefits and taxes.

Paperwork continues to increase because you have hired employees. The paperwork that personally annoys me the most is the paperwork related to payroll and taxes. When you are a one-man band, if you set up your corporate structure properly, you can just file a "Schedule C" on your personal income tax statements each April and be done with it. When you have employees, you have all sorts of new paperwork that you need to fill out and keep track of, from W-2s to quarterly payroll filings. You have to deduct certain taxes from each employee's paycheck (and any benefits if you are doing that). It takes time, and it is tedious. You can hire a service company to do it, but that costs money. Also, hiring a service to do your paperwork doesn't absolve you of the responsibility of making sure it was done right and not forgotten. Outsourcing of responsibility does not mean you no longer have any responsibility. You have to be on top of everything, because if you forget to do a particular filing, the government isn't going to blame your payroll service; they are going to blame you, the person whose name is signed on the dotted line for the business. (The Blame Game mentioned in the last chapter does not work with the IRS!)

In addition to governmental and tax paperwork, you will want to have new employees sign other paperwork, including confidentiality agreements and non-compete agreements, codes of conduct, mission statements, and more. You will have to write these or find someone to do it for you. Not only do you need to have the employees fill out these forms and agreements, but you also have to keep track of each form and agreement to make sure that they are current and being followed.

Then, depending on your size and industry, there are all sorts of other administrative things you need to do in relation to your employees, from complying with Occupational Safety and Health Administration workplace safety guidelines, to licensing and continuing education requirements if your industry is heavily regulated. You have to make sure you are complying with minimum wage requirements, workers' compensation laws, civil rights laws, child labor laws, environmental laws, Americans with Disabilities Act, labor laws, immigration laws, policies and laws designed to fight terrorism, and all sorts of other crazy things the government has thought up that suck up your time and resources. Some requirements are lessened if you are a small company; some are not. Unfortunately, this means that even if you have just a few employees, it may be close to a full-time job to deal with the all of the rules, regulations, and guidelines, not to mention the mountain of paperwork.

On-the-Job Training

Are you exhausted yet? Well wake up, because you haven't even started training your new employee! But before you can do that, you have to create procedures and systems that the employee can follow. You need to develop each procedure and break down each task to a level that is so basic and simple that virtually anyone can do it. That is the secret of the majority of successful businesses—they leave nothing to chance and everything to a clear procedure.

Once you create the systems, then you have to train the new employees and keep monitoring their progress. You need to tweak your procedures. You need to positively reinforce good work and find uplifting ways to change bad work. You have to be a shoulder to cry on when your employee breaks up with her boyfriend, and you have to be a stand-in if the employee gets sick. Then, you need to cross your fingers and hope that the employee stays for a while; otherwise, you will have to do this all over again with her replacement.

So, you have searched for the perfect employee, taken on the paperwork, abided by rules and regulations, incurred expenses, built a plan, and trained your new team member. After all of that, you will likely still have a mediocre employee. At the end of the day, many employees don't care if they do average work (and they definitely won't care as much as you do, because it is not their business). Ultimately, it is just a job to them, and if they don't want to be there, they can just leave; they have very little at risk.

Employee apathy can lead to bigger issues because your employee is a representative of your company. A rogue employee can damage a company in unimaginable ways.

Several months ago, my husband and I drove through a very well-known coffee chain on a Saturday afternoon. The attendant asked through the speaker, "What would you like today?" My husband ordered a black coffee. The speaker came on again, and we could hear giggles, which basically sounded like a few teenagers screwing around at work. The attendant replied, "I am sorry, can you repeat that?" Again, my husband ordered a black coffee. More giggles came through the speaker, and for the third time, the attendant asked, "What was that again?" My husband was getting annoyed and told the attendant that he wanted a black coffee and that he wasn't going to repeat himself again. The attendant apologized and asked us to pull around to the window.

The bad customer service was less than impressive, but what happened next was unthinkable. The attendant apologized again and after asking if we wanted any cream for the black coffee, mumbled something about it "being crazy in there" and gave my husband the coffee. When we got home, my husband removed the lid to pour some milk in the coffee and noticed something foreign floating in the top of the coffee. We inspected it, photographed it, and after it didn't dissipate in the scolding hot coffee an hour later, we were pretty sure that it was spit. Yes, the employee spit in the coffee and served it to my husband. I won't go into the details about how we handled the issue, but as you can imagine, this severely damaged our relationship with that business, one that we—and mostly everyone we know—patronized frequently.

The point is that it wasn't the business that spit in the coffee; it was a rogue employee acting on his own accord and against company policies. But our only recourse and relationship was with the company, not the individual employee. I hope this illustrates some of what you are getting into when you have other people to manage, some who don't care about the business even a fraction as much as you do and who may act in ways that are unacceptable to you.

The Literal (Pizza) Pie-in-the-Face Incident

By the way, my spit-in-the-coffee story isn't an isolated incident (gross, but true). In April 2009, two Domino's Pizza employees made a video while working one evening at a Domino's Pizza store. The disgusting video shows one employee putting ingredients up his nose and then on top of food to be served to the customer, as well as sprinkling other non-sanitary items (I won't mention them here, but feel free to Google the incident) on top of customers' food. These special employees, in their infinite wisdom, then posted the video to YouTube, which as you can probably imagine, made the rounds to millions of internet viewers. The brand exposure, which was obviously very negative in this case, was probably more than Domino's spends on television commercials in a month.

Patrick Doyle, president of Domino's USA, swiftly took to YouTube with his own video to apologize, explaining that it was an isolated incident in one store in North Carolina and expressing his gratitude to customers and dedication to regaining customer trust. In addition to talking about the action Domino's was taking—firing the two employees, pressing charges against them, and sanitizing the store from top to bottom—Mr. Doyle made the following powerful statement: "The independent owner of the store is reeling from the damage that this has caused, and it is not a surprise that this has caused a lot of damage to our brand. It sickens me that the actions of two individuals could impact our great system where 125,000 men and women work for local business owners around the United States and more than sixty countries around the world."

This is an incredibly powerful example of the employee issue. Two rogue employees again could cause incalculable brand damage to an established company with rigorous systems and procedures. When you think about starting a business and evaluate the risks and rewards of entrepreneurship, think about having employees and keep these two situations in the front of your mind.

Passing the Buck a Different Way (a.k.a. into Their Pockets)

If that wasn't enough stress, you also have to worry about your employees putting their hands in the cookie jar. Whether it is taking money from the cash register, not ringing transactions through the register and keeping the customers' money, shorting customers their due change, or stealing inventory, employees account for a large percentage of "shrinkage" in many businesses. You may have to install security cameras, you definitely have to build appropriate procedures, and most of all you need to keep an eye on your employees. I have heard of all kinds of stories regarding employee theft from entrepreneurs, from workers who would bag up inventory with the garbage, throw out the "garbage" and go back late at night to collect the goods and later sell them on eBay, to employees who were in charge of purchasing who ordered unrelated products and supplies for themselves.

There are employees who punch the time clock on behalf of other employees who come in late, to have the favor returned when they themselves leave early (in management classes this falls under the "exchange" principle). There are employees who steal the credit card numbers of the company's customers. You name it, it happens, and it happens more often than you would think.

Cash and inventory aren't the only items that can be stolen. Business secrets, customer lists, contract information, computer codes, and other prized business assets, tangible or intangible, can be taken by employees with access. In 2006, three people were arrested for trying to steal trade secrets from the Coca-Cola Company (including the formula for a new beverage) and sell them to PepsiCo (it was PepsiCo, by the way, that turned them in). If that can happen in a large company with tons of security, think of how vulnerable your small business is to theft.

The Burden of Responsibility

There is an additional burden to having employees, one that is emotional. That burden is a sense of responsibility toward your employees. The longer that your employees have worked with your company, the more a sense of family is engendered, making business decisions sometimes increasingly stressful.

I interviewed an investment banker recently who told me about one of his clients who was struggling due to some operational challenges in the business. The business had been around for more a decade and had around $75 million in sales. Due to recent issues, the sales started to decline, and the business was unprofitable. The investment banker paraphrased what his client told him about his sense of obligation to his employees:

> We are a very transparent business, meaning that we share everything with our employees so that they know how we are doing. This includes our financial statements. This is very easy to do when the business is doing well and growing. It has become increasingly more difficult as things are not going well. We had the first layoffs ever in the history of the company, which was very difficult for all. The employees are like my family and now I am responsible for these people not being able to provide for their families. The employees that remain are now very concerned about their jobs as well. Now, I have the stress of trying to return the business to profitability and managing the anxieties of the employees. If I fail, it will impact all of us.

While of course the employees can find other jobs if let go, having employees creates extra stress and burden for an entrepreneur in the form of feeling responsibility for the employees and their livelihoods.

So, you need employees to grow and to make more money, but you need to make sure that they are doing what they are supposed to be doing and also not doing anything they shouldn't. Remember how you wanted freedom and to be the boss? Was this the picture that you had in mind? I think that maybe you would have more freedom and authority teaching kindergarten.

PERSONAL BRAINSTORM

TARGET FOCUS—RISK/REWARD:
How Employees Affect Your Place
on the Job-to-Business Scale

If you don't have employees, or perhaps if you have just a few, you likely have more of a job-business than a business. Think about the following:

1. What are the benefits, issues, and risks of having employees?
2. If you plan to have employees, when do you plan to bring them on board?
3. What needs to be in place before you can take on any employees?

If you conclude that you don't want to take on employees in the near future, consider:

1. What limitations does the absence of employees create for your business?
2. Have you pigeon-holed yourself into a job-business instead of a business?
3. What additional risks and rewards do you have from a job-business versus a business?
4. Are the risks of creating the job-business worth the potential benefits?

Your plans to hire employees or not will affect what type of a business you have and add additional risks, issues, or rewards to your Entrepreneur Equation that you must consider.

28

Sometimes "Cash Flow" Doesn't Flow

IF YOU ARE INTIMIDATED by or think there are enough headaches surrounding the financial aspects of running a business, you are in for a lot of fun (and by fun, I mean more headaches). In the game of business, financial statements are the key tool to help you keep score. If you can't keep score, you shouldn't be playing the game—especially not professionally!

A lot of entrepreneurs are not proficient in any aspect of financial accounting. They particularly do not understand how to manage the cash flow of their businesses. Cash flow illustrates the actual cash impact of running your business on a day-to-day basis, rather than purely the profits and losses. Cash flow has a significant impact on whether your business is healthy and if you as the owner can take home any money—which isn't always the case, even when your business is showing a profit.

FINANCIAL LINGO

CASH FLOW—Where the cash in your business is coming from and going to (and sometimes where it's just sitting or waiting to come).

INCOME STATEMENT—Also known as a P&L (profit and loss statement) or a statement of earnings, this shows the company's expenses and revenues for a given period (such as week, month, quarter, or year) to determine if you have made any income or profits (this is "on paper" earnings, which is different than the change in cash in your business). The income statement includes sales for that period, as well as cost of goods sold, operating expenses (such as administrative costs), depreciation on assets, interest on any loans the business has or interest earned on investments, and sometimes income taxes.

STATEMENT OF CASH FLOWS—The statement of cash flows shows your sources of new cash coming into your business during a given period, as well as your uses of cash during that same period, ultimately demonstrating if your overall cash position is increasing or decreasing. It focuses on the actual change in cash, rather than income statement profits. It is generally organized by cash flow from operating activities, cash flow from investing activities, and cash flow from financing activities. Even if a business is profitable, negative cash flow can cause a business to fail.

WORKING CAPITAL—Your business's current assets less its current liabilities.

When many entrepreneurs write their business plans, as well as when they do their accounting, they focus on the income statement, which they may or may not really understand. The income statement shows for a given period of time (a month, a year, etc.) the value of the goods or services your business sold (your revenue or sales), the direct cost of those sales (the cost of goods), and then all of the sales, marketing, administrative, and other expenses you incurred while running the business during that period of time. Many entrepreneurs tend to look at their income statement profit literally as what they earned (or will earn) during the period, and they focus on that number as a good snapshot of the business and its health. However, the profit is different from the cash flow of the business, because the profit doesn't fully capture the money you need to spend on major purchases or take into account the timing of when you get paid or when you pay your suppliers and vendors.

Cash flow from a business includes the operating profits of the business (adding back in any non-cash depreciation) and subtracts any increases in what is called working capital (or if you are lucky enough to have a decrease, adds that decrease back), and also subtracts any increases in investing activities (such as purchases of property, plant, or equipment) in that period. This is the full information required for you to know how much money the business needs for that time period (which, if you raise money during that same period, will be referred to as a financing activity).

Your head is probably starting to spin. Just wait, it gets more fun.

Working Capital Starts with "Work" for a Reason

Working capital deals with the balance sheet of a business. A very cursory and basic explanation of working capital is that it is your business's current assets less its current liabilities. This includes assets that are considered usable in the short term, like accounts receivable (money owed to you for sales you make), inventory, and pre-paid expenses, less liabilities that are due in the short term, like accounts payable (money you owe to others).

Your eyes may be glazing over now because this is not easy stuff. Working capital definitely takes a lot of work to understand and to manage. Let me try to explain this further. In order for you to have goods to sell, it requires you to outlay cash. You may need to have the goods manufactured or buy supplies for you to make the goods yourself, and you may have one or several vendors or suppliers that supply you with the finished goods or material components. You, as a business owner, want to get the best payment terms (that means take as long as possible to pay your vendors and suppliers) to help you manage your cash flow. If you could be billed by your vendor thirty, sixty, or even ninety days after you received the goods or supplies, this would be fantastic for you. If your vendors agreed to extend payment terms to you, you wouldn't have to "come out of pocket" for the goods so far in advance of being able to sell them. However, getting favorable payment terms is particularly difficult for new businesses, as you have little clout and credibility—two of the Cs you left behind with your last job.

With your business being new, your vendors will be worried about you paying for the goods, so they will likely require that you pay for part or all of the goods upfront. So, you are starting in the hole outlaying cash. This is not captured on your profit and loss statement. While your money is being held by the vendor to make the goods, you may be able to work on making a sale to a retailer. If you sell to the end consumer, you have to wait until you have the goods in hand before you can sell them. When the goods or supplies are finally sent to you, then you can sell those goods to your customer (assuming you have a customer who has placed an order, otherwise it may take a while for you to make the sale of your goods once you receive them) and record it as a sale for the business. However, the cash that you have outlaid to manufacture and receive your inventory may be gone for quite some time before you make a sale.

Payment terms with your customers will dictate if you are going to get paid once you make the sale. Depending on their leverage (i.e., if your customer is a big organization like Walmart or Office Depot), your business's size, and how desperate you are to make the sale, it may take them thirty, sixty, or even ninety days to pay you. Some customers may try to not pay you at all (then you have to go tracking them down, which means longer before you get paid, if you get paid). You also have to hope that your customers don't go bankrupt themselves in the meantime (think Chrysler, Sharper Image, and Circuit City), or you will become a creditor, and it will take a long time for you to get paid even a fraction of what you are owed, if anything.

This timing cycle for using cash for working capital in your business isn't just related to purchasing inventory. If you sell a service, like consulting services, your customer may not pay the bill for thirty days or more. However, if you hire a service provider (like an accountant or lawyer), he may require you, as a small business, to pay a retainer fee up front.

As a new and growing business, you need even more money to manage the business because every vendor and service provider wants you to pay them right away, but your customers will want to take as long as possible to pay you. The diagram below demonstrates where you are when you start out—where the "X" is on the diagram. Your customers are taking a long time to pay you, but your vendors, suppliers, and service providers are requiring you to pay right away (and sometimes in advance). As you become a large company (think Walmart or McDonald's), you move to the plus sign, where you can dictate the terms because you are an important business with a lot of leverage. Then, you get more favorable terms of payment.

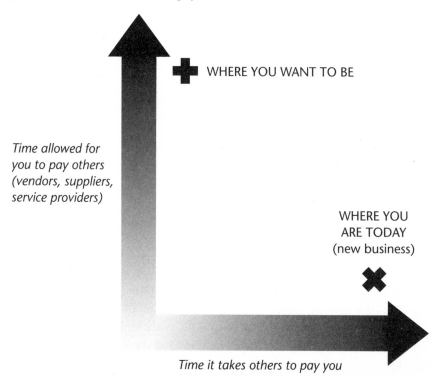

WHERE YOU WANT TO BE

Time allowed for you to pay others (vendors, suppliers, service providers)

WHERE YOU
ARE TODAY
(new business)

Time it takes others to pay you

It's not just working capital that you have to worry about. You may need to make large purchases of equipment, furniture, or other "property, plant, and equipment" for your business. This, too, impacts your business's cash flow.

Having to worry about the cash flow in your business isn't just relevant when you start a business. As you grow, you will need to purchase more and more inventory to meet growth demands, as well as more equipment to perform your services or run the business as it goes along. The more the business grows, for every dollar that your inventory, accounts receivable, prepaid expenses, and other current assets grow over and above the dollar growth in things you can put off paying for the same period of time (such as your accounts payable), that is another dollar that you have to finance in order for the business to grow. The same goes for every incremental dollar spent on property, plant, or equipment. This means that you either don't get to take those incremental dollars home (i.e., they come out of your paycheck to help finance the growth of the business) or you need to find other financing, such as a loan, to pay for them. Ultimately, this means that you are not getting paid as regularly. As the owner, you are the last to get paid, and if the business is going to grow, it is going to require more cash to support it. This cash is coming out of your pocket in one way or another.

A Cash Flow Illustration

Let me give you an illustration of how this cash flow stuff might work for a new business. You start a business that sells widgets. You need to have the widgets produced overseas; so you find a vendor to produce them who requires a 50 percent down payment before shipping the widgets and then 50 percent upon shipment to you. These widgets take sixty days to produce and thirty days by boat to arrive at your warehouse (which is a reasonable timeframe, although many types of goods can take even longer to produce and be received from overseas manufacturers). Once the goods finally arrive at your place of business, you send them to a retailer, Widget World, who has agreed to sell your widgets in its store. Widget World is a big, important customer, so it requests thirty days after the receipt of goods to pay you. You don't want to risk this important order, and therefore, you gladly agree. While you are waiting for Widget World to pay, you have more widgets produced from your vendors to fill future orders. Your business grows by 50 percent, so you need to order even more widgets than before. That sounds great, right?

It is great, because you are growing, but growth creates a challenge in managing your cash flow. You need to pay for the items before you sell them and with growth, that means that for every new order you place, you are paying for more and more items in advance.

Here is a timeline to show you what your widget business is in for:

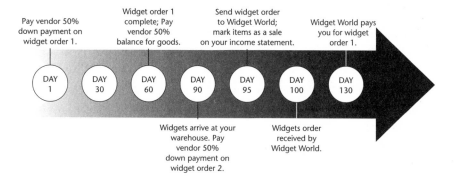

So, if it takes you a few days to process your products and then ship them on to your customer, by the time you are able to record a sale on day ninety-five, you have had to put out cash (starting day one) on both the full amount of inventory for that order, plus half of your next order, which is even larger because you are growing. You don't see a penny from the first sale (which happens officially when you ship the widgets to Widget World) until day 130. This is a typical cash flow issue that is not shown on your income statement and is what makes running the financial aspects of a business even more challenging.

Now, let's go wild and assume you are very successful at selling the widgets and that you sell $20,000 worth of widgets in your first sale to Widget World. You are making a healthy 40 percent margin on that sale, so your direct cost of the widgets is 60 percent or $12,000. That means you have to spend $6,000 on day one and $6,000 on day sixty to get the widgets from your factory. And your next order is for $30,000 of widgets (an incredible 50 percent growth rate that will cost you $18,000 to produce), so you have to put out another 50 percent upfront payment (or $9,000) for the second order on day ninety. You start $21,000 in the hole just from having your first order produced and placing your second order, and you aren't getting paid your $20,000 on the first order until day 130 from Widget World.

During that time, you will also have ongoing expenses for your business: rent, employees, utilities, insurance, postage, and so forth, will all be due. Once you get the money in from Widget World, you will have a very short window before your next payment is due on order two, and you will have to start thinking about order three. If order three is bigger (because you are growing) that incremental growth will need to be funded by the business, meaning less cash available to pay you.

So, even when you are doing well, managing cash creates an issue. If your cash profits from the business aren't enough to fund the businesses growth, and you don't take on financing in some form, you can't grow the business. If you use the profits of the business, or take on financing to grow, you are either delaying taking home profits or you're taking on liabilities. If you take on debt and the business has a blip along the way, then you can get into big trouble and be in violation of your bank agreements, which can cause them to put pressure on your business, charge you exorbitant fees, or even take drastic measures like seizing your assets.

The more asset-intensive your business is, the more susceptible you are to cash flow issues. However, in virtually every business there is a lag between your expenditures and the time you get paid. If you have to perform services, you still have to pay for rent, marketing, telephones, payroll, and other fees while you are working on a project and before you get paid by the client.

Why Timing (of Payments, That Is) Is Everything

Suzette Flemming, president of Flemming Business Services, knows the timing issue all too well. Her firm, which has provided accounting, bookkeeping, payroll, and tax services to businesses for more than fifteen years, couldn't avoid cash flow issues in the recent economic downturn. As an accountant, Suzette knew what to do to enhance her business's cash flow: require payment up front for all services.

However, she explains, "As the economy started to shift and my clients started having cash flow problems themselves, I let some of the pre-payments slide and would wait thirty or sixty days before knocking on clients' doors and asking for payment. This has affected my ability to do payroll and to pay my other bills on time to avoid paying late fees."

She also endured stress and worried that "squeaking too much" could cause her to lose clients but not "squeaking enough" could leave her without any money from the clients. Two of her clients have declared bankruptcy, putting her ability to collect anything for her services related to those clients in jeopardy.

If this sounds incredibly complicated to you, it is. Managing cash flow is one of the trickiest aspects to running a business, and even some of the biggest, most successful businesses in the world have gotten tripped up by mismanaging their cash flow, even though they did a good job managing every other aspect of their businesses.

UNDERSTANDING FINANCIAL ACCOUNTING, INCLUDING CASH FLOW MANAGEMENT, IS REQUIRED FOR YOU TO KEEP SCORE IN YOUR BUSINESS. IF THOSE SOUND LIKE THINGS YOU DON'T EVER WANT TO UNDERSTAND, THEN USE THIS REALITY AS PART OF YOUR PERSONAL SCREENING PROCESS RELATED TO STARTING A BUSINESS.

If you don't understand financials very well, take the time to really learn and understand this aspect of business, because it creates one of the biggest stumbling blocks out there. You need to put in the time in the financial arena if you are going to be in charge of your own company.

Cash flow and overall financial management also adds an increased layer of risk as you evaluate the potential upside of starting a business, because to grow the business and make more money, it is going to require you to give up more money, which may mean a longer payback period on your investment. As mentioned, in a normal job, you don't have to pay anything up front to be employed. Other than investing in some work clothing, and maybe a briefcase and transportation to and from work, there aren't a lot of upfront costs for having a job. To get a raise (growth in your current job), it doesn't require you investing more money the way it does to grow your business.

Understanding financial accounting, including cash flow management, is required for you to keep score in your business. If those sound like things you don't ever want to understand, then use this reality as part of your personal screening process related to starting a business.

EXERCISE 19

TARGET FOCUS—FINANCES:
Assessing How Cash Flows Impact Your Risk and Reward

1. First, make sure that your financial model has a cash flow statement. If it doesn't, enlist someone to assist you with creating one (they should help you, not do it all themselves, because you need to understand the impact of the cash flow on your business). I know you may cringe at this, but it is critical to understand how much money you need to run your business.
2. Once you have your cash flow statement in place, do what is called a "sensitivity analysis" on the assumptions. This means, change the assumptions and see how that changes your cash flow in your model. Some assumptions you want to change include the following:
   • Imagine that 10 percent of the people who owe you money delay paying you by a month. How does that affect your ability to operate your business?
   • Can you pay your bills on time, pay yourself, and/or grow under this scenario?
   • What if 20 percent or 30 percent of your customers delay paying you by a month?
   • What if it takes sixty days or ninety days extra to get payment?
   • What if some percentage of your customers (10 percent or 20 percent) never pay you?

Given that it is impossible to predict your financials with 100 percent accuracy, and that most entrepreneurs tend to be overly optimistic, take these sensitivities very seriously. How does this change in the potential financial reward of your business or the extra risk of having money tied up for longer periods in the business change the opportunity for you? Use your findings to further refine and review the risks side of your Entrepreneur Equation.

29

The You Show—
Even If You Have Tons of Friends,
You Are in This Alone

WHEN YOU START OUT, things are heavily dependent upon you. If you are up for being an entrepreneur, that is okay (and if you are not, then I hope you won't even attempt it). However, you may be misled into thinking that you have all kinds of allies, cheerleaders, and people who will help you succeed. Let's take a look at that.

Lots of Friends, Lots of Promises

When you decide to become an entrepreneur, you will have all kinds of people making all sorts of promises. A new business sounds exciting (in theory it does, and especially before any work has to be done), and everyone wants to be part of something exciting. Plus, people like to play the lottery, so in the several-million-to-one chance that you hit it big, they want to make sure that they have some association with the business so they can get some benefit out of it.

Have you ever been to a casino in Las Vegas and seen someone at the roulette wheel with a stack of cash and a bunch of friends surrounding him? He is placing bets, and his friends are chiming in, "Pick Black. No Red. Number seventeen!" They have nothing at risk, but they chime in anyway. They get the benefit of participating in the excitement without having any downside. Plus, if their friend wins big, maybe they will get taken out for a steak dinner.

When you start a business, you are that guy at the roulette wheel. You are taking the risk, and people you know will chime in uselessly because they have nothing at stake. People you know will tell you that they will help you with the new business. They will give you un-solicited, and often unhelpful, advice. They will offer to provide customer leads or make intro-ductions to low-cost vendors. They will tell you that they are going to patronize your business frequently and send all of their friends there. You will have tons of people making lots of great of-fers, and you will be pumped, as you have the equivalent of a volunteer fire department ready to make your business a success.

> WHEN YOU START A BUSINESS, YOU ARE THAT GUY AT THE ROULETTE WHEEL. YOU ARE TAKING THE RISK, AND PEOPLE YOU KNOW WILL CHIME IN USELESSLY BECAUSE THEY HAVE NOTHING AT STAKE.

You may assemble a world-class advisory board, have lots of moral support, and tons of friends, but let me tell you that whether your busi-ness succeeds will be 100 percent up to you. You will decide whether you sink or swim. Most of the people who made gracious offers to help will forget their offers (sometimes accidentally and sometimes inten-tionally) within five minutes of making them. Many of those who do remember making the offers won't follow through.

You will be going solo in your endeavor because you are the one tak-ing the risk. Being an entrepreneur and starting or buying a business requires serious commitments. And these commitments are enforced, legally, financially, emotionally, and otherwise, upon you. It is going to be your money invested, your personal guarantees for any debt (potentially risking your house or other major assets), and your name on every dotted line of every piece of paper you sign. Regardless of the number of friends you have, unless they are co-signing your loans or other legal documents, you will be standing alone.

It's Your Name on the Dotted Line

From the day you sign your first legal document—perhaps your certificate of incorporation or even earlier, your retainer agreement with the law firm who is going to draft those documents—you are claiming responsibility for everything related to the business. You signed the contract, and you had better understand everything that contract says, because you are legally responsible for it. Even if your lawyer reviews it and says its fine, you need to make that judgment yourself. For the lawyer, the worst thing that happens is that it isn't fine and you have to pay her more money to help get you out of whatever situation in which you find yourself. For you, the worst thing that can happen is that you can lose or owe significant amounts of money and risk losing your business or your financial security.

I have seen entrepreneurs sign engagement letters with service providers, retail and corporate leases, tax audits, and vendor contracts without being able to fully and correctly explain the contract's contents. How does somebody risk their business, their financial security, thousands to hundreds of thousands of dollars, and potentially their homes, on something they don't understand? It is like gambling with the title to your house. Would you take the title to your house to the roulette wheel and bet it on black? I hope not. That isn't an educated decision—it is just gambling. You need to make sure that you don't do the same thing in your business. You need to remember that it is your name on the dotted line and that it is your butt— and bucks—on the line.

You're the HBIC or BMOC,
So You Need to Know What's Going On

Your responsibility and risk doesn't end during your entire tenure as owner of your business. Do you remember how everyone scoffed when the CEO of Enron, Kenneth Lay, pleaded ignorance to his company's massive sham? The response was that he was in charge and therefore, he should know what is going on in the company. In that case, he wasn't even an entrepreneur behind the company—he was a hired gun, but he was the CEO and held responsible. When you are CEO of your own company, you need to know everything that is going on in your business because not only are you in charge, it is your money, your business, and your future on the line.

This carries over into every aspect of your business. You can hire accountants to help you with your books, but ultimately you are responsible for the numbers. The accountants' accounting is only as good as the information provided to them. Previously, I referenced the phrase "garbage in, garbage out." I have seen that on many a company's books. There are a lot of companies who hire accountants to put numbers into QuickBooks or some other accounting program for them. However, because the owner doesn't understand the numbers or the financial side of the business, the financial statements are dead wrong.

I have seen financial statements prepared by CPAs that have told a completely misleading story. I have seen unprofitable businesses that looked profitable because the accountants just used the information given by the company and didn't really evaluate the "garbage" they were putting into the financial statement format.

One example was a major company that I was referred to by a well-known and intelligent lawyer (yes, if you have noticed the trend, I receive a lot of referrals from lawyers). This company sold gift products and had been approached by several competitors who wanted to buy the company. Based on the financial statements, the owner, the competitors, and the lawyer all thought that the business was worth millions of dollars. I was thrilled, as it is always more fun (and frankly much easier for me) to work with companies that are doing well than those who are doing poorly. As you can guess, I get hired by a lot more of the latter, which may just be a function of probability, given that the majority of businesses don't earn a profit over their lifetimes.

This is another long story, so I will keep it to the highlights. When I evaluated the financial statements, I noticed something odd. The company sold a lot of gift certificates. Every time the company sold a gift certificate, instead of recording it as a "liability" (i.e., noting that the company took a customer's money that day and in exchange, had to provide goods to the gift certificate holder in the future), it was marked as a sale at the time the gift certificate was sold. That is a huge problem—and by problem, I mean *error*—because that transaction didn't generate revenue; no products were sold. There was no associated cost to the gift certificate. There would be when it is used by the holder; that is when the revenue from the certificate should have been booked.

For those of you not that familiar with accounting, let me break this down in a different way. Day one, the company sells a gift certificate for $100. On day one, the company owes the holder of the gift certificate $100 worth of merchandise in the future.

The holder doesn't redeem that gift certificate until six months later. If that holder picks an item that retails for $100 but costs the company sixty dollars to produce, the company makes forty dollars in gross profit from that sale on that day when the sale is made. If the holder picks a product that retails for $100 but costs the company seventy dollars to produce, then the company makes thirty dollars in profit on that day instead. The company's profit depends on what the certificate holder buys with that $100 gift certificate, on the date that the purchase of the goods is made by the certificate holder.

In this case, the company on day one erroneously recorded a sale of $100 from the gift certificate. There was no direct cost of the gift certificate that day since nobody had used it yet, so the company recorded $100 in profit on their books as well! That would be a nice business, but that business obviously doesn't exist.

The entrepreneur clearly didn't understand this, and gave the information about the business's sales to his accountants' CPAs who had been in business for more than thirty years! The accountants took the entrepreneur's information and prepared financial statements, assuming that they were getting good information. So, the financial statements showed the company with a ton of revenue and no offsetting costs associated with it. Every gift certificate showed up on the income statement at 100 percent profit. When merged with the rest of the business, it looked like the business was fabulously profitable. However, when you took out the certificates and recorded them properly, the business was in fact *losing money*. The company wasn't charging enough for their products to cover their costs, and they couldn't see that because of the accounting error. Their business, which everyone—including the lawyer and the CPAs—all agreed was worth millions, was basically worthless.

> THE COMPANY WASN'T CHARGING ENOUGH FOR THEIR PRODUCTS TO COVER THEIR COSTS, AND THEY COULDN'T SEE THAT BECAUSE OF THE ACCOUNTING ERROR. THEIR BUSINESS, WHICH EVERYONE—INCLUDING THE LAWYER AND THE CPAS—ALL AGREED WAS WORTH MILLIONS, WAS BASICALLY WORTHLESS.

At the end of the day, do you know whose problem that was? It wasn't the accountants. They just arranged the numbers. It was the entrepreneur's issue, whose name was on every contract, whose money was on the line, whose name was on the dotted line (oh, and who also had a liability of several million dollars from unredeemed certificates). Several years after we discovered this error for them, the business owner was still dealing with the consequences.

Now, you may be thinking that the way around shouldering the entrepreneurial burden by yourself is to get a partner. In *The Art of the Start*, Guy Kawasaki advocates finding a "soulmate" with whom to start your business. I generally believe that partnering is easier in the tech world than in other industries (but is still not a layup). Finding a partner is a great idea in theory, but it's very tough in practice. Plus, it is not advisable to manage by committee, and it is not possible for two people to be accountable for any one thing.

Having an equal partner for your new business is the business equivalent of getting married. If you partner with someone you know and trust, you have the preexisting relationship dynamic issues to worry about, not to mention the longevity of your personal relationship if things go south in the business. If you don't know the person well, you are now entrusting your investment and livelihood to another person who could have all kinds of issues. If that person gets the business in trouble, you will still be held responsible and accountable. Do you want to give someone else the ability to put your business and financial security at risk? At the end of the day, if your name is on a contract, even if someone else's is there too, you are still 100 percent responsible for it, and any implications that come as a result.

As a recap, your name is on the dotted line, so everything related to the business affects you, and you need to be on top of it all. If an employee is stealing from the business, he is stealing from you. If you aren't paying attention, and funds are misappropriated, it is your loss alone. If you get bad legal advice, you are the one that is going to pay for it. So again, make sure you understand how serious of a commitment it is to have your name on the dotted line.

Oh, and remember those people who said they were going to help you in your business but never were to be heard from again? If you succeed, these people will in fact come out of the woodwork. They will be your best buddies, want to get free or reduced-cost goods and services, and accompany you to your luxury skybox (one can dream) to watch a basketball game. Success always finds leeches.

But if the going gets tough, don't count on any of them to help bail you out. Even if the tough times follow the good ones, even if you had success and they partook in it, you will face the tough times all by your lonesome. Ask any failure how popular he is, and he will likely tell you that he is quite lonely.

The Risk of Being the Key Man (or Woman)

A few business risks relate directly to you being the person in charge. This is sometimes referred to by large companies as "key man" issues.

This means, God forbid, if something happens to you (the "key man," HBIC, or BMOC in your business), or even to the perception of you, the business can significantly suffer since you are so important to the business and its success.

Most people don't like to think about worst-case scenarios, especially when it involves something bad happening to them personally. Unless you are a major hypochondriac—or comedian Richard Lewis—you probably don't spend a lot of time thinking about your own demise or all of the bad things that could happen to you. Not surprisingly, most business plans include a lot of discussions about the upside but don't address contingency plans for when things go in the other direction.

When you have a job working for someone else, in the case of an accident or illness, you may not be able to work for a while. If your job isn't there for you when you return, you have the option to seek a similar job or even a different job. The only thing lost is your paycheck (that is, the only thing related to your job that you have lost). If you have racked up some major medical bills, you may be thrilled at the prospect of having a steady paycheck to return to in order to help pay those down.

The game changes when you own a business. While employed, you may feel badly if you are ill and can't finish a client project or something for your employer because you are unable to work. However, the burden of your absence doesn't fall on you. It is up to your employer to fill in the gap by finding someone else to finish your project for the client or getting the deadline extended to keep the business going. When it is your business, it doesn't matter if you are fighting cancer or in a coma, the business remains your (and your family's) responsibility. If you are unable to finish the client project because you are stuck in the hospital with tubes shoved into you, who is going to run it in your absence? This issue is obviously exacerbated if you don't have any employees (another reason to not create a job-business).

So, what is your Plan B? If something happens to you, who is going to open the business each day? Who is going to solicit new customers? Who is going to pay the rent and the payroll? Who is going to be responsible for keeping the business going and staying afloat while you are gone? The more that falls on you (which, especially in the first couple of years and really, for most of the entrepreneurial business, is a whole lot), the bigger this risk is. Ask yourself, can the business run without you? If the answer is "no," then what is at stake?

If and when you recover from your illness or accident, when you own your business, you don't go back to a job with a standard paycheck; no, you go back to fixing a business that may now be hemorrhaging money (assuming it is still in existence after your extended absence). You may have difficulty paying your medical bills because your cash is tied up in keeping the business going. You are trying to muster the strength to make a full recovery from your illness, plus you have to deal with the stress of the business. Sound pleasant? I don't think so. In evaluating the risks and rewards and best case and worst-case scenarios, be sure to think long and hard about whether you are prepared to encounter that risk.

Your being the key man can affect the business just by a change in others' perceptions of you. If someone wrongfully accuses you of a crime or unethical act, even if it is untrue, it can affect your business.

What if an even worse scenario happens? What if you unexpectedly die? Can your family or loved ones run the business, or will there be anything for them to sell and recoup your investment? Do they have a substantial amount at risk, such as having their house used as the business's collateral or having all of the family's savings tied up in the business? You need to take into account what is on the line for them as well.

Martha, Martha, Martha

A great example of how one person can be so important to a business, its success, and its value is Martha Stewart. Martha Stewart's company, Martha Stewart Living Omnimedia, is publicly traded. When I worked at Banc of America Securities, we were one of the investment banks that participated in the company's IPO. I was on the team that helped secure that transaction for Banc of America Securities. All of the investment banking underwriters involved in the IPO realized that Martha Stewart was key to the success of her business. Even though it was a large company, her name was attached to it, and she was important to the brand. When the company filed the documents related to its IPO (called the S-1 registration statement), the investment bankers included this issue as a "risk factor" for the business. Below is what was written in the Martha Stewart Living Omnimedia IPO filing to warn potential investors about this risk:

> THE LOSS OF THE SERVICES OF MARTHA STEWART OR OTHER KEY EMPLOYEES WOULD MATERIALLY ADVERSELY AFFECT OUR REVENUES, RESULTS OF OPERATIONS AND PROSPECTS.
>
> We are highly dependent upon our founder, Chairman, and Chief Executive Officer, Martha Stewart. Martha Stewart's talents, efforts, personality, and leadership have been, and continue to be, critical to our success. The diminution or loss of the services of Martha Stewart, and any negative market or industry perception arising from that diminution or loss, would have a material adverse effect on our business. While our other key executives have substantial experience and have made significant contributions to our business, Martha Stewart remains the personification of our brands as well as our senior executive and primary creative force.

This risk was proven to be significant a few years later. Martha Stewart Living Omnimedia's stock was close to twenty dollars per share in early 2002 when the news broke about Martha Stewart's alleged securities fraud (for those of you asleep during the early 2000s, she was accused of selling an unrelated stock based upon illegal "inside information"). The issue of Martha—the founder and key person at her company—potentially going to jail sent the stock to a low of approximately six dollars per share, and it didn't recover for several years, well after she was convicted and served time in jail.

The value of the business significantly declined and was seriously impacted by this unforeseen issue affecting Martha Stewart. In fact, that company has never really been the same since that incident, and while it is has had its ups and downs, at the time of writing this book, the stock was trading at just over three dollars per share. Martha Stewart herself valued the cost of the scandal at "[probably] more than a billion dollars."[1] Overall, an issue affecting one person, Martha Stewart, had a huge impact on the entire business, even though it was a very large business with other talented individuals helping to run the company. If that business can be affected in such a major way, imagine what could happen to your business.

What if the Worst-Case Scenario Happens to the Business Itself?

What if the worst-case scenario isn't you, it is the business? Can you financially and emotionally withstand a worst-case scenario? What if nobody comes to your store, wants your goods, or desires your services? What if an employee steals a significant amount of money or inventory from you that can't be recovered? What if your goods, which you source overseas, are captured by pirates (hey—it happens), and you can't service your customers? What if a customer sues you or spreads the word not to do business with your company? What if the product you sell injures one or more of your customers and/or you have to do a massive product recall? These are all possible issues (okay, the pirate one is a bit far-fetched, but your goods could easily be lost in transit or delayed in customs) that create more risks when you own your own business. Is the extra benefit you get from having your own business worth the risk of the worst-case scenario?

I am not trying to scare you or provide outlandish "what-ifs." These are very real issues facing business owners that aspiring entrepreneurs never factor into the equation. You need to be sure you are up for the whole range of scenarios, including the good ones and the bad ones. Nobody panics too much when things go better than expected, but there is a whole lot of panicking in the face of a crisis. When you evaluate the risks required to start a business and the potential reward you stand to earn from that business, make sure to factor all of the risks, including the worst-case scenarios.

As a business owner, if you are barely making what you did at your day job, having to face all of the aforementioned risks will put that risk and reward equation way out of whack. Now, if you realistically have the capabilities to start the next Google, then the extra risks might very well be worth it. But remember, for every Google there are millions of sole proprietorships and small businesses that are barely cutting it.

ENDNOTES:

1. Martha Stewart, interview by Cynthia McFadden, *Nightline*, ABC, November 19, 2009.

Assembling Your Entrepreneur Equation, and a Few Reminders in Case You Get Sucked in by the Hype

IN THIS FINAL SECTION, you will put together all aspects of the screening process for one final sanity check. Chapter 30 will take you through every part of your Entrepreneur Equation so that you can fully assess the risks, issues, and rewards given your particular circumstances and the opportunity you are evaluating to see if they are in balance and create a worthwhile trade-off for you. Chapter 31 will remind you of the realities of entrepreneurship with a few parting words of wisdom. Finally, Chapter 32 gives you a "cheat sheet" for reference and quick reminders.

30

Finalizing and Evaluating Your Entrepreneur Equation

IF YOU HAVE GOTTEN this far and are still considering whether to pursue a new business opportunity today, you should do a final evaluation of your situation, the opportunity, and the overall risks and rewards as the final step in your screening process. You will look at (1) your motivation, to see if the realities of entrepreneurship will likely bring you the rewards you are seeking; (2) your timing, to see if you are best positioned to take on entrepreneurship today or if it would lessen the risks and/or increase the rewards by waiting; (3) your personality, to see if the path of entrepreneurship plays to your particular strengths, and; (4) your opportunity, to see if there are enough rewards in the business model. Then you will evaluate all of these qualitative and quantitative risks and rewards in your personal Entrepreneur Equation to make your ultimate entrepreneurship decision.

EXERCISE 20

TARGET FOCUS—THE OVERALL ASSESSMENT:
Putting Your Entrepreneur Equation Together

Now it is time to assemble all of the exercises you have completed to create your personal Entrepreneur Equation. So, what is your Entrepreneur Equation? It is simply the trade-off between the risks and rewards of a particular business opportunity for you, based on your personal current goals, opportunities, and circumstances. For the equation to make sense for you, your potential rewards need to greatly outweigh the potential risks in total.

Now that you have a clearer understanding of entrepreneurship, the current competitive environment, and what is required to start and run a business, you can compile and evaluate your risks and your rewards. These risks and rewards should reflect your personal situation and objectives today, as well as the specific business opportunity you are evaluating.

Divide a piece of paper into two columns, one labeled "My Risks Today" and the other "The Rewards of the Opportunity." Below are the areas you will be evaluating on each side of your equation:

My Risks Today:
- Timing risks (current finances, experience, responsibilities)
- Personality risks
- Risks related to the particular opportunity I am evaluating
- Capital risks (the amount you are investing, loans you are taking out, any lost salary)
- Risks of the opportunity cost of any investment
- Other financial and qualitative risks

The Rewards of the Opportunity:
- Qualitative and quantitative rewards from my motivation
- Qualitative and quantitative rewards of the particular opportunity I am evaluating
- Other qualitative and quantitative rewards of business ownership

Go back to the various exercises and brainstorms you have completed, using the questions below to help you revisit the exercises. Use the answers to help you fill out and then review the risks and rewards of your equation on your piece of paper.

1. **Your motivation**
   - Are you being motivated by the type of factors that will create success?

2. **Your timing**
   - Is it the right time for you to fully engage in a new business opportunity, given:
     - Your personal financial situation,
     - Your current experience,
     - Your current responsibilities, and
     - Your network?
   - Is there anything you can do over the next several months or years to give yourself a better chance of succeeding, such as prototyping or testing the business on a small scale or supplementing holes in your industry and business knowledge, skills, and experience?

3. **Your personality**
   - Do you have a personality whose character traits are consistent with business ownership?
   - Will you be happier being creative and entrepreneurial while working in another person's business where they are taking the risk or filling the "Santa" role?

4. **Your particular opportunity**
   - Is the opportunity you are evaluating a jobbie, job-business, or business?
   - How does that create new risks or limit rewards for you?
   - Does your opportunity have enough competitive advantages to compete effectively in the current über-competitive business environment?

- Does the opportunity you are evaluating create enough of a financial return to be an attractive business?
- Will you find more enjoyment in your passion if you are not dependent upon it for a paycheck?

5. **The risks and rewards for you**
   - What risks and rewards will be created by your new business?

6. **Other issues**
   - What other issues will your businesses create that you need to factor into your risk and reward equation?

What you have now is your Entrepreneur Equation, with all of your specific risks and all of the opportunities' potential rewards. Now, for the million-dollar question: looking at your Entrepreneur Equation, does the business opportunity have enough rewards to justify the personal, financial, and qualitative risks you will be taking on? Do the potential rewards *significantly* outweigh the risks you will be taking and issues you will be enduring? Regardless of your answers to any specific exercise, if this trade-off equation is out of balance, *you should not pursue the new business.*

Go back to further evaluate your Entrepreneur Equation. As you look at the risks in your equation, is there anything you can do to minimize them and stack the odds more heavily in your favor? How about enhancing the rewards to make the trade-off more enticing? Reducing risks and increasing rewards can rebalance your Entrepreneur Equation to make a given business opportunity more worthwhile for you to pursue.

Remember, the components of your Entrepreneur Equation uniquely apply to you and your circumstances, and may shift over time. Evaluating your Entrepreneur Equation will be an ongoing process and your equation will change any time your objectives, opportunities, or personal situation changes. My goal has been to help you ask the right questions and provide some reality about what you are in for so that you can make an informed decision regarding pursuing a new business and properly assess the risks and rewards at any given point in time. Your circumstances in terms of your personal makeup, your experience, your finances, your responsibilities, and the particular opportunity you are evaluating will impact how much risk is appropriate given the potential rewards of business ownership.

31

A Momentary Lapse of Reason

W E RECEIVE SO MUCH information in our lives that our memories are sometimes too short. This is probably why throughout history, the same failures always repeat themselves in different eras; pain is temporary, and when it wears off, it is easy to forget.

Just when this book was starting to make sense to you, when you were finally realizing all of the hard work, the trade-offs, the risks, and the issues that were involved in starting a business, something happened. You turned on *The Oprah Winfrey Show* and caught a segment on business successes. You saw Oprah interview a single mom who had no money, no experience, and six young kids and created a multimillion-dollar business selling scented hand puppets out of her basement.

Wait, you're thinking. *If she can do it…*

There are a few thoughts I want to reiterate. My first thought is, sure, it is possible. However, *possible* and *probable* are not the same thing. There are people who win the Powerball multi-state lottery from time to time and take home more than $100 million dollars. The chances of that are really slim, and it sure isn't a good investment strategy to put all of your money into the Powerball lottery, but it is possible to win big, and some lucky one-in-a-few-dozen-million bastard will do it.

My second thought would be that maybe you didn't get the full story. I know a gentleman who recently sold his business for $20 million. Are you impressed? You shouldn't be, because he and his partners invested $35 million to get the business to the point that it was worth $20 million. Overall, they lost $15 million in that business, even though part of the story included a sale of the business at a $20 million value. But I didn't tell you that part of the story, so you just assumed that the $20 million number was impressive. You can't determine if a business is successful just because it is called profitable, has a certain level of sales, or was sold for a certain amount of money. You need the gritty details.

The Rest of the Story

Remember, you don't always get the full story, like the widely held beliefs about Bill Gates's start. Maybe the lady on Oprah was a single mom without a dime but happened to have a rich uncle that financed the business. Maybe she had to raise so much capital that that by the time her creditors or equity partners were paid out, not much was left for her. Maybe she had a friend or mentor that had the exact experience, contacts, or relationships that she was lacking, and she used them heavily. Or maybe she was just that several-dozen-million-to-one lottery winner.

If you find your mind wandering, your memory getting short, and yourself enduring a momentary lapse of reason, go back to the *Let's Make A Deal* curtains and your personal Entrepreneur Equation. How much would you be willing to risk for the potential reward at the end of the day? Certainly you wouldn't spend hundreds of thousands of dollars of your savings on Powerball lottery tickets (if you would, you should put down this book immediately and go directly to Gamblers Anonymous).

Just because something *can* happen, doesn't mean it is likely to or that the odds make sense or that the risk justifies the reward. You could marry a supermodel or become a ruler of an island nation, but you probably wouldn't want to bet your savings and your salary on it. Keep that in mind the next time *Oprah, Forbes,* or Yahoo! News profiles some rags-to-riches business story. Also, keep in mind that the devil is in the details. They may not be telling you the whole story and just because you hear some statistics, that doesn't imply anything about the overall success of the business or the financial rewards of its owners. Chrysler was a multibillion-dollar business. If you heard about a multibillion-dollar company, you would think it was successful. In 2009, that company went bankrupt. One data point doesn't always relate to the others.

32

The Cheat Sheet

THIS BOOK HAS A NUMBER of screening processes and sanity checks you can use to help you understand if you should own your own business today. If you were too lazy to read this entire book, then you pretty much failed the first screening process. You have to have the patience, be willing to do the research, and put in the work to make a business happen. As I have said, if you fail to prepare, you prepare to fail. Reading this book is not that much work, particularly compared to what you face as a business owner. So, if you can't make it through the screening processes right now, use that fact as a good reason to keep your day job.

On the other hand, perhaps you did read the book, and you want a handy guide to be able to quickly remind yourself why entrepreneurship is so challenging and may not be worth pursuing (and to give you a sanity check when you conceive your next "big idea"). Remember to keep asking yourself not "Can I be an entrepreneur?" but rather, "Should I be an entrepreneur, given my personal circumstances, goals and opportunities?" Continually revise your Entrepreneur Equation, which will also shift as your personal situation and business opportunities do.

Whether you have read the book or not, here's a brief summary of each of the chapters highlighting some of the realities, risks, and rewards to consider as you evaluate whether business ownership is for you (either today or ever):

CHAPTER 1

The American Dream and our business landscape have changed substantially over the past eighty years, yet many entrepreneurs are approaching business with an outdated perspective.

CHAPTER 2

Every career path that has a lot of risk (and potential rewards) associated with it has a screening process; entrepreneurship didn't until now. This book serves as that initial screening process for you as an aspiring entrepreneur.

CHAPTER 3

Experts have been doling out all kinds of advice on how to make your business successful for decades. However, the assumption may be wrong. Maybe you weren't meant to run a business, either today or—depending on your personality and priorities—ever. Plus, the entrepreneurship game has changed. There are more lucrative career opportunities, and there is also more competition in business today, which makes running a business a less-attractive opportunity with less upside potential than it was even twenty years ago.

CHAPTER 4

Entrepreneurship has nothing to do with being good at producing a good or a service or having a technical skill. Being an entrepreneur means that you are good at running a business, and that means doing less of any single thing and much more of a lot of different things (many of which you may find really annoying, like marketing and accounting). You also need to know if you are creating a job or a business. If you have no employees and the business is virtually synonymous with you, then you have a job. However, this is a job you have to pay for the pleasure of working at, with lots of risk attached to it. That may not be so smart.

CHAPTER 5

When you start your own business, contrary to popular delusions, you are not in control, and you have no freedom. You are controlled by your customers (without whom you do not have a business), plus a whole host of other people, from your employees to your investors to your landlord, all with their own agendas. Crazy enough, you actually have fewer people with control over you when you have a job versus when you own a business.

CHAPTER 6

Your ego may make you want to go into business for the wrong reasons. You will encounter more rejection from potential customers in any business than in any job or job search. Also, having a good story to tell at cocktail parties is not a great reason to start a business.

CHAPTER 7

Ideas are not businesses. Good business ideas fail, and bad business ideas succeed. It is all about executing a viable business model. Everyone loves business ideas, but they are worthless (unfortunately) without work behind them.

CHAPTER 8

Hobbies are fun because we pursue them at our leisure. When you pursue them as a business, they become work. Also, if you know a certain hobby well, it doesn't mean that you can run a business related to it. If your business doesn't run full-time or generate the minimum wage on an hourly basis, then it is not a business, it is a "jobbie," a hobby disguised as a business or a job.

CHAPTER 9

When you own a business, you have more, not less, contact with people. If you are a loner, a business is not a solution to your problems.

CHAPTER 10

Who else are you responsible for that may be affected by your business decisions? Will your kids be happy if you have to decide to use their college funds to grow your business? Remember, you can't make two things your number one priority.

CHAPTER 11

You need to have experience to make your business successful, both in your industry and in business. If you can't invest the time to learn an industry and business skills, why are you investing your personal savings?

CHAPTER 12

You may not have the time to start a business. If you start it when you work for someone else, they may own the business by default. If you try to fit it in after working, eating, sleeping, and showering, it may take you forty years to launch.

CHAPTER 13

Sometimes who you know is more important than what you know in business. If you don't have good contacts and resources, it will be hard for your business to succeed.

CHAPTER 14

If you have issues with money, including not having money, not having financial responsibility, or having an ultra-conservative approach to money, running a business is going to be extremely challenging for you.

CHAPTER 15

Business ownership is a roller coaster, not a merry-go-round. The highs and the lows are amplified because you have everything at risk.

CHAPTER 16

Sometimes things are fun for a day but lose a lot of excitement as time goes by. Imagine yourself running your business for a decade. Will you still enjoy it when it is no longer shiny and new?

CHAPTER 17

Impatience and business goes together like a hungry tiger and a wounded bunny. One will kill the other.

CHAPTER 18

To succeed, focus on your core competencies. If your core competencies don't include being a strategic visionary or being able to wear a lot of hats at the same time, don't put yourself in a position to do either.

CHAPTER 19

Hoping, wishing, and dreaming don't make a business. The "secret" to a successful business is hard, focused work.

CHAPTER 20

Raising capital is difficult, necessary, and ongoing. The more you need money for your business, the less able you are to find it. You will always underestimate how much you need and how long it will take you to get it, probably by a factor of one-and-a-half to two times.

CHAPTER 21

Now is the most competitive business environment in all of history. There are more products and services than we need, split amongst a fairly static group of people and resources. Today, there are fewer opportunities to make the upside potential from a business than there were years ago, if you can even break through the noise to get potential customers' attention in the first place.

CHAPTER 22

Sometimes, you are too smart for your own good. If you are great at doing certain tasks, it doesn't mean you can teach others to do them as well as you. You can't do everything by yourself either—there are only twenty-four hours in a day. Plus, if the business is fully dependent upon you, then you have a job, not a business.

CHAPTER 23

Buying a business is not a shortcut for entrepreneurship. Sometimes, you are just buying someone else's problems. You will always be at an information disadvantage when you purchase a business. Because people are greedy and won't sell their business if they know the next year will be even better, assume that whatever business you are evaluating will have imminent issues ahead and possibly its best years behind it (people don't tend to sell when the cash is sure to continue to roll in).

CHAPTER 24

Winning the genetic lottery doesn't automatically pass down an entrepreneurship gene to you. Just because you have a business that has been in your family for years doesn't mean that you can run it well (or will want to).

CHAPTER 25

Is the risk of the business worth the reward? Would you risk $990 for a chance at $1000? No, because there is not enough upside. You need to evaluate your business opportunities in the same way you would play *Let's Make a Deal* with your own money on the line.

CHAPTER 26

When you leave your job, you give up a lot of things you don't even think about. From paper clips, freshly brewed coffee, and benefits like vacation time, to credibility, clout, and contacts, don't overlook all of the advantages you gain from working for someone else.

CHAPTER 27

Employees are necessary for growing your business, but they create all sorts of new problems for you.

CHAPTER 28 Managing the financial health of your business requires you to not only manage and understand profits and losses, but also working capital, investment needs, and cash flow. This is very complicated and is a factor that trips up even large, well-run businesses. If you want to play the game, you need to know how to keep score.

CHAPTER 29 Your business is the "You Show." No matter who else you think will help you, at the end of the day, it is your name on the dotted line. And what happens in the worst-case scenario? If you are the only one that knows what is going on and you get the swine flu, get hit by a bus, or die, then what happens? What is at risk when you have your own business?

CHAPTER 30 The risk and reward trade-off in starting a business will be personal to you and your circumstances. However, the potential rewards from your business opportunity need to greatly outweigh the risks you will take on and the issues you will endure. If they don't, you should not pursue that particular opportunity.

CHAPTER 31 There will always be a story about someone with rags-to-riches success. That person is either beyond lucky (the dozen-million-to-one lottery winner), or perhaps you aren't getting the full story. Just because a business generates millions of dollars in revenue, doesn't mean it is profitable. There are billion-dollar businesses that have gone bankrupt.

That's it. I hope that you were able to get a better understanding of why entrepreneurship is so different and challenging in today's environment than it was generations ago and why the risks of starting, buying, franchising, and generally owning a business may not justify the potential rewards. If you decide to keep your day job, I am sure you will be motivated to focus on your core competencies and find a way to be entrepreneurial without having to become an entrepreneur. Or perhaps you will go the "jobbie" route and test out a business concept on the side to see if it has legs before pouring your life savings into it. If and when you do start a business, you should now be prepared for wearing many hats and feel confident that you have evaluated that the upside potential far exceeds the risk that you will be taking in terms of your money, time, and effort.

Whichever route you choose, I am sure we will be connecting again soon. I will be the one telling you that you have "spinach in your teeth" so that you can remove it, smile, and enjoy the rest of your day.

Okay, then. Lucy Van Pelt is officially closing shop for the day.

Index

About the Author

CAROL ROTH is a business strategist, deal maker and *New York Times* best-selling author. She has helped her clients—who've ranged from "solopreneurs" to multinational corporations—raise more than $1 billion in capital, complete more than $750 million worth of mergers and acquisitions transactions, secure high-profile licensing and partnership deals, and create seven-figure customer loyalty programs.

Carol is a frequent radio, television, and print media contributor on the topics of business and entrepreneurship, appearing regularly on Fox News Channel, MSNBC, Fox Business Network, and WGN-TV Chicago, among others. Her blog at CarolRoth.com was recently named as one of the Top 10 small business blogs online and she was named a 2011 Top 100 Small Business Influencer by Small Biz Trends. Carol is also a contributing blogger to outlets like *The Huffington Post*, AllBusiness.com, and Crain's Chicago Business/Enterprise City, and is the only business strategist with a fashion doll made in her likeness.

Carol holds a bachelor of science degree from the Wharton School of Business at the University of Pennsylvania, where she graduated magna cum laude. She currently resides in Chicago, Illinois, with her husband, Kurt, who is also an investment banker (and her former business partner). They have no children, pets, or plants, and are avid sports fans (particularly of NFL football). Carol is also a recovering toy collector, recently trading in a portion of her collection for a more sophisticated toy (a Simpsons pinball machine).

For more information on Carol, visit www.CarolRoth.com.